The Virtue of Loyalty

THE VIRTUES: MULTIDISCIPLINARY PERSPECTIVES

Series Editor

Nancy E. Snow
*Professor of Philosophy and Director of the Institute for
the Study of Human Flourishing,
University of Oklahoma*

Justice
Edited by Mark LeBar

Humility
Edited by Jennifer Cole Wright

Integrity, Honesty, and Truth Seeking
Edited by Christian B. Miller and Ryan West

The Virtues of Sustainability
Edited by Jason Kawall

The Virtue of Harmony
Edited by Chenyang Li and Dascha Düring

The Virtue of Loyalty
Edited by Troy Jollimore

The Virtue of Loyalty

Edited by
TROY JOLLIMORE

OXFORD
UNIVERSITY PRESS

OXFORD
UNIVERSITY PRESS

Oxford University Press is a department of the University of Oxford. It furthers
the University's objective of excellence in research, scholarship, and education
by publishing worldwide. Oxford is a registered trade mark of Oxford University
Press in the UK and certain other countries.

Published in the United States of America by Oxford University Press
198 Madison Avenue, New York, NY 10016, United States of America.

© Oxford University Press 2024

CIP data is on file at the Library of Congress
ISBN 978-0-19-761265-1 (pbk.)
ISBN 978-0-19-761264-4 (hbk.)

DOI: 10.1093/oso/9780197612644.001.0001

Paperback printed by Marquis Book Printing, Canada
Hardback printed by Bridgeport National Bindery, Inc., United States of America

Contents

Series Editor's Foreword

Typically, having a virtue means being disposed to having certain kinds of perceptions, thoughts, motives, emotions, and ways one is inclined to act. The end of the twentieth and the beginning of the twenty-first centuries have seen an upsurge of interest in the topic of virtue. This is true not only in philosophy but also in a variety of other disciplines, such as theology, law, economics, psychology, and anthropology, to name a few. The study of virtue within disciplines is vitally important, yet the premise of this series is that the study of virtue in general, as well as of specific virtues, can be enhanced if scholars take into account work being done in disciplines other than their own.

Cross-disciplinary work can be challenging. Scholars trained in one field with its unique vocabulary and methods do not always move seamlessly into another discipline and often feel unqualified to undertake the task of serious cross-disciplinary engagement. The upshot can be that practitioners of disciplines can become "siloed"—trapped within their own disciplines and hesitant to engage seriously with others, even on important topics of mutual interest.

This series seeks to break the silos, with fifteen volumes on specific virtues or clusters of virtues. For each book, an introduction by the editor highlights the unity of writings by identifying common themes, threads, and ideas. In each volume, the editor seeks to include a chapter from a "wild card" discipline, a field one would not expect to see included in a collection of essays on a particular virtue. We do this both to highlight the diversity of fields in the study of specific virtues and to surprise and challenge readers to broaden their horizons in thinking about virtue.

The audience for this series includes practitioners of different disciplines who seek to expand their thinking about virtue. Each volume contains chapters that are accessible and of interest to scholars from many disciplines. Though the volumes are not comprehensive overviews of the work on virtue that is occurring in any given field, they provide a useful introduction meant to pique the curiosity of readers and spur further engagement with other disciplines.

Nancy E. Snow
Professor of Philosophy
University of Kansas

Contributors

Heidi Cobham completed her doctoral research in philosophy at the University of Sussex in 2023. She has worked as a doctoral tutor on the Philosophy, Politics, and Middle East module at the University of Sussex.

Constance Flanagan is the University of Wisconsin–Madison School of Human Ecology Vaughan Bascom Professor Emerita in Women, Family, and Community.

Mathew A. Foust is Professor of Philosophy and Chair of the Department of Philosophy and Religion at Appalachian State University.

Margaret Gilbert is the Abraham I. Melden Chair in Moral Philosophy and Distinguished Professor, Philosophy School of Humanities.

Diane Jeske is Professor and Director of Graduate Studies at University of Iowa, Department of Philosophy.

Troy Jollimore is Professor of Philosophy at California State University, Chico.

Leah Kalmanson is Associate Professor and the Bhagwan Adinath Professor of Jain Studies in the Department of Philosophy and Religion at the University of North Texas.

John Kleinig is Emeritus Professor of Philosophy in the Department of Criminal Justice, John Jay College of Criminal Justice, and in the PhD Program in Philosophy, Graduate School and University Center, City University of New York.

Sharon Krishek is a Senior Lecturer in the Philosophy Department of the Hebrew University of Jerusalem.

Sanford Levinson holds the W. St. John Garwood · and W. St. John Garwood, Jr. Centennial Chair in Law at the University of Texas.

Tony Milligan is Senior Researcher in the Philosophy of Ethics, Cosmological Visionaries project, Department of Theology and Religious Studies, King's College London.

Alisa Pykett is an Action Researcher and Evaluator at the University of Wisconsin Population Health Institute.

Introduction

Troy Jollimore

Although loyalty structures our lives, it is often easy to forget how significant and profound its influence is. Like many virtues, loyalty operates largely by silently setting horizons and limits within which we make our choices and conduct our affairs. (Perhaps, when speaking of this structuring effect, we should speak of our *loyalties* rather than of *loyalty*.) Each day affords opportunities for betrayals and violations of intimate trust that we do not even consider committing. When we *are* tempted, our loyalty-based commitments become active and enter our consciousness: we become aware of ourselves as loyal agents, people with commitments we are strongly reluctant if not entirely unwilling to violate. Perhaps we see our very identities as being wrapped up with and to some degree constituted by such commitments. Of course, this is not to say that loyalty is never violated. Like every virtue, we sometimes fail to live up to its demands. And like every virtue, loyalty has its limits. Sometimes other reasons or needs, including those arising from other, competing loyalties, are more compelling. And sometimes it is difficult to be confident which consideration is the most compelling. The discomfort and even pain that can arise in such situations is itself a testament to how much our loyalties mean to us. The prospect of a life entirely without loyalties would for most of us be extremely unattractive. Indeed, we might wonder whether such an existence would be a recognizably *human* life at all.

Troy Jollimore, *Introduction* In: *The Virtue of Loyalty*. Edited by: Troy Jollimore, Oxford University Press.
© Oxford University Press 2024. DOI: 10.1093/oso/9780197612644.003.0001

Loyalty and the virtues

The twentieth and twenty-first centuries have witnessed a renewed focus on the virtues as an approach to ethics. In a sense, this development constitutes a return to the roots of Western ethical thought. In ancient Greece and Rome, the virtues were central to thinking about how we ought to live and about what constitutes a good life for human beings. And the truth is that, while beliefs about specific virtues and their natures (and sometimes even their names) have changed, the virtues have continued to play a substantial role in everyday moral thinking, where commendations grounded in positive character traits like honesty, generosity, humility, and compassion, and criticisms grounded in negative character traits like dishonesty, cruelty, arrogance, and selfishness, tend to be both common and significant.

Our ethical evaluations of others frequently make use of and refer to particular virtues and vices. Virtues and vices are essential to many of our attempts to understand and interpret other people and their behavior. We see people as possessing certain characters and dispositions that endure over time, from which their decisions and patterns of action arise. Of course, there are other ways of attempting to interpret people's behavior. One might, for instance, view a person as an agent with certain set goals and interpret her actions as attempts to achieve those goals. The virtue framework is, then, one among a number of frameworks that we can apply to human beings and their actions in the process of interpreting and evaluating them. But it is a central and significant framework, one we could hardly imagine doing without. Moreover, there is considerable intersection and interaction between these frameworks. Often, for instance, an understanding of an individual's goals, or of why she selects some strategies for achieving those goals while ruling out others, presupposes that we understand her moral character to a considerable degree; and this may include understanding her to be virtuous or vicious in certain ways.

Virtue elements, then, are essential to our understanding of other human beings. But they are also highly salient in our practical, first-personal moral thinking. Everyday moral thinking frequently treats virtues as possessing the power to justify action, or to explain why a particular action or decision would be right or wrong. "It was the honest thing to do" strikes many people as a perfectly good explanation of why a given person chose not to tell a lie or hide some fact, or of why they were right to make that choice. By the same token, "That would be cruel" seems to many people sufficient in itself to show that the action being considered is something that should not be done. Unlike, say, the consequentialist or the Kantian, who would say that to *really* know whether the action was right or wrong we would need to perform some other sort of investigation—evaluating its effects on overall outcomes, perhaps, or determining whether it is universalizable—a great many people, in the course of their ordinary moral lives and conversations, are perfectly content to end their moral deliberations with statements that directly refer to some virtue or other and do not presuppose or require any further justification in terms of some independent moral notion or value.

Loyalty and morality

These general trends about the virtues are observable, and in certain respects amplified, in the particular case of loyalty—a moral notion that, as the philosopher Philip Pettit has claimed, "is at the heart of common-sense morality."[1] As we observed, many of the evaluations we direct toward other people are connected with loyalty. We praise people for being good friends and blame them for being inconstant, unreliable, "fair-weather" friends. Many people care deeply whether candidates for political office are genuinely

---

[1] Pettit 1998, 163.

patriotic; in some cases, being labeled a traitor can end a political career. We make wedding vows in which we pledge ourselves to a romantic and life partner for better or worse, for richer or poorer, in sickness and in health. And most of us, at some time or other and in some form or other, have experienced the pain of betrayal and learned, via that experience, a great deal about why betrayal is bad and, hence, why loyalty is admirable and virtuous.

Indeed, betrayal is frequently viewed as an especially serious moral crime or sin (a fact expounded on by John Kleinig in his contribution to this volume).[2] A great many people view being unpatriotic, or being an unfaithful spouse, as highly significant moral failings. In the United States, treason is one of the few non-homicide crimes that can earn a death sentence. The disloyal—the Benedict Arnolds of the world, the Judases, the Macbeths—are often regarded as among the worst of moral criminals. Dante, indeed, reserved the lowest circle of Hell, the ninth, for those guilty of treachery.

As one would expect, such views play powerful roles in the motivations and deliberations of the typical moral agent. Under ordinary circumstances it would take a great deal to get most of us to consider betraying our country or some individual person we cared about. Moreover, the motivational and justificatory structure here is like that of the other virtues. The fact that an action would be a betrayal is *itself* taken to be a strong reason, and frequently a sufficient reason, for refraining from it. Similarly, the fact that some action is required by loyalty to a partner, friend, child, or other significant party is likely to be viewed, in itself, as generating a requirement to do it.

Of course, consequences or other impartial moral considerations might still turn out to be relevant in other ways. Perhaps the best available overall account of the justification of loyalty (or any other virtue) will make at least some appeal to that trait's contribution to

---

[2] See Kleinig, Chapter 4, this volume.

the goodness of human life or the functioning of human societies. Impartial moral principles might also set limits on what loyalty can require or what people can permissibly do in its name. Many of the philosophical and theoretical questions concerning loyalty—and many of those considered in the essays in this book—concern how it ought to be placed in the context of broader morality: for instance, how it relates to deontological prohibitions, to desirable or undesirable outcomes, and indeed to other virtues, as well as when it ought to take precedence over these potentially competing moral considerations, and when it should cede its authority to them.

Some of the most pointed of these questions are those that ask whether, in the final analysis, loyalty can be reconciled with the demands of impartial morality at all, and—a related but importantly distinct question—whether loyalty is a genuine virtue at all. We have already seen that in the view of many, the conclusion that a given action is required by loyalty can appropriately put an end to moral deliberation before that deliberation gets a chance to consider questions concerning broader outcomes and general welfare or utility. This naturally invites the question of whether loyalty can motivate and justify actions which have horrific consequences or which are inherently morally awful, a question around which much of the most urgent and spirited discussion of loyalty's status as a virtue revolves.

If the question is whether loyalty can *appear* to justify immoral and even evil actions, and whether it has in fact motivated people to act badly in its name, the answer is clearly yes. Loyalty's ability to move people to perform or participate in immoral behavior has frequently been noted by its critics. Arthur Koestler claimed that "No historian would deny that the part played by crimes committed for personal motives is very small compared to the vast populations slaughtered in unselfish loyalty to a jealous God, king, country, or political system."[3] The philosopher Alasdair MacIntyre, who

---

[3] Koestler 1978, 77.

defends the moral value of patriotism, nonetheless acknowledges that it is a "permanent source of moral danger."[4] More personal loyalties may raise similar concerns. While Aristotle seemed to suggest that only perfectly virtuous people could participate in true friendship, it seems clear that some form of friendship can exist between people of less than ideal virtue. (If you need to be convinced, there are several quite entertaining films that take this as a theme, and which might persuade you. I particularly recommend Joel and Ethan Coen's *The Big Lebowski* [1998] and Alexander Payne's *Sideways* [2004].) Such friends may well ask each other to perform actions that conflict with the demands of impartial morality, and it is at the very least not obvious that all such demands can be immediately written off as illegitimate.[5]

These particular forms of moral danger are connected to the fact we observed earlier, that judgments about loyalty are frequently taken to put an end to moral deliberation and to prompt decisive and immediate action. To some extent, as we have noted, this feature is common to many if not all of the virtues. But it is perhaps more perilous when attached to loyalty, as here it tends to be attended by significant pressure to stop thinking, to act immediately and single-mindedly, precisely as a means of demonstrating the depth and intensity of one's obedience and commitment.

Here especially we can see how the fear of being accused of disloyalty, of being labeled a traitor, can easily distort an agent's moral thinking and push them to perform acts they would ordinarily oppose. In the process, judgment and conscience can be suppressed, if not switched off entirely. Against the background of such considerations, loyalty might strike us as too closely linked to obedience and servility to function as a genuine virtue. We might find ourselves focusing on such examples as Mr. Stevens, the

---

[4] MacIntyre 1984.
[5] For discussion see, for example, Cocking and Kennett 2000; Nehamas 2016, 136–137; and Diane Jeske, Chapter 2, this volume.

overzealously loyal butler in Kazuo Ishiguro's novel *The Remains of the Day*, who ultimately regrets the devotion he has shown to his employer, the Nazi sympathizer Lord Darlington:

> His lordship was a courageous man. He chose a certain path in life, it proved to be a misguided one, but there, he chose it, he can say that at least. As for myself, I cannot even claim that. You see, I *trusted* him, I trusted I was doing something worthwhile. I can't even say I made my own mistakes. Really—one has to ask oneself—what dignity is there in that?[6]

It might seem, too, that the question of whether any particular loyalty is good must be settled solely by a moral evaluation of object of the loyalty. (Note, by contrast, that we do not ordinarily think that the moral goodness of kindness or honesty is generally contingent in this manner on the moral worthiness of the particular persons we are being kind to or honest with.)

Perhaps, though, it is a mistake to think that loyalty requires obedience or makes us servile. It may be more plausible to think that at least sometimes the loyal thing to do, when the object of your loyalty has lost their way, would be to help them find it again, even if this means criticizing them or being firm with them. As various social critics, activists, and gadflies have reminded us, dissent can be patriotic. John Kleinig observes that "the well-established idea of a 'loyal opposition' should give pause to the suggestion that loyalty requires complaisance or servility."[7] Such themes make their way into this volume as well. Tony Milligan and Heidi Cobham examine a fictional marriage (from a novel by Iris Murdoch) in which the husband, Paul, holds a deeply deficient conception of loyalty, which he sees as being centered on obedience and servility. Leah Kalmanson points out that the requirement that loyal advisors

[6] Ishiguro 1989, 243.
[7] Kleinig 2022.

"remonstrate" with their leaders rather than blindly going along with ideas and actions they believed to be profoundly wrong has been emphasized in many Chinese writings about loyalty. My own chapter also puts forward the idea that being loyal to someone who is guilty of a wrongdoing need not involve affirming, let alone becoming an accomplice to, their misdeeds. Such thoughts may go a considerable distance toward relieving the worry that loyalty amounts to nothing more than an objectionable demand for servility and abject obedience.

That said, while it is a mistake to accept simplistic assumptions about the kind of devotion and dedication loyalty requires, it would surely also be a mistake to regard the possibility of conflict between loyalty and the demands of impartial morality as merely incidental. It is, rather, part of loyalty's essence. The very notion of being on some side or other, and being "true" to that side through thick and thin, seems in tension with the idea that one should always strive to be on the *right* side, to join and support those whose actions are morally justifiable and supportable. George Orwell once wrote that "The essence of being human is that one does not seek perfection, that one is sometimes willing to commit sins for the sake of loyalty." Perhaps Orwell overstated the case; *sins* is a strong word. But it is not obvious that he did, or that he overstated by much.

Thus, loyalty seems to raise moral concerns that do not arise with respect to such character traits as patience, honesty, or compassion, and may seem potentially hazardous in ways that these other putative virtues do not. Loyalty, assuming that it is a virtue, would appear to be a highly complex virtue, and one about which we may well have complex and conflicting feelings. It is not, or so it would appear, an appropriate object of unalloyed admiration, but something that seems at least sometimes to call for a more nuanced and ambivalent response.

This is not to say that loyalty should be viewed purely as a source of moral hazard. That view is also excessively simplistic. If nothing else, it excludes the real possibility that in some cases of conflict between loyalty's demands and those of impartial morality, it is loyalty that gets things *right*. Consider the consequentialist demand that we always maximize the overall good, as determined from an impersonal point of view. In some cases, one might think, this would require us to sacrifice the life of a friend or lover in order to save two strangers—or, more schematically, to betray someone close to you in order to prevent a larger number of equivalent betrayals among people unrelated to you. Such a demand strikes many of us not only as excessively demanding but as morally wrongheaded. In at least some such cases, perhaps, it is impartial morality, rather than loyalty, that constitutes the source of moral peril.

The chapters

The essays in this book explore various aspects of this central and highly significant virtue, often paying considerable attention to the conflicts and dilemmas we are faced with as a result of our loyalties. Because loyalty is not confined to a single dimension of our lives, many different kinds of relationships and objects of loyalty are considered. Several of the chapters focus on personal loyalties such as friendship and romantic love, while others are concerned with loyalty toward states or other political communities and, in particular, toward the documents, such as a constitution, that might govern and express the political ideals and principles of such a community. A number of chapters examine cases in which loyalty's demands seem to conflict with the demands of impartial morality or of other virtues. Other authors examine the processes by which loyal traits and characters are formed, or survey some views regarding loyalty found in non-Western traditions, or delve into the specific nature of betrayal as a moral phenomenon. The result is a broad, though not comprehensive and by no means conclusive, portrait of a complex and significant moral phenomenon.

A glance at the list of contributors and their respective disciplines might give the reader the impression that this volume is somewhat less diverse than other volumes in Oxford's *The Virtues* series. While it is true that most of the chapters here are authored by people who identify as philosophers, I would suggest that that impression is misleading. Loyalty has come to be an active and contested topic of philosophical debate in recent years, and the variety of approaches taken to loyalty *within* philosophical discourse manifests significant diversity and variety. The philosophers included here approach the topic of loyalty from a diverse array of backgrounds and interests, and bring to the topic a wide range of assumptions, strategies, and argumentative approaches. They disagree not only in the answers they propose and defend with respect to questions that arise in connection with loyalty but also about what the important questions are, what kinds of methods should be pursued in trying to answer them, and how we ought to conceive of what would count as an adequate or satisfying answer. These are deep disagreements indeed, and the result, I think, is a book that represents many different ways of thinking about a topic that turns out to have many different faces.

Full-fledged virtues are not present at the beginning of life, nor do they appear spontaneously out of nowhere. Chapter 1, developmental psychologist and human ecologist Constance Flanagan and applied community researcher Alisa Pykett's "Developmental Foundations of Loyalty in Childhood and Adolescence," considers the early character traits that develop into loyalty or into traits that support and forge connections with loyalty. Flanagan and Pykett argue that the development of loyalty as a virtue is deeply rooted in and strongly influenced by family relationships and in extrafamilial trust-based relationships such as friendships. As Flanagan and Pykett write, "the capacity to be loyal to a cause depends on the formation of an autonomous moral self whose trust in others and in herself is grounded in relationships of care in infancy, is inspired and practiced through imaginary and role play, is clarified through friendships, and honed and polished in collective action with others in community groups." In deploying the concept of role play to help account for the ways in which the sentiments and behaviors associated with loyalty are learned, honed, and strengthened, the authors draw on Josiah Royce's suggestion that we learn loyalty-exhibiting behavior by "imitation" (a theme we will encounter again in Mathew Foust's chapter). On their account, such processes of imitation encourage the development of self-consciousness and assimilation into a larger social and moral community, one that serves as the object of and setting for many of one's future loyalties.

Flanagan and Pykett are especially concerned with friendships between young persons and the opportunities for developing and testing loyalties afforded by friendships. Chapter 2, philosopher Diane Jeske's "Loyalty and the Selves We Are as Friends," explores some of the difficult issues raised by this sort of loyalty, and it is one of several chapters to pay close attention to the dilemmas posed by conflicting loyalties. Responding to E. M. Forster's famous statement that he would rather betray his country than his friend, Jeske recognizes a common impulse to agree with Forster but urges us to be cautious when dealing with such sweeping statements absent any particular context. In some situations, after all—where a friend has committed a serious wrong—it might well be better to betray one's friend than to betray one's country. Why, then, are so many of us so strongly inclined to endorse Forster's sentiment? Jeske suggests that this has to do with the fact that friendship provides a unique kind of good by opening a space in which people can be intimate and authentic with one another, that the loss of this space cannot be compared with the kind of loss brought about by betraying one's political commitments, and that this loss is real, and serious, even in cases in which betraying one's friend is justified all things considered—when, for instance, such a betrayal is morally required.

The topic of dilemmas is perhaps inseparable from that of loyalty and will recur throughout this volume. In Chapter 3, "Loyalty

Dilemmas," philosopher Margaret Gilbert picks up the theme of dilemmas posed by conflicting loyalties, while also asking whether a proper view of loyalty requires us to hold that it is a moral virtue, and whether the dilemmas of loyalty are properly understood as moral dilemmas. "When is loyalty virtuous," Gilbert asks, "and when not?" She argues, against many accounts of loyalty, that the obligations of loyalty are not moral obligations, but rather instances of what she refers to as "directed obligations of joint commitment." Her consideration of the moral status of loyalty recognizes that a significant issue involves unquestioning or "blind" loyalty. As Gilbert argues, "people are blindly loyal just in case they choose to fulfill their loyalty obligations even in circumstances in which morality requires them not to do so." Blind loyalty is not, she argues, a virtue, for on her account, exemplifying loyalty as a virtue is a matter of giving loyalty-based obligations "their proper place in one's practical reasoning."

The specter of betrayal is central to both Jeske's and Gilbert's chapters. In Chapter 4, "Betrayal," philosopher and criminal justice expert John Kleinig places that concept at center stage, in order to demonstrate that an adequate understanding of what makes being betrayed so bad will shed light on what makes loyal relationships so valuable and significant to us. In Kleinig's view, understanding the nature of betrayal—and hence of loyalty—requires recognizing that there are different kinds of betrayal, and that these different kinds invoke different moral considerations and invite very different responses. He considers five kinds of case: a participant in organized crime who becomes a police informer; a police officer who believes a fellow officer has wrongfully killed a civilian; a married man who leaves his wife and children for a new romantic partner; a citizen of a capitalist country who begins surreptitiously working for an ideologically opposed country; and an employee of a pharmaceutical corporation who becomes aware that his employer is making false and potentially harmful claims about its products. In each of these cases the agent is placed in a kind of practical dilemma, in which they are subject to competing weighty claims and may well feel that no choice is completely defensible or morally clean: no matter what they choose, they will have betrayed either some person or some important principle (and, in some cases, both). Kleinig's discussion sheds considerable light on the particular psychological states and motivations that arise in and motivate situations involving betrayal, and he is particularly interested in the question of distinguishing "corrupt" and hence morally criticizable motivations for betrayal from defensible justifications.

Perhaps more than most putative virtues, loyalty faces many challenges from skeptics and critics who deny that it is in fact a genuine virtue. Chapter 5, my "Is Loyalty Redundant?," considers and responds to one of those challenges. The Redundancy Argument claims that any legitimate reasons for meeting loyalty's demands must be grounded, not in loyalty itself, but in other sorts of moral facts, leaving loyalty itself no substantial role to play. Focusing on cases involving a friend who has been accused of some wrongdoing, I argue that the Redundancy Argument takes an excessively narrow view of the kinds of responses loyalty can support: we can acknowledge, for instance, that loyalty may not obligate us to participate in a friend's criminal activities, or to hide a criminal who happens to be a friend from the law, but it does not follow from this that loyalty is irrelevant to agents who find themselves in such situations. The chapter concludes by suggesting that these considerations are not limited to friendship or other personal relationships, but may also apply in broader political contexts, such as patriotic loyalty to one's country.

In Chapter 6, "Loyalty and the Reception of Buddhism in China," religious studies scholar and philosopher Leah Kalmanson traces the complex development of various strands of Buddhist and Ruist thinking about attachment to and alienation from specific persons and communities, and asks how these ideas helped to shape the history of Buddhism and people's responses to it. Thus, this chapter contributes to our understanding of the psychological sentiments that relate to loyalty and how these sentiments have been understood and debated in various cultural contexts. Kalmanson's examination of Buddhist and Ruist views regarding the resolution competing loyalties has clear connections with several of the other chapters, including the response to the Redundancy Argument I develop in Chapter 6. Consider the disagreement between Kongzi (commonly known as Confucius) and one of his critics about whether it is more virtuous to defend one's father, who has stolen a sheep, or to report him to the authorities. The Ruist view, she writes, suggests that "in such cases, children must find ways to remain true to overarching ethical principles, without damaging the parent–child bond, and without failing to be a loyal son or daughter." Similarly, Kalmanson notes the importance in these traditions of the idea of remonstration—the idea, that is, that genuinely loyal behavior might involve a degree of criticism and resistance, rather than blind obedience, directed toward the object of one's loyalty.

The idea that we learn to be virtuous by imitating the virtuous is a common theme in virtue ethics, going back at least as far as Aristotle. In Chapter 7, "Exemplars of Loyalty," philosopher Mathew Foust returns to the work of Josiah Royce, focusing in particular on Royce's claim that imitation functions as a significant means to instill and hone behaviors that exhibit and express loyalty. Foust places Royce in conversation with recent work by Linda Zagzebski, exploring the role of exemplars in moral theory, suggesting possible points of contact between Zagzebski and Royce, and identifying possible tensions or disagreements. Foust's chapter also addresses a question that dogs philosophical discussions of loyalty, and which arises in one form or another in many of the chapters in this collection: Is loyalty by nature a thoroughly local and partialistic virtue, or can its demands be reconciled with those of a broader, more impartial morality?

Chapter 8, "Loyalty to the Constitution," finds law professor Sanford Levinson poses probing questions about loyalty attachments to ideas, ideals, bodies of law, and documents—here, in particular, the US Constitution—that illuminate a number of more general issues: the role of sentiments in loyalty, the nature of loyalty's interactions with impartial morality, the kinds of dilemmas that may confront political subjects as a result of their various and conflicting loyalties, and the means that states may permissibly make use of to encourage the formation of loyalty and to demand displays or proofs of loyalty. Levinson's discussion centers on the practice of requiring university professors, lawyers, and many others to take an oath of loyalty to the US Constitution. That this practice is broadly accepted and often unremarked on is, in his view, unfortunate, as he sees such a requirement as not only conceptually unclear but indeed potentially dangerous. The failure of conceptual clarity is rooted largely in the fact that it is not obvious precisely what it means to support and uphold a document that contains provisos allowing its own alteration almost without limit—a fact that, Levinson observes, raises the question, just what is it that we pledge allegiance to when we pledge allegiance to a country's constitution? In reflecting on this question, the chapter explores a kind of real and potentially serious ethical dilemma many people, including Levinson himself, must confront in the course of their actual lives.

In Chapter 9, "Love and Loyalty," philosopher Sharon Krishek focuses on personal loyalties between romantic intimates and draws from a literary example to make her case. Loyalty, Krishek writes, is not strictly speaking a necessary component of romantic love, but it is necessary if such love is to endure and flourish. Love, on her Kierkegaardian view, is rooted in a correspondence between the selves of the lover and the beloved—a correspondence that is largely a matter of positively influencing each other, and which is crucially formed by seeing the beloved as they are. As she writes, "What it takes to recognize (and deepen) the correspondence . . . is a clear appreciation, a *clear vision*, of the beloved." Krishek uses the story of a married couple, Bernard and June, from Ian McEwan's novel *Black Dogs* to illustrate the kind of failure of love she has in mind. Here, as she writes, the lovers betray each other not by replacing the beloved with a person—a substitute lover—but by adopting a set of rigid ideas that prevents them from making genuine space for each other. Their disloyalty is thus a matter of failing to meet the conditions that would allow them to truly see each other, and hence make their love endure. "Loyalty, then," Krishek suggests, "is the atti-tude that enables the lovers to experience, through clear-sighted vision of the respective beloved, the metaphysical correspond-ence between them; particularly when they cease to experience it spontaneously."

Finally, in Chapter 10, "A Dubious Virtue," philosophers Tony Milligan and Heidi Cobham cap off our volume by returning to the question of whether loyalty is a virtue and, if so, what kind of virtue it might be. Milligan and Cobham argue that we can re-gard loyalty as a genuine virtue while rejecting the implausible view that loyal actions are always morally admirable and that the commitments of loyalty never lead us morally astray. In developing their account, they focus on an example drawn from Iris Murdoch's *The Bell*, a novel centering on Paul and Dora, whose troubled mar-riage exemplifies some of loyalty's darker aspects. Unlike Bernard and June in *Black Dogs*, Paul and Dora's problem is not a lack of loyalty to each other, but rather a defective conception of loyalty, one that is unacceptably rigid, too focused on servility and obedi-ence, and as a result disconnected from important realities about human needs and human flourishing. It is appropriate, perhaps, that this collection should conclude with a reminder that merely caring about loyalty is, in itself, not enough; what matters, as with any difficult topic of significance, is that we think well about it, and do our best to achieve—or, at least, make progress toward—a gen-uine understanding.

Bibliography

Cocking, Dean, and Jeanette Kennett. "Friendship and Moral Danger." *Journal of Philosophy* 97:5 (2000): 278–296.

Ishiguro, Kazuo. *The Remains of the Day*. New York: Knopf, 1989.

Kleinig, John. "Loyalty." *The Stanford Encyclopedia of Philosophy* (Summer 2022 edition), Edward N. Zalta, ed. https://plato.stanford.edu/archives/sum2022/entries/loyalty/ .

Koestler, Arthur. *Janus: A Summing Up*. New York: Random House, 1978.

MacIntyre, Alasdair. "Is Patriotism a Virtue?" The Lindley Lecture, University of Kansas, 1984.

Nehamas, Alexander. *On Friendship*. New York: Basic Books, 2016.

Pettit, Philip. "The Paradox of Loyalty." *American Philosophical Quarterly* 25:2 (1998): 163–171.

1

Foundations of Loyalty in Child and Adolescent Development

Constance Flanagan and Alisa Pykett

A person is not born loyal: loyalty is a virtue that is learned. Josiah Royce emphasizes the developmental work involved in nurturing capacities for loyalty to a cause when he states that the training of the young for such devotion is a "long and manifold task."[1] In this chapter we look at the developmental foundations and relational processes through which the virtue of loyalty is learned and nurtured. We begin with definitions of loyalty drawn from the work of the authors of several chapters in this volume,[2],[3] as well as from Royce's definition of loyalty as devotion to a cause.[4] Following that we argue that the capacity to be loyal to a cause depends on the formation of an autonomous moral self whose trust in others and in herself is grounded in relationships of care in infancy, is inspired and practiced through imaginary and role play, is clarified through friendships, and is honed and polished in collective action with others in community groups.

First, loyalty refers to allegiance, fidelity, or faithfulness *to someone or something beyond oneself*—a person, organization, community, nation, or cause. It is based on self-transcending (as opposed to self-enhancing) values.[5] For Royce, loyalty was "the

---

[1] Royce 1908, 120–121.
[2] Foust 2012.
[3] Jollimore 2013.
[4] Royce 1908.
[5] Schwartz 2013.

Constance Flanagan and Alisa Pykett, *Foundations of Loyalty in Child and Adolescent Development* In: *The Virtue of Loyalty*. Edited by: Troy Jollimore, Oxford University Press. © Oxford University Press 2024. DOI: 10.1093/oso/9780197612644.003.0002

willing and practical and thoroughgoing devotion of a person to a cause."[6] To commit in this way presupposes a level of freedom and self-determination that is learned through the course of development. Although we presume that adults have both the free will and practical experience that inform their choices, including devotion to a person or cause, children have many decisions about the beliefs and persons to whom they are loyal made for them. For example, parents decide if and where children will worship. Laws dictate certain ages when schooling is compulsory and social norms determine the truths to which students pledge allegiance. In this chapter we will argue that practice in negotiating with authorities during the child and adolescent years is part of the "long and manifold task" whereby individuals learn self-determination and autonomous decision-making that ultimately enable their loyalties to be freely chosen. Even young children try to negotiate bedtime, and adolescents challenge curfews. But it is in late adolescence and early adulthood when commitment to a cause or religious or political belief rises to the level of loyalty to a cause, "freely chosen."

Second, loyalty is practical. According to Mathew Foust, although affection may figure in loyalty, it is never enough. The loyal person must act. Feeling or even expressing compassion for the suffering of others might soothe one's conscience, but it does not test one's character. Mere private devotion to a leader or a cause is insufficient for promoting that cause or for revealing one's character. Action, by contrast, takes courage; it is public and reveals to others what one stands for. Such public action can exact a cost, in criticism or loss of relationships. And therein lies a lesson about the sacrifice one is willing to bear to be loyal to a cause.

Third, loyalty is social in two senses. It entails some form of self-sacrifice for the good of another, a group, or for the common good.[7] Although one can be personally enriched or grow through a

---

[6] Royce 1908, 9.
[7] Jollimore 2013, 1.

cause, personal enrichment or self-enhancement as the sole motivator of one's actions is insufficient as a basis for loyalty. Loyalty also is social insofar as it is achieved through social relationships and processes—in communities with others—families, friendships, teams, community-based organizations. Not only does the loyal person recruit others to her cause through example (fellow servants of a cause) but the cause itself unifies individuals in a common commitment.

Finally, loyalty is aspirational insofar as one dedicates herself to a hoped-for future. A person might be loyal to a leader or a cause that improves her own lot in life, or she can dedicate herself to a cause that promises a better world than the one with which she is familiar. In other words, loyalty to a cause is motivated in part by placing one's hopes in attaining the vision that the cause represents (e.g., a more just world, more inclusive and egalitarian communities). In summary, loyalty combines individual self-determination with communion in shared dedication with others to a cause, simultaneously, "satisfying our basic desires to pursue private passion (by choosing our cause) and to conform to the customs of a community (by serving a cause in communion with fellow servants)."[8]

Developmental prerequisites of loyalty

What, then, are the developmental prerequisites for being loyal? To be capable of sacrifice to a cause, one has to develop (1) an autonomous secure sense of self capable of self-determined choices; (2) a positive orientation to and sense of responsibility for the well-being of others; (3) an identification of one's self with groups who share similar beliefs, ideals, aspirations; and (4) a faith that the ideals to which one aspires and the cause to which one is loyal can be achieved through collective action with fellow servants of the cause.

[8] Foust 2012, 61.

Early roots

The earliest roots for these capacities are founded in a secure sense of self in infancy. Here we draw from Erik Erikson's theory of psychosocial development in which he argues that during each phase of life, humans develop particular ego strengths (at times he calls them virtues) by resolving particular tensions that exist between oneself and one's world at that particular stage.[9] Resolving these tensions is the developmental task if the child is to grow and mature. The tension to resolve in infancy is learning to trust—others, the world, and oneself. Although at times Erikson conflates hope with trust, referring to hope as "the earliest and most indispensable virtue inherent in the state of being alive," he nominates trust as the foundation for the capacity to act as a human being—to explore the world, to learn from it, and to learn about oneself through that exploration. A sense of basic trust is a "pervasive attitude toward oneself and the world derived from the experiences of the first year of life."[10]

Social relationships make that possible: infants learn to trust the world and to trust their own ability to explore it through the reliable, dependable responsiveness of caretakers who meet their needs. The infant is assured that she belongs to a community of 'others'—people who care about and are 'there' for her. This assurance is the basis for the child's orientation to the world, that is, her belief that it is a place safe to explore. And exploring increases her confidence in her own instincts. The knowledge that there are others who care so much for you and who are there for you engenders a self-confidence, a sense of worthiness about, a faith in oneself. Erikson describes it thus: "By trust I mean an essential trustfulness of others as well as a fundamental sense of one's own trustworthiness."[11] In

---

[9] Erikson 1950.
[10] Erikson 1950, 96.
[11] Erikson 1950, 96.

addition to an emerging awareness of one's independent self, an infant is learning that the world is a place where people are benevolent. If an infant's needs are not satisfied, if caregivers are absent, neglectful, unpredictable, then the child will feel more anxious about exploring the world and doubtful about her capacities. Over time, relationships may not be freely chosen but rather sought out in order to fill a void.

The infant's attachment to caretakers and her belief that humans are benevolent are foundations for a positive pro-social orientation to humans. Positive views of humanity are necessary, although not sufficient, bases for becoming a caring, helpful person who responds to the needs of others. Love and affection alone can also lead to indulgence and a child's sense that she is the center of the universe. This is why discipline from caretakers, including reminders to share one's toys and to respond with empathy to a playmate or sibling's distress, are needed to teach children ego-transcending values. Loyalty involves a willingness to forego self-gain for the benefit of others.

Imitation, self-consciousness, and role play

Royce uses the word *imitation* to explain the process whereby children become both self-conscious and aware that they are part of a larger community, claiming, "for whatever else we teach to a social being, we teach him to imitate."[12] But by imitation he does not mean mirroring or repeating the acts of another. His discussion of imitation reveals that it is a dynamic process of exchange and co-creation between social beings. He explains, "an act of imitation . . . is essentially the construction of something that lies, in a technical sense, *between* the acts of my model, and what were formerly my own

---

[12] Royce 1903, 279.

acts ... (for) *I never merely repeat his act*."[13] In an earlier discussion, he elaborates on the child's reconstructive process: "One may also call our judgments imitative processes, whereby we reconstruct our views of objects by putting together *successive ideas of our own.*"[14] In other words, the child observes others' actions but is an agent, not a mirror. She re-creates what she observes and, in the process, becomes aware that she is in relationship with but independent of those whom she imitates. The act is social, agentic, a creative expression of herself and her relationships.

Through such processes the child becomes conscious of herself as an agent. But Royce goes further, alluding to the obligation of adults to make the child aware of her agency, self-determination, and unique talents. In the exchange and relations of social imitation, adults are "obliged at the same time to teach him (the child) to assert himself, in some sort of way, in contrast with his fellows, and by virtue of the arts which he possesses."[15] Through such exchanges, a child learns to be self-conscious as she recognizes a contrast between her consciousness and some consciousness external to her consciousness.[16]

Royce also uses imitation and self-consciousness in discussions of role play. He contrasts the crying baby's inability to be self-conscious with the child "who struts about, playing soldier, or shyly hides from strangers, or asks endless questions merely to see what you will say, or quarrels with his fellows at play, or shrinks from reproof, or uses his little arts to win praise and caresses, he is self-conscious."[17] But role play deserves more discussion as a practice through which the child tests her courage and character. By playing 'house' and assuming a parent's role with dolls

[13] Royce 1959, 70, italics added.
[14] Royce 1903, 279.
[15] Royce, 1903: *Outlines of Psychology*, 279.
[16] Foust 2012, 86.
[17] Royce 1898, 208.

or younger siblings, a preschooler is exploring and developing his schema of what a 'good' parent is obliged to do. A loyal parent assumes responsibility—feeds a hungry baby and cuddles one who is crying. Loyal (aka good) parents make sacrifices for their child; a child engaging in this sort of role playing is play-acting her readiness to live up to those standards of a good parent. In a similar vein, a preschooler playing a super heroine is holding up standards of courage, testing the limits of bravery and sacrifice she is willing to take for the 'cause' of slaying monsters or bad guys. Whether play-acting at being a good parent or at vanquishing a villain, the child is forming schema about moral concepts such as courage, fidelity, and responsibility; she is facing her fears and assessing her moral fiber. Imagining the person she could be and play-acting that role speaks to the aspirational aspect of loyalty. In her own way the preschooler is imagining how she might contribute to a more perfect world.

Learning loyalty through families

The family is the most basic group to which a child belongs— the first experience of being part of a group of people that are bound together. Perhaps because families are the settings for our earliest relationships, strong emotional bonds tend to be formed and it is typically family members whom we expect to "be there" for us. Young people may behave in a certain way out of respect for their family or to represent them well, but contextual and cultural differences impact young people's beliefs about loyalty to family. For example, in adolescence it is common for youth to assume more freedom and authority over decisions. In the process many will assess how loyal they feel to the beliefs and values handed down by parents. This process of individuation, however, is not as strong in Latinx families. Both Latinx parents and adolescents report that the youth feel a strong sense of loyalty, responsibility, and obligation to their families that includes obedience and respect for parents and elders in positions of authority.[18,19,20]

Learning loyalty through friendships

As children mature, they learn about loyalty through peer relations, especially friendships. The egalitarian nature of peer relations is an important contrast with the asymmetrical power relations that exist between children and adults. Freedom and choice figure more prominently in peer relations than in parent–child relations. But friendships offer unique lessons in loyalty insofar as qualities of faithfulness, loyalty, and intimacy are even more characteristic of friendships than of peer relations.[21] Friendships are relationships that are co-created through mutual obligations and self-sacrifice. Friendships are reciprocal; they cannot be one-way. Friends hold one another accountable, and the bonds of friendship depend on each living up to the standards of loyalty they hold for one another.

Friendships are co-created and co-maintained. They demand that parties in the relationship are loyal to one another, that they keep promises, that they make good on what they agree to do. There is a tacit moral tie that is essential to a friendship. A friend has a right to expect loyalty from you and, if you betray her, she has a moral complaint against you. A 'friend' who doesn't keep promises or a 'friend' who doesn't believe that she has obligations or owes anything to the relationship is not loyal and is thus not a friend.

Friendships are a testing ground for our own character. Friends are there for us when we need them—in turn, we want to live up to the standard of being a 'good friend.' When we break a promise,

[18] Calzada, Fernandez, and Cortes 2010.
[19] Fuligni, Tseng, and Lam 1999.
[20] Marin et al. 1987.
[21] Newcomb and Bagwell 1995.

we lose not only the respect of our friends but also respect for ourselves. Being there for a friend shows that we care. Being true to our word means doing the things we said we would do, even if we don't feel like it. Thus, there is an element of sacrifice learned if we care enough for the relationship. We do what we don't feel like doing—because we value our friendship and because we hold ourselves to a moral standard of dependability. In friendships we come to value certain virtues (loyalty, reliability, empathy, a cooperative spirit, honesty, and authenticity) as standards that humans—or at least good people—should live by. If you are a good friend, these also become standards that define who you are. Being a loyal friend speaks to our character: I am a person who keeps her word. I am authentic, not two-faced. I do what I promise.

Beyond a specific friendship, the honesty that friends express to each other—the truth and trust that bind their friendship—adds to the stock or spread of loyalty. As Foust explains, such behaviors increase the confidence that humans place in one another, thus facilitating the spread of loyalty.[22] If we were to lie, not only do we undermine the link or unity between ourselves and the person to whom we are dishonest, but we decrease the confidence that humans place in one another, thus encumbering the spread of loyalty. According to Royce, honesty is the duty that humans owe to one another as humans. He explains, "When I speak the truth, my act is directly an act of loyalty to the personal tie which then and there binds me to the man to whom I consent to speak. My special cause is, in such a case, constituted by this tie. My fellow and I are linked in a certain unity—the unity of some transaction which involves our speech one to another."[23]

In friendships, children also learn about vulnerability and its relationship to sacrifice. Friends are not always reliable. Sometimes they forget what they promised. Typically, such omissions can be forgiven.

[22] Foust 2012, 64.
[23] Royce 1908, 140.

But friendships, especially in adolescence, evolve as teens' interests change. A friend can decide she does not want to hang out with you anymore. Although it hurts, that may also be an occasion for learning that loyalties have to be freely chosen. Vulnerability is also learned in friendships because of their intimate character. We trust friends with our most intimate secrets, our deepest hopes and fears. This is an indication of the deep trust that characterizes the relationship. But those revelations leave us open to the possibility of betrayal. In Chapter 4 of this volume, John Kleinig discusses the relational dimension of betrayal and how a betrayal can feel like an attack on one's own identity, given that a particular identity is being called into question.[24] As Kleinig observes, betrayals may sometimes be forgiven, but in some cases they will lead to a permanent alteration of and perhaps even the end of the relationship in question.

Conflicting loyalties, identity formation, and purpose

What if a friend asks us to keep a secret that could bring harm to others? To join in an activity that is not, in our view, a good cause? At times, friends can ask us to do things that are at odds with our principles. Such loyalty dilemmas in childhood or adolescence teach lessons relevant to loyalty dilemmas later in life, forcing us to confront such questions as: Who are the people/values/causes/ groups with which I identify? How should I act when my loyalty to one (e.g., person) is in conflict with my commitment to another (e.g., value)? When faced with conflicting loyalties, we learn "that the loyal life calls for adaptation."[25]

Jollimore points out that "loyalty may be a single virtue but because we have multiple loyalties it tends to attach us to a plurality of

---

[24] See Kleinig, Chapter 4 of this volume.
[25] Foust 2012, 63.

values, some of which may conflict with others."[26] When faced with conflicting loyalties, a person "has to decide which of his loyalties to act on, and which of his loyalties he would betray. To decide this is to decide to attach oneself to one among many roles that one plays in life, and thus to decide, in a deep sense, *who one really is.*"[27]

Deciding who one really is describes the developmental task of identity formation in the late adolescent and young adult years. This is a time in life to 'take stock'—of who one is, what one values and stands for, and where one's life is or could be headed. All of these questions are part of the overarching question, what is my purpose in life? When he says what he intends to do with his life, his purpose, a person reveals his identity.[28] Purpose is an aspiration to do something meaningful with one's life and typically emerges in adolescence.[29] Research on a sense of purpose has identified three dimensions: a goal or intention that is aspirational and gives direction for the future, a desire to contribute to something larger than the self, and meaningful engagement toward achieving the goal.[30]

Insofar as loyalty to a cause is an abstraction, it requires the cognitive capacities to imagine abstract entities, a capacity that emerges in adolescence. Further, a high level of self-discipline and self-control must also be mastered if one is to be capable of the self-sacrifice that loyalty to a cause demands. Finally, although the terms *loyal* and *legal* have similar roots, the loyal person does not merely obey the laws. If that were the case, the civil rights movement in the United States would not have challenged and altered the course of segregation which had been the law in many states. In this case loyalty to the cause of civil rights for all people was seen by activists as a moral justification for disobeying laws that denied those rights to Black people. At the same time, the fact that activists

---

[26] Jollimore 2013, 48.
[27] Jollimore 2013, 39, italics added.
[28] Foust 2012.
[29] Damon 2008.
[30] Damon, Menton, and Bronk 2003.

disobeyed laws was perceived by many at the time as being *disloyal* to the United States. The activists' decision to defy the law alludes to the importance of self-determination in deciding on a cause: "I, and only I, whenever I come to my own, can morally justify to myself my own plan of life. No outer authority can ever give me the true reason for my duty."[31] Loyalty to a cause is a sustained commitment; it cannot be hot and cold.[32]

However, a young person needs time to explore and reflect before fully committing to a cause or plan of life. She does so by joining groups or organizations, studying religious traditions and engaging in spiritual practices, volunteering for causes, and so on. Because they need time to explore before firmly deciding their commitments, Erikson proposed a moratorium on consolidating identity too early in the process. Ultimately, after a time of exploration, most young people tend to commit—to relationships, religions, beliefs, and causes. Commitment itself is a developmental process, and it is not surprising that Erikson nominates fidelity as the special virtue that emerges through the struggles of youth:

> Fidelity is the ability to sustain loyalties freely pledged in spite of the inevitable contradictions of value systems. It is the cornerstone of identity and receives inspiration from confirming ideologies and affirming companions. In youth, such truth verifies itself in a number of ways: a high sense of duty, accuracy, and veracity in the rendering of reality; the sentiment of truthfulness, as in sincerity and conviction; of genuineness, as in authenticity; the trait of loyalty, of 'being true'; fairness to the rules of the game; and finally all that is implied in devotion—a freely given but binding vow; with the fateful implication of a curse befalling traitors.[33]

---

[31] Royce 1908, 31.
[32] Mathew Foust, Chapter 7 of this volume.
[33] Erikson 1964, 125.

Learning loyalty through groups

Studies have overwhelmingly found that the need to belong is an important motivating factor in human behavior—people seek out human interaction and work to keep those ties intact.[34] A sense of belonging to the community is linked to improved mental and physical health across different ages, while lacking a sense of belonging can negatively impact well-being.[35] So it is not surprising that people, motivated in part to fulfill the need to belong, seek out different groups and consider how their behaviors impact continued participation in those groups throughout their lifetimes.

Groups, organizations, and teams provide settings for young people to explore, reflect upon, and practice loyalty to an entity beyond themselves. Children as young as five consider loyalty to a group to which one belongs a norm that good people follow. In a study that examined children's perspectives on the character of individuals based on whether they remained committed to their team even through failure, children were aware of the commitments expected of people who belonged to a group and felt that individuals should be loyal to the groups to which they belonged.[36] They evaluated a hypothetical individual who remained loyal to his/her 'losing' group as 'nicer, more trustworthy, more moral, and more deserving of a reward' compared to a hypothetical individual who abandoned her group and joined another 'winning' group. In sum, even for kindergartners, disloyal behavior is evaluated unfavorably and loyal behavior positively.

In a lecture on training for loyalty, Royce posited that "true and systemic loyalty" is the domain of the mature person and cannot be fostered before adolescence.[37] According to Royce, precursors can be laid in childhood, and adolescents can experience a limited

[34] Baumeister and Leary 1995.
[35] Michalski et al. 2020.
[36] Misch, Over, and Carpenter 2014.
[37] Royce 1908, 259.

form of "natural loyalty" (as opposed to social aspect of loyalty) through fraternal organizations and sports teams. These settings are not immune from misguided training for loyalty, as too much focus on winning at any cost as opposed to fair and ethical play in the game can harm the developmental process. The number and range of group activities available to children and adolescents have increased greatly since the early 1900s, but teams, groups, and organizations remain key settings for fostering the development of loyalty.

Through belonging to groups beyond one's family, young people start to experience different worldviews and ways of enacting those views. For example, schools provide an opportunity for students to feel like they are part of a larger institution that includes students of different ages, teachers, staff, and the community. Adolescents' very faith in humanity (their beliefs that people in general are trustworthy) is positively impacted by their sense that students at their school feel a solidarity with the institution.[38] Physical cues demonstrate loyalty to the school through clothing, cheers, and competition with other schools in sports and possibly academic-focused endeavors such as debate. However, it is also important to note that due to existing educational disparities and the experiences of young people of color who may feel *unwelcome* in their school, many students do not have the opportunity to develop solidarity with their own schools.

Studies have found that, compared to youth who are not involved in any community clubs or extracurricular activities at school, adolescents who are involved in at least one club have higher levels of social trust.[39] Compared to their uninvolved peers, they have more positive views of humanity and fellow citizens and are more likely to say that most people in their community are benevolent, care about making their communities a good place to live, pitch

---

[38] Flanagan and Stout 2010.
[39] Flanagan, Gill, and Gallay 2005.

in to solve community problems, and are open and welcoming to newcomers.

Sports teams

Non-school groups and teams provide settings for young people to experience and practice loyalty to an entity outside of their own families or circle of friends and out in the community. Participating on or supporting a sports team provides many developmental opportunities to practice loyalty. As a fan or supporter of a team, young people learn to remain loyal to a team even when that team is losing. Again, physical cues and concrete experiences reinforce a sense of solidarity and belonging—fans wear team gear to signal their loyalty, they share chants and songs, they join in with the mass of people at the games, and they observe more experienced fans and imitate and adapt their loyalties.

As a player on a team, a young person learns that individuals make sacrifices for the good of the team—they play a position that is not preferred, they struggle through difficult training and challenge themselves to grow for the good of the team, or they make an extra run or dive for their teammate even though they are tired. They are asked to remain loyal to the team whether they win or lose and whether they play or not. All of the players are held accountable for the successes and setbacks of the team. They have to show up, to train, to take care of their bodies, to make sacrifices for the good of a group that transcend their own individual self-interest. In doing so, they can experience the sense of belonging and solidarity with teammates. Sports teams can be particularly useful for young people because at least some of the goals are self-evident—to improve as individual players and as a team and to win matches. Sports teams also expose young people to conflicting loyalties as they may have to make decisions about attending a game or attending an event with families or friends. The sports milieu also presents conflicts between engaging in "fair play" or taking unfair actions to win, which echoes Royce's claims about the importance of emphasizing fair play when dealing with youth sports teams. As young people become more autonomous, they need to sort out these conflicts and decide, as mentioned in an earlier section, which loyalties and/or values to act upon in a particular situation.

Community and social issue groups

While participating in groups focused on positive youth development or sports teams can help young people practice many elements of loyalty, especially self-sacrifice and enacting loyalty through behaviors of commitment and trustworthiness, participating in groups with an explicit commitment to community or wider social issues provides a particularly rich environment for young people to experiment with being loyal to a cause. Royce calls this the social aspect of loyalty, differentiating it from the "natural loyalty" of sports teams and fraternal organizations.[40] Being loyal to a cause may differ somewhat from being loyal to a team or a school as it may require a commitment to a more abstract idea, such as racial equity or environmental justice, or a commitment to a political party. We say that this form of loyalty *may* require commitment to a more abstract idea because commitments to social causes and political parties can be intertwined with commitment to the people who are working for those causes or parties, particularly for young people. For example, people will conceive of and enact their loyalty to a particular political party, that is, Democrats or Republicans, in different ways. Some people might be loyal to the values of the party while others are loyal to a particular political figure or to the party itself, standing by the party's side regardless of shifting values and tactics.

---

[40] Royce 1908, 257.

Loyalty to a cause also pushes young people's thinking and connection farther out into the widening circles of the ecological social structures—beyond the individual self, family, school, and immediate context and into the societal or political level. As young people wade into larger circles of the world with increasing levels of autonomy, they develop their own worldviews and begin to consider who they want to be in the world. Young people learn about the larger macro systems through concrete experiences in community settings (e.g., institutions, organizations, community groups, youth groups in community organizations) that serve as microcosms of public life—"mini-polities" where they can try out different civic actions, grapple with others on public issues, and form a civic identity in relation to others.[41] Participating in these settings helps young people develop a sense of belonging and mattering to a community. Community settings are key mini-polities for young people to (1) learn about societal structures, (2) examine their own worldviews through exposure to others, (3) develop their civic identities, (4) develop loyalty to causes of emergent importance to them, (5) experiment with the enactment of loyalties, (6) experience conflict of loyalties and the resultant decision-making process, and (7) gain exposure to moral exemplars of loyalty.

In a recent study, Jasko, Szastok, Grzymala-Moszczynska, and Maj found a relationship between engaging in group political action on behalf of one's social values, gains in feelings of personal significance, and the willingness to self-sacrifice for the cause in the future.[42] The authors proposed that gains in feeling *personally significant* (through participation in collective action) predict future self-sacrifice to a cause. While based on a Polish sociopolitical context with adults, the findings point to the possible role that acting on behalf of social values that are important to young people has on their feelings of personal significance and their willingness

---

[41] Flanagan 2013, 8.
[42] Jasko et al. 2019.

to commit to a cause. In considering the development of loyalty, young people's exposure to different community organizations and groups provides opportunities for them to explore and experiment with the social values that are important to them and experience the positive feelings of personal significance through collective action, which, in turn, could increase their loyalty toward a specific cause or group. By participating in different kinds of groups, young people discover the social values that are most important to them and the kinds of groups, ideas, and causes that deserve their chosen loyalty.

Young people find their way into programs and groups in community settings through various paths—they seek them out based on overlapping interests, a friend invites them and they have fun so they keep coming back, a group with which they are already involved takes on a project with an explicit social or political issue, or, in some instances, they are seeking some way to address harms they have suffered or injustices that they observe. In other words, young people's pathways into groups can be arbitrary or intentional, but their participation can result in a commitment to a cause regardless of the method of entrée. As they engage more with the group, they often have more responsibilities in that group—they are held accountable for their commitments and contributions to the group or the cause. They identify as a member of that group, working on a particular issue in a particular way. For example, a young person involved in a youth organizing effort to address educational disparities in a local community center becomes loyal to the *cause* of educational equity and the *strategy* of community organizing. The support and solidarity with the other group members is key for young people to maintain their loyalties to the group and the cause, which is not surprising given the importance of peer relationships in adolescence and young adulthood. As discussed earlier in this section, the gains in feelings of personal significance can also help maintain their commitment to a particular group.[43] With the current level of economic and social precarity for young adults, these feelings of personal significance and group solidarity are vital.

Community settings also provide exposure to moral exemplars of loyalty, especially as new members get acquainted with the community group. While community organizations and groups have both adult and youth leaders, peers can be particularly powerful exemplars of loyalty since young people can relate to someone their own age and see how they can take certain actions of loyalty immediately (and not in the distant future of adulthood). In other words, young people can see how someone *like them* behaves if they are loyal to a cause or a group. Witnessing other young people enact loyalty to a cause also prompts questioning of one's own civic identity and commitments in the world. With active identity formation occurring in adolescence and young adulthood, young people are primed to learn from and adapt the practices of moral exemplars. For example, a student might join the gay-straight alliance at their school and see a peer exhibiting loyalty to the group and a commitment to shifting the school culture despite sacrifices of time and pushback from other students. At the same time the identity fluidity of adolescence and young adulthood coupled with the power of belonging to a group also makes young people more susceptible to joining groups that could cause harm. Erikson discussed this vulnerability and potential for harm. The need to belong for someone who does not have a strong sense of self can lead to decisions to join groups and follow leaders that are not necessarily freely chosen or well-informed. For example, a young person who has not been able to find a sense of belonging in other spaces may be recruited into and develop loyal attachments to extremist or radical groups.

Often part of developing a civic identity requires "questioning" loyalties to people, ideas, or institutions that young people connected to strongly in earlier parts of their lives. They may

[43] Jasko et al. 2019.

experience tension between loyalty to their families or the institutions that their families value and new institutions or ideals/people. For example, a young person may decide to support a different political party than their parents, or they may become devoted to a cause that is in direct conflict with their religion's or their parents' beliefs, such as access to reproductive health services or participation in a gay-straight alliance. Or they may develop loyalty toward the cause of environmental justice but live in a town whose economy depends on mining. These shifts of loyalties may precipitate the loss of a strong sense of belonging in one group for a tentative sense of belonging in a new group. These conflicts of loyalties help young people develop their own identities and experience their own threshold for discomfort in loyalties; however, they can also come at a cost to young people.

As young people start to learn more about social issues and think about how to address them as an individual and as part of a group, they are exposed to different efforts to address social issues. They are also exposed to different *strategies* for addressing these social issues, including service, voting, working within the system, activism, and more radical forms of disruption of the social order. Loyalty to a cause or an idea intersects and sometimes conflicts with loyalty to a particular way of behaving as a member of community or one's own sense of civic duty or civic identity. For example, many young people had to navigate loyalties to school and their identities as students with conflicting loyalties to environmental justice and the youth climate strike or the student walkouts to stop gun violence. Loyalty is at the heart of making choices to support issues *and* particular strategies to address those issues.

These questions of loyalty to strategy also relate to broader considerations about loyalty, political engagement, and democracy. Young people's earliest exposure to political loyalties comes from their families, for example, a parent who always votes Republican or Democrat and will tolerate a certain level of dissonance/conflict with other ideas to which they are loyal in the name of loyalty to that party. In school in US contexts, students are socialized, and in many cases required, to express loyalty to the country through actions such as reciting the Pledge of Allegiance or standing for the national anthem before events.

Aspirationally, civic education (which ranges widely from school to school and may not even be offered in some schools) aims to teach young people, in a nonpartisan way, about how US democracy works; to foster democratic dispositions; and to develop democratic skills such as perspective-taking, understanding differences, and deliberation. On one hand, there is an aspirational loyalty to a robust democracy that values differences, seeks input, and collectively works to provide the best opportunities for the well-being of people living here. On the other, there is the less complex loyalty to a particular party winning at any cost, regardless of harm done in the process. Loyalty to a particular party without consideration of loyalty to a robust and fair democracy leads to intense polarization where loyalty is enacted by blanket dismissal or attacks of people in different parties or the parties themselves. This distinction is reminiscent of Royce's distinction between emphasizing fair play versus winning at any cost.[44] Royce suggests that coaches who train young athletes to win at any cost as opposed to engage in fair play on the field with respect for their opponents do the young people harm. How are young people in the United States learning to engage with others from different backgrounds, different viewpoints, and different needs, developing loyalty to a robust and just democracy that requires the long-haul work of engagement and participation? While exceptions exist, we would argue that young people, especially young people in the current political landscape, are more often socialized into and exposed to pathways that lead to loyalty to a party at any cost over loyalty to a robust democracy.[45] The

[44] Royce 1908.
[45] See Hess and McAvoy 2005 for a discussion on navigating political issues in classrooms.

political landscape has become so contentious and party-focused that many schools avoid classroom topics and conversations that may be construed as political, which hampers the development of loyalty to a robust democracy and diminishes how "freely chosen" a young person's loyalty actually is. In the current context, it is imperative to have spaces where young people can practice democracy and develop a sense of loyalty to a robust and just democracy.

Conclusions

In this chapter we have traced the long and manifold developmental tasks through which a dependent child matures into an autonomous adult capable of loyalty to a cause. Throughout we have emphasized the importance of relationships, with persons and groups, that provide a sense of belonging and a set of values and beliefs that ground the young person. Insofar as loyalty to a cause must be self-determined and intelligently chosen, the child must have ample opportunities for exploration, creative expression, and critical reflection. Insofar as loyalty demands self-sacrifice, self-transcending values that direct attention to and responsibility for the needs of others must guide the child's development. Relationships with families, friends, classmates, and teammates lay the foundations in which a young person learns to balance autonomy and solidarity with a community of fellows. It is in adolescence and young adulthood when the capacities to be loyal to a cause reach fruition. It is then that a person is capable of determining that a cause is good, not just for herself, but for humanity. At this time of life when one takes stock of the world and one's place in it, linking one's own well-being with that of a larger community by identifying oneself with a cause has the effect of enlarging one's life and providing a direction for the future.[46]

[46] Jollimore 2013.

Bibliography

Baumeister, Roy, and Mark Leary. "The Need to Belong: Desire for Interpersonal Attachments as a Fundamental Human Motivation." *Psychological Bulletin* 117:3 (1995): 497–529.

Damon, William. *The Path to Purpose: Helping Our Children Find Their Calling in Life*. New York: Free Press, 2008.

Damon, William, Jenni Menton, and Kendall Cotton Bronk. "The Development of Purpose During Adolescence." *Applied Developmental Science* 7:3 (2003):119–128.

Calzada, Esther, Yenny Fernandez, and Dharma Cortes. "Incorporating the Cultural Value of *Respeto* into a Framework of Latino Parenting." *Cultural Diversity and Ethnic Minority Psychology* 16:1 (2010): 77–86.

Erikson, Erik. *Childhood and Society*. New York: W. W. Norton & Co., 1950.

Erikson, Erik. *Insight and Responsibility: Lectures on the Ethical Implications of Psychoanalytic Insight*. New York: W. W. Norton & Co., 1964.

Flanagan, Constance. *Teenage Citizens: The Political Theories of the Young*. Cambridge, MA: Harvard University Press, 2013.

Flanagan, Constance, Sukhdeep Gill, and Leslie Gallay. "Social Participation and Social Trust in Adolescence: The Importance of Heterogeneous Encounters." In *Processes of Community Change and Social Action*, edited by Allen Martin Omoto, 149–166. Mahwah, NJ: Psychology Press, 2005.

Flanagan, Constance, and Michael Stout. "Developmental Patterns of Social Trust between Early and Late Adolescence: Age and School Climate Effects." *Journal of Research on Adolescence* 20:3 (2010): 748–773.

Foust, Mathew. *Loyalty to Loyalty: Josiah Royce and the Genuine Moral Life*. New York: Fordham University Press, 2012.

Fuligni, Andrew, Vivian Tseng, and May Lam. "Attitudes Toward Family Obligations among American Adolescents with Asian, Latin American, and European Backgrounds." *Child Development* 70:4 (1999): 1030–1044.

Hess, Diana, and Paula McAvoy. *The Political Classroom: Evidence and Ethics in Democratic Education*. New York: Routledge, 2005.

Jasko, Katarzyna, Marta Szastok, Joanna Grzymala-Moszczynska, Marta Maj, and Arie Kruglanski. "Rebel with a Cause: Personal Significance from Political Activism Predicts Willingness to Self-Sacrifice." *Journal of Social Issues* 75:1 (2019): 314–349.

Jollimore, Troy. *On Loyalty*. New York: Routledge, 2013.

Marin, Gerardo, Fabio Sabogal, Barbara Vanoss Marin, Regina Otero-Sabogal, and Eliseo Perez-Stable. "Development of a Short Acculturation Scale for Hispanics." *Hispanic Journal of Behavioral Sciences* 9:2 (1987): 183–205.

Michalski, Camilla, Lori Diemert, John Helliwell, Vivek Goel, and Laura Rosella. "Relationship between Sense of Community Belonging and

Self-Rated Health across Life Stages." *SSM-Population Health* 12 (2020), https://www.sciencedirect.com/science/article/pii/S235282732030313X

Misch, Antonia, Harriet Over, and Malinda Carpenter. "Stick with Your Group: Young Children's Attitudes about Group Loyalty." *Journal of Experimental Child Psychology* 126 (2014): 19–36.

Newcomb, Andrew, and Catherine Bagwell. "Children's Friendship Relations: A Meta-analytic Review." *Psychological Bulletin* 117 (1995): 306–347.

Royce, Josiah. *Outlines of Psychology: An Elementary Treatise with Some Practical Applications.* New York: Macmillan, 1903.

Royce, Josiah, *The Philosophy of Loyalty.* New York: Macmillan, 1908.

Royce, Josiah. *Studies of Good and Evil: A Series of Essays upon Problems of Philosophy and of Life.* New York: D. Appleton, 1898.

Royce, Josiah. *The World and the Individual (1899–1901 Gifford Lectures).* New York: Dover, 1959.

Schwartz, Shalom. "Value Priorities and Behavior: Applying a Theory of Integrated Value Systems." In *The Psychology Values: The Ontario Symposium Vol. 8,* edited by Clive Seligman, James Olson, and. Mark Zanna, 1–14. New York: Psychology Press, 2013.

2

Loyalty and the Selves We Are as Friends

Diane Jeske

Introduction

E. M. Forster famously stated, "If I had to choose between betraying my country and betraying my friend, I hope I should have the guts to betray my country." As with most pithy, quotable claims, this assertion about the priority of the virtue of loyalty to a friend over the virtue of loyalty to a country is appropriately general and sweeping. The claim might call forth images of a German citizen during World War II hiding her Jewish friend in her attic in defiance of her country's edicts, or of Huck Finn protecting the escaped slave Jim in the face of laws requiring him to send Jim back into slavery. But just a little more reflection suggests that matters are not as clear-cut as Forster's assertion would have them be. For suppose that your friend is a white supremacist who has been suckered into believing all of the far right-wing conspiracy theories about the deep state and stolen elections. A few days after the storming of the US Capitol, you recognize your friend among the rioters and recall some claims your friend once made to you about assassinating various public officials—claims that, at the time, you took as hyperbole. You have very good reason, then, to believe that your friend poses a threat to elected officials. Should you follow the lead of the courageous German hiding her Jewish friend and of Huck Finn protecting Jim? Or should you alert law enforcement officials to the identity of the

Diane Jeske, *Loyalty and the Selves We Are as Friends* In: *The Virtue of Loyalty*. Edited by: Troy Jollimore, Oxford University Press. © Oxford University Press 2024. DOI: 10.1093/oso/9780197612644.003.0003

individual seen in the photos of the invading mob? Should you prioritize being a loyal friend or being a loyal citizen? Does one or the other of these virtues win out here?

What these contrasting narratives—the German hiding her Jewish friend and Huck Finn, on the one hand, and the friend of the rioting conspiracy fanatic, on the other—suggest is that we really need more information than can be given to us in an admittedly elegant quotation. In a conversation with Forster, we might urge him to provide us with more information about his friend, his country, the nature of his friendship, and the nature of the situation that has led to the need for him to make a choice between betraying either his friend or his country. In the cases of Nazi Germany and the antebellum southern United States, the conflict has been forced upon our protagonists by the highly unjust laws that threaten extreme harm to their friends. In the case of the protagonist who sees her friend in pictures of the mob, the conflict is the result of her friend being a violent nutjob. These certainly seem to be important differences between the cases.

Some philosophers of friendship will insist that my example of the white supremacist member of the mob is misleading. I have described that person as the friend of the protagonist of my example, but, according to those who take a page from Aristotle on friendship, such a morally flawed person cannot be anyone's friend, and, thus, whatever relationship the protagonist stands in to him it is not one of friendship. But this Aristotelian response is unsatisfactory to many of us, especially to those of us who are also morally flawed and have loving relationships with other morally flawed persons. Both we and our friends can find ourselves in trouble resulting from our own (morally and/or rationally) bad choices, and it is perhaps at such times that we most hope that at least our friends will still be there for us.

The question remains, however, how far our loyalty to our friends ought to extend and how it ought to be limited by other legitimate concerns. Good friends, it seems obvious, exhibit the virtue of loyalty to each other. But good citizens also exhibit the virtue of loyalty to country and compatriots. Forster's quotation sets up a conflict between loyalty to country and loyalty to a friend, but in many real-life situations, there are more than two relevant factors. Even with Forster's example, we need to consider that each of us most likely has more than one friend, and that in betraying our country we might thereby betray the interests of our other friends (and family, and colleagues, and neighbors) who are also co-citizens. Life rarely presents us with straightforward either/or choices, and it is simply not clear that being a virtuous and loyal friend is always compatible with being a virtuous and loyal citizen, daughter, sister, and so on.

I do, however, think that Forster's quotation hints at something extremely important, something about why the virtue of loyalty is such an important element in being a good friend: disloyalty to a friend constitutes a loss for *both* friends, a loss that differs in kind from that involved in disloyalty to one's country. The intimacy constitutive of friendship creates a space in which the friends can be open and be their 'authentic' selves together. Within a friendship, we are in fact selves that we can only be within the 'culture' of that relationship, selves that, at least in close friendships, and particularly in long-term friendships, play a crucial role in the narrative that we tell ourselves to make sense of who we are and of the course of our lives. Disloyalty poses a threat to that unique subculture of two, and, thus, to the selves whose identities importantly involve membership in that subculture. In doing so, it disrupts the narrative of our lives and has the potential to cause a permanent injury to the self, an injury that can never fully be healed.[1] Thus, even when disloyalty is the correct choice, perhaps both morally and rationally, not only is the friend who is betrayed harmed, so is the betrayer: both parties suffer an irreparable loss. Having and acting on

---

[1] Kleinig also speaks of betrayal as wounding our identity in his chapter in this volume (Chapter 4, 108).

the dispositions constitutive of the virtue of loyalty, then, seems imperative for preserving that space of friendship in which, and only in which, the selves we are as friends can exist and flourish.

In what follows I will begin by examining the nature of friendship. Then I will consider what is involved in loyalty in order to show why it is peculiarly important in friendship. In the concluding section, I will briefly suggest how disloyalty to a friend can be more costly than disloyalty to one's country. I will also argue, however, that the cost to the self of the betrayal of a friend does not settle how one ought to act in such cases of conflict: what being a virtuous and thus loyal friend demands may not be decisive as to the right action. Rationality and morality may very well be on the side of disloyalty to a friend—in some cases, at any rate, it will be; but the inevitable loss incurred reveals much about both friendship and loyalty.

Friendship, intimacy, and the self

Friendship is a complex relationship between two people that requires, by its very nature, a certain amount of time in order to be established. Friendship necessarily involves a certain history between the two parties, and so the claim that Jerry and Elaine are friends implies that Jerry and Elaine have had certain kinds of interactions in the past. Further, friendship requires a history of more than one or two discrete interactions. In this way, the relationship between friends is different from, say, a contractual relationship. Whereas two people can be contractually bound via a single act, two people cannot be friends via a single act: friendship needs to be established over time through a complex series of interactions.[2] How much time is needed for the establishment of a

---

[2] In this way, then, friendship differs from marriage. In order to be married, all that is required is that the spouses consent to and acknowledge their consent to the terms of the marriage contract.

friendship will vary from case to case, depending on the characters and personalities of the two would-be friends, the circumstances in which they find themselves, and the nature of their interactions.

Obviously, not all histories of interactions can be partly constitutive of a friendship. I have histories of interaction with a lot of people who are strangers (we happen to ride the same bus every day), acquaintances (we live in the same building and greet each other at the mailboxes and the dumpster), colleagues, and even 'enemies' of a type (the neighbor who is constantly complaining about any small noise from my condo or the colleague who makes me want to stuff a rag in her mouth at department meetings). What renders a history of interaction apt for constituting friendship is what it expresses, and what it expresses is dependent upon the attitudes and desires of the persons interacting.

Philosophers of friendship have consistently agreed with Aristotle (and, it seems to me, common sense) that friendship is characterized by mutual attitudes of concern of a certain sort. First, that mutual concern must be of a certain relative strength. After all, I have a certain level of concern even for strangers: if I hear about a fatal accident on the interstate, I feel sorry for the victims and for their families. However, if I were to learn that one of the fatalities was my friend, I would feel sorrow and grief to a far greater extent. Friends care about each other to a greater degree than they care about just any person qua person. The moral saint who loves all equally is no one's friend.

Again following Aristotle, it is taken as a truism in philosophical discussions of friendship that friends care about each other for their own sake. Caring about another for her own sake is contrasted with caring about her only instrumentally, or as a means to an end. Suppose, for example, that Elaine only cares about Jerry because he has a great sense of humor and so is always able to make her laugh. In such a scenario, we might think, Elaine doesn't really care about *Jerry* but only about her own amusement, and Jerry happens to be a means to such amusement. She cares about Jerry's well-being only to the extent that such well-being is a precondition of Jerry's being able to amuse her, and she will cease to care about him when she gets free season tickets to the local comedy club. Friends must intrinsically desire each other's well-being or happiness, where to intrinsically desire something is to desire it as an end.[3] It is not sufficient to act in a certain way toward one's 'friends': one must do so from the correct motives, and from a settled disposition to have such motives. In other words, one must exhibit virtues of care, as it were, with respect to one's friends.

It is important to see that caring about another for her own sake does not imply that one will care about that other person no matter what changes she or you might undergo. Intrinsic desires need be no more permanent than instrumental desires. And it does seem that our intrinsic desire for another's well-being is usually caused and sustained by our beliefs about our friend, although intrinsic concern can in some instances be quite intransigent. But, for many of us, finding out that a friend has betrayed us in some terrible way, or committed a heinous crime, will lead to our concern eroding or disappearing entirely.

It is this differential concern for each other for their own sakes that must be expressed in their history of interaction for that history of interaction to be of the right sort for friendship. A history of using each other for their own ends or of undermining each other's well-being would obviously not be sufficient for friendship. But even merely friendly interactions are not enough, if those friendly interactions do not express a concern for each other that goes beyond what one demonstrates for any person with whom one comes into contact. Such expressions of concern do not need to be of a

---

[3] Matters can get complicated. It may be the case, for example, that what causally sustains Elaine's concern for Jerry for his own sake is her enjoyment of his sense of humor. Thus, when Elaine no longer enjoys Jerry's company, her intrinsic desire for his happiness may gradually dissipate. However, purely instrumental concern can morph into intrinsic concern: interaction guided by self-interested aims can lead to empathy and engagement that then lead to an intrinsic desire for the other's well-being.

grand sort, such as donating a kidney or giving large financial gifts. Many friendships are constructed out of small gestures of caring, such as giving birthday gifts, sharing jokes intended to provide amusement, recommending books and movies that the other will enjoy, cheering each other up on a day-to-day basis, and so on. Friendships often deepen when more significant acts of caring occur, such as when one friend supports another through the grief of losing a parent. But the groundwork for those grand gestures of care is laid in the small daily acts of care that are the bread and butter of most friendships.

It is important that friends not only interact with each other, but that they *want* to be together, to share their lives and experiences with each other. Of course, they need not want to spend every moment of their lives with each other, and there might even be times when they just want to get away from each other.[4] However, differential concern alone, without a desire to be together in some way, is simply not enough for friendship. All of our synonyms for 'friend,' such as 'buddy,' 'pal,' and 'chum,' all convey a sense of the persons involved being companions of some sort. Aristotle claimed that friends wish to live together, and, in ancient Greece, that made sense, in so far as being in each other's physical presence was the only form of companionship available. We now have other ways of 'being together,' and throughout the pandemic many people have relied on technologies such as Zoom to allow them to be in the company of friends. But there are other ways of being companionable. Throughout the pandemic, a close friend and I have texted each other throughout the day, starting with a 'good morning' and ending with a 'good night.' Both of us live alone, and this texting has provided us with a sense of connection to each other, a way to feel that we are not really alone. Our texts vary in content from daily

---

[4] Friends can often differentially annoy each other as well as have differential mutual concern. In part, this is a result of that concern and of mutual dependence and knowledge. My brother, for example, can annoy me like no one else can, in part because he has known me so well for my entire life.

minutiae to greater anxieties and fears. This sharing gives our lives a dimension and meaning that they would not otherwise have.[5]

I have said that friends must have and express a differential concern for each other for the other's own sake. But friends regard each other with more than just concern: they like or love each other. Some such positive attitude seems to underlie friends' desires to share their lives, and it usually plays an important role in initiating and maintaining the interactions that come to constitute a friendship. But not just any sort of positive attitude is relevant to friendship. We may or we may not admire, respect, or be proud of our friends, and we can certainly have such attitudes to people who are not our friends. Of course, we can also like or love people who are not our friends, but these attitudes of liking and loving take on a special role in the context of friendship, as we will see in the later discussion of friendship and loyalty. How to analyze the concept of love and of its relationship to attitudes of liking and of concern is a large task, and not one that I can undertake here, so much of what I say about love and similar attitudes[6] will draw primarily on our intuitive understandings.

The final element of friendship to be considered is mutual understanding or knowledge. It seems obvious that friends have a differential knowledge of each other—that is, a knowledge that goes beyond what just anyone would have. But what amount and kind of knowledge is relevant to friendship is a difficult matter. A bare outline of facts as might appear on a detailed Wikipedia page would not be the kind of knowledge we expect friends to have of one another. And certainly friends don't need to know everything about each other: whether Elaine shares her kinky sexual fantasies and

---

[5] I do not want, however, to downplay the importance of being in the physical presence of a friend. The pandemic has brought home to many of us how nothing can really compensate for the loss of being together in the same physical space. For more on the importance of physical presence to friendship, see Jeske 2019.

[6] Even calling love an attitude is controversial. Are dispositions to behave part of love or merely standard causal results of love? This is just one question about the nature of love that I will be setting aside.

lax flossing routine with Jerry is not determinative of whether they are friends. Elaine may reveal aspects of herself to Jerry that she does not reveal to George and vice versa. What friends reveal to each other is a function of the nature of their relationship and of the types of interactions they choose to express their concern for one another. What they know about each other will sometimes come from express revelations but will also sometimes come via inferences from behavior and context.

It is important to stress that friends will have an understanding of each other that is a result of their interactions and care for each other. Having such an understanding is more than a matter of being able to recite a list of facts. After all, if I had a stalker who was attentive to my daily moves and who sought out all of the information that she could find about me but who never interacted with me, her picture of me would not approach the kind of understanding that a friend has. Friends have a conception of each other that is developed through a lens of care and affection. I don't mean that friends will look at each other through rose-colored glasses, but, rather, that they seek to understand one another because they care about each other and want a fuller picture so as to be able to effectively put that care into action. Through their interactions they are better able to empathize and sympathize with each other. Importantly, friends attempt to understand us in part by taking account of our own self-conceptions. Sometimes friends are well positioned to help us to revise those self-conceptions, to soften our harsh critiques of ourselves, or to provide bracing and constructive corrections. As Dean Cocking and Jeanette Kennett (1998) have persuasively argued, friendship results in each friend having a conception of herself that she would not have had without the friendship. So, in a very real sense, who we are and who we understand ourselves as being is partly constructed via our friendships.

In this section, I have discussed various features that characterize friendships: a mutual differential concern for each other for the other's own sake, a desire to share experiences (to be, in some way, 'companions'), some positive attitude or attitudes such as love, liking, or affection, and a knowledge that constitutes an understanding conception of the other. But friendships will vary in the extent to which they exhibit these features, and I leave it open as to whether a friendship will necessarily include all of them. I am inclined to believe that we cannot offer necessary and sufficient conditions for a relationship's qualifying as a friendship, but can only describe paradigmatic features of a friendship. However, this claim is not important for my discussion of loyalty and friendship, because I will be focusing on clear paradigms of friendship.

Now that we have a robust picture of the nature of friendship, it is time to consider loyalty so that we can then see how significant the virtue of loyalty is to friendship.

Loyalty and its demands

Benedict Arnold was a traitor to the cause of the American colonies during the War of Independence: initially a military hero of the colonial cause, he turned his coat from Continental Army blue to British red and has thus become a byword in America for treachery and disloyalty. But he was not welcomed with open arms by the British, because, as we all know, however much we might be glad of someone's coming to what we view as the right side, no one likes a traitor.[7] We despise persons who lack the virtue of loyalty, it seems, even when we think that being disloyal is somehow the correct choice, even when we think that the object against which the traitor turns is not worthy of loyalty. As we will see in the next section, this is particularly true in the case of disloyalty to friends.

John Kleinig (2014) says that 'loyalty' "is now used . . . to refer to persevering commitment to some associational object" (14), that it

---

[7] See Kleinig's discussion of the "instrumental turncoat" in this volume (Chapter 4, C4P14).

"is a practical or realized disposition to deny oneself for the sake of an associational other" (19). In so far as loyalty is a settled disposition or trait of character, it can be considered a virtue. Associational others, according to Kleinig, are those with whom one in some way identifies oneself (2014, 19–20), those persons or groups of persons that I in some way view as *mine*. They are persons or groups of persons to whom I stand in some sort of special relationship. Standard examples of associational others are my co-citizens, my colleagues, my family members, my teammates, my fellow battalion or squadron members, and my friends. Thus, to be a virtuous citizen, colleague, and so on, is, in part, to have and to act on the virtue of loyalty.

Some of these associational others are such that we have deep and meaningful special relationships with them. In some cases, our emotions and sentiments are deeply implicated, as is true with respect to friends and family and members of an army squadron. But other cases may not involve such deep emotions. Consider a case in which I have been a regular patron of a locally owned donut shop and have come to know the owner, chatting with him when I am there buying donuts. Then a Dunkin Donuts opens, and it is more conveniently located on my way to work and has tastier donuts. I think that this is a case involving a demand for loyalty, and that I have an obligation to continue patronizing the local shop.[8] I would certainly feel guilty if I started regularly buying Dunkin donuts, and I think that the owner of the local shop would be justified in feeling betrayed. This may not be a serious betrayal, but it is a betrayal nonetheless. Importantly, it would reveal something about my character. At the very least, it would provide evidence for the claim that I do not have the virtue of loyalty considered as a global trait, although I might exhibit it in certain contexts: I am not

---

[8] And this obligation is in addition, it seems, to any I might regard myself as having to support local business.

steadfast in my choices and commitments, and will forgo them for the slightest benefit to myself.

Importantly, loyalty to another person or persons need not involve the judgment that the object of one's loyalty is in some way superior to other potential objects of such loyalty (see Oldenquist 1982, 192 and Ewin 1992, 406). Many Americans, however, have thought that loyalty to their country requires believing that the United States is the greatest country that exists or has ever existed. I do not, however, think that this is right. I can have a 'persevering commitment' to my country while yet believing that it is flawed, perhaps even deeply flawed. In such a case, my disposition to make sacrifices on behalf of my country might take the form of attempting to remedy its flaws, perhaps by aiming at ensuring that more just policies are enacted.[9] To return to my simple example of the donut shop: I can be loyal to my regular donut shop even while acknowledging that Dunkin has better donuts at a better price. In the case of friendship, surely we can be loyal without thinking a friend is the greatest friend ever: after all, not all of our friends are our 'besties,' and we may not even have a best one of our friends. Something or someone can matter deeply to me without my believing that anyone who does not value it or them as highly as me is somehow making a mistake.

Ewin quite rightly says that "the loyal person sticks in there in the bad times as well" as the good (1992, 411). For example, the US citizen who moves to Canada and applies for Canadian citizenship during the Trump administration because she often vacations in Europe and thinks that Europeans will treat her better if she is not associated with Trump in any way is clearly being disloyal: she is motivated by a desire to avoid a certain image in the eyes of others, and she allows that motivation to override any commitment to

---

[9] Does this form of loyalty to country deserve the name of 'patriotism'? This is a conceptual issue with which I am not going to engage. See Keller 2005 for discussion of such issues.

improving her country.[10] The paradigm of loyalty to a sports team is the Chicago Cubs fan, who stands by a losing team season after season. As Cohen says, "[t]he loyal friend [or American or Cubs fan] is not vigilant for better options" (2003, 321). These examples reveal not only the ways in which loyal citizens or fans are not fair-weather fans or citizens, but also something about how they view their objects of loyalty: they cannot easily disassociate from them without some loss to their sense of who they are. In fact, we might think that to actually have the virtue of loyalty, one must see oneself not only as committed to the object of one's loyalty but also see the object of loyalty as bound up with one's conception of oneself.

This loss of a sense of self is crucial. In recent years it has become familiar to see philosophers claim that we are partially constituted by our relationships.[11] Those who make this claim sometimes seem to mean it in the strong, metaphysical sense—that is, that we would literally not be the same people if we did not have the relationships that we do.[12] I do not think that such a claim is intelligible. However, it is certainly true that our relationships shape the kinds of people we are and the way that we conceive of ourselves. And those relationships in which we seem to owe the other the strongest loyalty are also the ones in which our self-conceptions are the most implicated. My sense of who I am crucially involves descriptions that tie me to certain others in special ways: I am an American, I am a philosophy professor, I am a daughter, I am a friend. To betray my country, my colleagues, my family, or my friends would require a radical reconceptualization of my self-understanding. In an article

---

[10] This is clearly a case that involves what Kleinig calls a 'corrupt motivation,' in so far as this American-turned-Canadian clearly acts in a purely self-serving way (this volume, Chapter 4, C4P392).

[11] This claim formed the basis for some communitarian political philosophy, as in the work of Michael Sandel.

[12] Or at least not those relationships which they regard as identity-constituting. I assume that they would think that I could still be metaphysically the same person even if I had always purchased my donuts at Dunkin.

on friendship with animals, Fröding and Peterson claim that "we must maintain our friendships so as not to lose track of ourselves" (2011, 60). The same can be said of other special relationships such as those to colleagues and co-citizens.

This is not to say that it is always a bad thing to force ourselves to reorient our self-understandings. If one's political party has shown itself to be willing to support a demagogue, then it might be a good thing to realign oneself politically. If one's partner is abusive, then it might be a good thing to forsake that partner and one's relationship to her. Nonetheless, such abandonment of one's previous commitments will be painful and, at least temporarily, psychologically disorienting. As I will show in the next section, this is true in cases of friendship in a particularly poignant and potentially devastating way.

But what does loyalty to some 'associational other' demand of us? Ladd seems quite right in saying that loyalty is not a matter of "mere blind obedience to every wish of the person who is the object of loyalty" (quoted by Ewin 1992, 404). If my friend and I are at a party and she wants me to do cocaine with her, it does not seem that I am being disloyal if I decline, no matter how much she wants me to join her. In fact, it seems that loyalty to my friend might require that I try to dissuade her from doing what I regard as foolish and potentially dangerous. But if she ignores my counsel and decides to try cocaine, loyalty would seem to demand that I stay by her side and make sure that she makes it home from the party safely. So it might seem that a loyal friend is one that is committed to her friend's well-being and makes decisions from the perspective of that commitment.

We all know, however, that how we conceive of a friend's well-being may not match the way in which the friend conceives of her well-being. It is also true that a friend may herself prioritize someone else's interests, such as those of her child or lover, above her own. In such cases, it becomes even more difficult to determine what loyalty to the friend demands. Should I make my decisions based on my friend's beliefs about what it is for her to live a good life, even if I think she has radically mistaken beliefs? Or should I act on what I sincerely believe is best for her even if she will resent my interference, interference which she regards as misguided, even if well-intentioned? Should I be willing to focus on persons other than my friend if that matches my friend's own priorities? These are difficult questions that I am going to set aside.[13]

Difficult situations will inevitably arise when a friend is making choices that one regards as bad for her long-term well-being. Does loyalty demand that one support the friend in her harmful choices or does it require interference? In situations such as this, loyalty to a friend seems quite different from loyalty to one's country. If the United States is enacting unjust or misguided policies, it seems that the loyal citizen is allowed and, I would argue, required, to intervene in an attempt to change those policies. But friends, unlike countries, are agents with wills of their own, and, arguably, for agents of that sort, making their own choices is part of their good. However, it does seem that it is a prerogative of friendship that friends have greater paternalistic license with respect to each other than do other persons. (See Fox 1993 and Chan 2000 for further discussion of paternalism in close personal relationships.) Friends are intimate with each other, and such intimacy requires a certain degree of shared decision-making, and a certain ceding of the range of one's independence: one is answerable to one's friends to a greater extent than one is to other persons. After one does something wrong or foolish, a friend is required to have a good answer to the question, "Why didn't you stop me?" in situations where other persons are allowed to merely shrug and throw up their hands. The good of friends is interwoven, and so it is inappropriate for someone who is making seriously bad choices to say to her friend, "What business is it of yours?" When people

---

[13] See Daniel Koltonski 2023 for an overview of these issues.

are friends, the other's well-being is peculiarly and deeply their business.

I am not going to attempt to spell out what the demands of loyalty to friends are, in part because what is demanded will be a function of the nature of the particular friendship. I agree with Kleinig, though, that "[n]ot every associative obligation will be an obligation of loyalty. . . . Obligations of loyalty have as their social context an environment in which parties to the association are likely to encounter internal or external inducements to endanger or harm interests that are integral to the association and whose resistance will be costly" (2014, 24). The paradigm case of a demand of loyalty to a friend would be where one refuses to divulge something a friend has told one in confidence but which is such that only by divulging it can one avoid a harm or secure a benefit to oneself. A paradigmatic case of disloyalty would be one in which, in virtue of one's special insights into a friend's nature, one manipulates a friend into doing something that one wants her to do (see Tsai [2016] for how intimacy makes people vulnerable to exploitation).

The cases in the previous paragraph involve a conflict between the needs of the friend and of the friendship with one's self-interest (as conceived independently of the friendship). But protecting a friend and one's friendship with her can also conflict with one's reasons to promote the greater good, because, of course, the problems of two people "don't amount to a hill of beans in this crazy world," in the immortal words of Rick in *Casablanca*. Suppose, then, that I use my insight into my friend's character in order to manipulate her into undertaking a very risky assignment for the resistance for which she is peculiarly well suited and which, if successful, will result in many lives being saved. If my reason to promote the greater good outweighs my reason of loyalty to my friend, then, Kleinig claims, I am not being disloyal to my friend when I get her to undertake the mission. According to him, "[d]isloyal conduct is constituted by deviation of a more mundane kind—when some form of narrow self-interest, self-advancement, or self-assertion motivates the departure" (2014, 25). But surely if I reveal a friend's confidence not for my own self-interest but for the rather minor interest of a third party, I am still being disloyal to my friend. Admittedly, in such a case, my balance of reasons supports being loyal to my friend, where it does not do so in the case of the resistance mission. But my reasons of self-interest can also potentially outweigh my reasons to be loyal to a friend: perhaps I stand to achieve my lifelong ambition by revealing some minor secret told to me by my friend. I think that in the case of manipulating my friend into undertaking the covert resistance mission, I have betrayed her, but I was justified in doing so. Similarly, I think that I can be justified in betraying my friend for some sufficiently large benefit to myself. Where Kleinig claims that "[t]here are limits to what loyalty can demand" (2014, 25), I think that it is, rather, that there are limits to the extent to which we are justified in meeting the demands of loyalty.[14] When I tell the police where to find my Capitol storming friend, I have done what I ought to do, but it remains the case that I have betrayed my friend. What it is to be a virtuous friend is determined by the nature of the friendship and of the needs of the friend. The wider world, however, forces us to consider factors beyond our friendships and our friends, so acting on the virtues of a friend is not always overall permissible. But in such cases, we have still failed qua friends and failed to exhibit the virtue of loyalty to the friend.

And such betrayals come with a cost, even when they are justified betrayals. The nature of friendship makes disloyalty to a friend particularly poignant and difficult, as we will now see.

---

[14] In practice, this difference may not amount to much, in the sense that Kleinig and I might agree about what an agent ought to do in various situations. The only difference is that in some situations, Kleinig will say that the agent was not being disloyal in virtue of her action being justified, whereas I will say that the agent was justified in being disloyal.

Friendship and betrayal

Friendship is characterized by the intimacy between the parties. Friends have special knowledge of each other, a history of concerned interaction, mutual attitudes of affection and concern, and a desire to be 'companions' in some sense. Being intimate with someone in this sense renders one vulnerable: in opening oneself up to another, one allows that other access to one's desires, temptations, fantasies, and weaknesses. These aspects of oneself that one usually strives to keep hidden render one peculiarly susceptible to manipulation and exploitation (see Tsai 2016). This is especially true when one's most tender emotions are implicated: friends know how to play not only upon knowledge of us that most people do not have, but they can do so knowing that the other cares about and loves her, and such care and love can be manipulated. Kant warned that "it is very unwise to place ourselves in a friend's hands completely, to tell him all the secrets which might detract from our welfare if he became our enemy and spread them abroad," or "who might be capable of sending us to the gallows in a moment of passion" (1930/ 1963, 208). Friendship requires trust both to be developed and to be maintained. This kind of vulnerability to manipulation and unwanted revelation of private aspects of oneself is certainly an important part of what makes loyalty in friendship so important. However, I am going to focus on a different aspect of friendship and why it renders betrayal within that relationship so serious.

Each of our friendships constitutes a different realm in which we move. As I said earlier, our friendships play an important role in creating our understandings of who we are and also in creating who we in fact are. It is commonplace but very significant that we often say of our time with a close friend, "I can just be myself." But, importantly, we can sincerely and truthfully make that claim about our time with multiple friends, even though who we are with each friend is most likely different. I think that I can just be myself with each of my two closest friends, but it is nonetheless the case that who I am with each is not the same. Who I am with a friend is not some fact independent of our relationship, where that relationship involves both a history of interaction and current attitudes and dispositions. So it is not as though there is some pre-friendship 'authentic' self that is somehow elicited in the context of a good friendship: the self that I can be when with a friend is a self partially constructed by the friendship.

And this is often an important difference between well-functioning and dysfunctional friendships. In the former, we can own the selves that are constructed through the relationship, while in the latter, the selves that are created can feel confining and inhibiting. It is rather like the distinction between a perfectly tailored set of clothes and ill-fitting hand-me-downs: the former allow us to move in natural ways and flatter us, while the latter are either constricting or we feel lost in them. After all, we do not come to friendships without a self. In fact, it is not uncommon for us to say of first meetings with those who eventually become good friends, "I felt like I could be myself right from the beginning." We often mean that we felt that we could be open, act naturally, identify with what the other was saying and recognize reciprocal identification, and felt a sense of trust that opened the door to a deepening intimacy. And as that intimacy deepens, the selves that were brought into the friendship develop and change in response to the interactions between the friends.

Think about how it can be awkward for one to bring together two of one's friends that have not previously met or who do not know each other well. In such situations, I can feel as though I am acting: all of the naturalness and sense of authenticity that I have in interactions with each friend one-on-one dissipates. In trying to be the self that I am with each friend while in the presence of the other creates a sense of performance, as though I am trying to play two characters at once. In a very real sense, in such encounters, one is trying to exist in two private spaces at the same time, or is trying to layer a new third private space on top of the other two. In either case, this is not an easy feat. Sometimes the two friends gel and that third private space becomes reality, but that cannot always be achieved.

There is another way to think about the private space of friendship. My friend with whom I have texted throughout the pandemic has been my friend for over thirty years. Given our long-standing friendship and our unique knowledge of one another, we have a shared language and imagery that we can use to share our lives with one another, and thus can communicate in ways that we cannot with others. In this sense and others, friendships constitute subcultures with two members. Subcultures have unique histories, identities, values and norms, traditions, and so on. And close friendships, especially those that are long-standing, have all of these elements. We have already seen the important role that history plays in creating affection and knowledge. Friends also have expectations, both derived from the larger culture and unique to themselves, the result of negotiation, both explicit and tacit, over the years. They have shared references and inside jokes that will simply be meaningless or totally not funny to outsiders. In an important sense, then, they have unique identities within the friendship, just as people understand themselves as members of ethnic, religious, or shared-interest subcultures. We can express ourselves within the friendship in ways that we cannot express ourselves outside of the friendship. Thus, the virtues appropriate to a friend are in part a function of that particular friendship, its history and norms. As Simon Keller (2023) argues, what it is to be a good friend is not something that can be determined independently of the particular people and the particularities of their relationship.[15]

The devastation wrought in one's life by the loss of a good friend poignantly illustrates the nature of such subcultures. I was very close to my mother and considered her to be my best friend. I lost

---

[15] Keller argues that this shows that being a good friend is not a virtue. Because I have not here analyzed the concept of a virtue, I will not address that part of his argument.

her quite suddenly in 2018, as she died just one week after a diagnosis of ovarian cancer. One of the most painful aspects of my grief has been the way in which my life feels truncated. In long-term friendships, in particular those we develop with our parents, we share imagery, language, rituals, and traditions that incorporate and draw upon experiences over a long course of our life. That friend has seen us grow and develop, and, in the case of parents, that growth and development has taken us from children to young adults to middle-aged adults. The self that we are with such long-term friends draws upon every stage of our lives, and so helps us to understand the narrative of our lives, to make sense of how we have gotten to where we are. When we lose such a long-term friend, that unique space of our subculture is no longer available to us, and so we can no longer be the self that we were when with that friend. That is a devastating loss that leaves a permanent scar on the self. This is why friends and friendships are irreplaceable. As I stressed in the discussion of the nature of friendship, friendship cannot occur at a moment; it is a relationship that essentially involves a history of interaction that is expressive of concern. And the special knowledge involved in friendship is inextricably entwined with that interaction, not something that can be relayed independently of the experiences involved.

I certainly do not intend to paint a portrait of the space in our lives created by friendship that casts it in a permanent rosy glow. Inevitably in long-term friendships, the interactions will include conflict, arguments, hurt feelings, renegotiations of expectations, and temporary withdrawals. But the persistence of the relationship and of the mutual differential concern through the ups and downs, the periods of lesser and of greater closeness, and the perceived slights and neglect makes the sense of security that friends have with one another that much stronger. It creates an assured reliance on that private space and culture created by the friendship, and a sense that the self that has been created by the friendship and that lives in that space and identifies with that culture is safe and is a permanent part of one that is deeply cherished and beloved by the other party to the relationship.

I think that it is probably quite clear at this point why the virtue of loyalty, that "persevering commitment" in Kleinig's words, is so important when the "associational other" is a friend. In being loyal to a friend, we are acting to protect not only the friend's well-being as understood independently of us and of our friendship, but we are also, and perhaps most importantly, acting to protect that part of the friend that relies on the private space and culture created by our friendship. By consistently exhibiting loyalty, by instantiating that virtue, we create in our friend a trust that our private space will always be available to her. In taking advantage, say, of knowledge of my friend in order to manipulate her into achieving a goal I have, be it trivial or significant, I have violated that private space, disrupted the security of our shared culture, and quite literally attacked the self that she is as a result of and within the friendship. This is why grief is appropriate and common both when a friend dies and when a friend engages in an act of betrayal. The death of a friend causes a permanent loss of the space in which we can be the self we are within that friendship, while betrayal puts it under threat and renders it unsafe. And, of course, betrayal has these negative effects not only on the one betrayed but on the one who is disloyal. That shared private space and culture created by friendship depends on both friends for its existence, and its loss or a threat to it is a loss or a threat to both parties.

Recall that long-term friends play a key role in our construction of the narrative of our lives. Betrayal by a friend, if it is of a serious nature, will force a reevaluation of that narrative in so far as it forces a reevaluation of the meaning of our interactions with the friend. Given that one had understood the self that one is in the friendship as safe, cherished, and beloved in the space of the friendship, reevaluating the relationship is inevitably going to be painful. And the self of the friendship can only be understood in relation to the other, so reinterpretation of the relationship forces one to rethink who the self of the friendship is. At least with grief over the loss of a loved one to death, one can retain one's understanding of the self that was constructed by the friendship. But with betrayal, the grief involves a loss of the past as well as a loss of the future. Just as a first encounter with a person is only the start of a friendship if certain kinds of later interactions occur, so the nature of a friendship might only be determined by how it ends or how the parties treat each other at some later time. Thus, when one is betrayed by a friend (or when one feels forced to betray a friend), one will inevitably reinterpret past interactions in light of that betrayal. Friendships, perhaps, are organic wholes, such that their value is not merely the sum of the value of their parts: when they end via betrayal, the value of what has gone before may no longer add up in the way that it did before.

Conclusion: damned if you do, damned if you don't

To conclude, let's return to Forster's conflict of loyalties, where one must choose between betrayal of one's country and betrayal of one's friend. Of course, there are many permutations of such a choice, some of which involve one's country being unjust (one is in Nazi Germany and one's friend is Jewish, one is Huck Finn and one's friend Jim is a runaway slave), some of which involve one's friend being immoral (one's friend is a conspiracy theorist who took part in the storming of the Capitol), and others involve both or neither of one's friend and one's country being unjust or immoral. But I want to consider a case where, it seems to me, the balance of your reasons supports betraying your friend: all things considered, you ought to be disloyal to your friend. So let's return to the case of the friend whom you spot in pictures of the Capitol being stormed. You recall claims that the friend made about killing various politicians, claims that, at the time, you wrote off as being in jest. You have watched your friend gradually being seduced by conspiracy theories about the deep state, with such seduction crystallizing with propaganda regarding massive fraud in the 2020 presidential election. This radicalization of your friend is fairly recent relative to the thirty plus years in which you have been friends, and, in recent years, you have steered away from discussing politics in order to avoid conflict. But now you cannot avoid facing the fact that your friend has become dangerous and that no amount of rational argument is going to convince her that her beliefs are propaganda-generated fantasy. So you alert the FBI to the identity of the individual in the photos of the mob.

As I said, I think that, in this case, in betraying your friend, you have done what you ought to do: reason here supports disloyalty to your friend. But you will never be the same after this action, not just because of your inevitable feelings of guilt, resentment, and self-doubt. In an important sense, you have to rethink who you now are, because for the past thirty odd years, you have been Harry's friend, and an important part of your self has been created by and is called forth in the private space of your friendship with Harry. All of the trust and care that has been devoted to creating and maintaining that space and culture where the two selves involved in the friendship can flourish has led to a situation where you have taken advantage of Harry's openness and vulnerability to you to promote aims, worthy that they are, that he does not share with you. You each cherished and loved the other, and crafted your interactions to express those mutual attitudes. And it all culminated in your exploiting that achievement of loving intimacy to take action that will ruin Harry's life.

Both you and Harry will inevitably have to deal with the injury to your identities caused by the loss of the friend and of the friendship. As I said in the previous section, this kind of grief, unlike the grief caused by death, forces us to reshape not only our futures but also our pasts. We cannot simply carry forward the idea of the friendship as it was, somehow separated from the betrayal that ended it.

We have to reevaluate that part of us that was created and nurtured by the friendship, and try to understand the narrative of our lives now involving this abrupt ending. Importantly, we simply no longer have the space to be the selves that we were with each other. We have lost our membership in that subculture of two, and so have lost that part of our identities.

This is not the case with betrayal of one's country. I certainly do not want to minimize the role that our citizenship can play in our lives and how wrenching being disloyal to one's country can be, even when your country is unjust, as in the case of Nazi Germany or the antebellum United States. But with friendship, the dislocation caused by disloyalty is a dislocation of the self that is a unique creation of the two people involved. It is the loss of a private space and culture where one is cherished as the unique individual that one is, where one is understood in a unique way as a result of a history that can never be replicated.[16]

When one is disloyal to one's country, in most cases, the country will continue to exist, and one can hope to at some point once again become a loyal citizen. But disloyalty to a friend, even when justified, does not allow for such comfort. The friendship just is the intimacy between two people, and threatening the private space of that intimacy is to threaten the friendship, no matter what the basis or justification of that threat might be. And any such threat is a threat to an aspect of the self that cannot be replaced or recreated. Disloyalty to a friend will always involve a cost and it is cost to which grief is the only apt response, because it is a cost for which there is no compensation.[17]

---

[16] Kleinig (Chapter 4, C4P31) discusses Judith Shklar's view that desertion is the crucial aspect of betrayal. If this is so, then in friendship, the desertion is of a particular person rather than of a group of which a particular person may be a member. Such a personal desertion is inevitably going to be felt as more deeply destructive of one's sense of self, in so far as one's whole self, rather than merely an aspect of it, is implicated.

[17] I would like to thank Richard Fumerton, Tracy Isaacs, Troy Jollimore, and the audience of a Zoom colloquium organized by the Center for Advanced Studies, LMU, Munich, in July 2021, for helpful comments on earlier versions of this chapter.

Bibliography

Chan, Sin Yee. "Paternalistic Wife? Paternalistic Stranger?" *Social Theory and Practice* 26:1 (2000): 85–102.

Cocking, Dean, and Jeanette Kennett. "Friendship and the Self." *Ethics* 108:3 (1998): 502–527.

Cohen, Andrew. "Examining the Bonds and Bounds of Friendship." *Dialogue* 42:2 (2003): 321–344.

Ewin, R. E. "Loyalty and Virtues." *The Philosophical Quarterly* 42:169 (1992): 403–419.

Fox, Ellen. "Paternalism and Friendship." *Canadian Journal of Philosophy* 23:4 (1993): 575–594.

Fröding, Barbro, and Martin Peterson. "Animal Ethics Based on Friendship." *Journal of Animal Ethics* 1:1 (2011): 58–69.

Jeske, Diane. *Friendship and Social Media: A Philosophical Exploration.* New York: Routledge, 2019.

Kant, Immanuel. *Lectures on Ethics.* Translated by L. Infield. Indianapolis: Hackett, 1930/1963.

Keller, Simon. "Are You a Good Friend?" In *The Routledge Handbook of the Philosophy of Friendship*, edited by Diane Jeske, 301–310. New York: Routledge, 2023.

Keller, Simon. "Patriotism as Bad Faith." *Ethics* 115:3 (2005): 563–592.

Kleinig, John. *On Loyalty and Loyalties: The Contours of a Problematic Virtue.* New York: Oxford University Press, 2014.

Koltonski, Daniel. "Friendship and Practical Reason." In *The Routledge Handbook of the Philosophy of Friendship*, edited by Diane Jeske, 223–232. New York: Routledge, 2023.

Oldenquist, Andrew. "Loyalties." *The Journal of Philosophy* 79:4 (1982): 173–193.

Tsai, George. "Vulnerability in Intimate Relationships." *The Southern Journal of Philosophy* 54, Spindel Supplement (2016): 166–182.

3

Loyalty Dilemmas

Margaret Gilbert

Introduction

Like love, loyalty may be blind—impervious—to important aspects of its object or its circumstances. So, when is loyalty virtuous, and when is it not? In this essay I approach this question from a particular angle. I focus on what I refer to as *loyalty dilemmas*.

In terms that will be explained, I shall assume that the primary site of loyalty is a relationship, not necessarily personal, of two or more people, and that to act loyally is to fulfill the applicable *role requirements* of a relationship to which one is a party. That the primary site of loyalty is a relationship is generally acknowledged in discussions of the subject.[1] In referring to a relationship between "two or more people," I have in mind two or more human beings, and my focal example will be of this sort. I do not mean to deny that social groups or collectives can have loyalty obligations or that they can act so to fulfill them.

I shall assume, further, that—qua party to the relationship in question—one is in some sense *obligated* to fulfill these requirements. I refer to the relevant obligations as one's *loyalty obligations*.[2] So, more fully, *loyal action* is a matter of fulfilling one's loyalty obligations.

---

[1] See, e.g., Fletcher 1993, 5; Jollimore 2013, x, xvii, referring to "a community to which one belongs" in addition to "personal relationships"; Kleinig 2014, 2, referring to "associational contexts."

[2] Cf. Jollimore 2013, 31.

Margaret Gilbert, *Loyalty Dilemmas* In: *The Virtue of Loyalty*. Edited by: Troy Jollimore, Oxford University Press. © Oxford University Press 2024. DOI: 10.1093/oso/9780197612644.003.0004

One faces a loyalty dilemma in my sense when there is a clash between one's loyalty obligations such that the fulfillment of one excludes the fulfilment of at least one other. I shall focus on the case where two of one's loyalty obligation's clash.

It may be assumed that the obligations that clash in loyalty dilemmas are moral requirements. I call this the *moral requirement assumption*. There are two possible versions of this assumption. First, it may be understood that each of the clashing moral requirements is an *all-things-considered* moral requirement.[3] Second, it may be understood that each of the clashing requirements is a moral requirement *all else being equal*.

I shall argue that there is a way of understanding loyalty dilemmas that does not appeal to moral requirements of either kind. It invokes obligations of a different sort. I argue, further, that loyalty obligations are best understood as obligations of that sort. Taking this point on board, I consider its implications for the question: when is an act of loyalty virtuous?

To communicate the gist of my argument in the space available, I must pass relatively quickly over some of the relevant ideas. Where appropriate I refer the reader to fuller discussions in the footnotes.

Preliminaries

A focus on friendship

It is generally agreed that friendship is a primary site for loyalty.[4] Another central case is citizenship. I shall initially focus on friendship, saying something about citizenship toward the end of my discussion. My concern in both cases is not so much with the nature of

---

[3] As I indicate in due course, I find it hard to contemplate this as a real possibility, but it has been mooted.

[4] See, e.g., Kleinig 2014, 147: "friendship, the quintessential locus for loyalty."

the relationship in question as with the kind of obligation a person takes on as a result of being someone's friend, or being a citizen.

i. Role requirements

Without reference to any particular friendship, one might say: "A friend doesn't speak ill of a friend behind their back." Or, more positively, "Friends help friends in need." I take such statements to specify the *role requirements* of friendship. I take such requirements to be institutional requirements, the institution in question being that of friendship.[5]

There can, of course, be disputes as to what the role requirements of friendship are. Further, distinctions have been made between friends generally and "good" or "close" friends, and between good or close friends and "best" friends. I shall focus on friendship as such and make what I take to be plausible assumptions about the content of some of the role requirements of friendship. The general thrust of my discussion will not be affected should someone wish to dispute these particular assumptions.

There may be relationships that correspond to no established type and for which there are no generally recognized role requirements. Consider, for instance, the relationship referred to when someone says, "We're not exactly friends, but we're not just acquaintances either." With respect to questions about loyalty, I believe such relationships can be treated along the lines I shall indicate for those with established role requirements. To keep things simple here, I set them aside.

ii. Those who are friends are in some sense obligated to fulfill the role requirements of friendship

---

[5] I take institutions generally to be systems of rules that are blueprints for behavior. For further discussion, see Gilbert 2018a, 30–36, and Chapter 13.

Suppose that—as they both understand—Rob and Rena are friends. I take it that, absent special background understandings, both Rena and Rob are in some sense *obligated* to fulfill the role requirements of friendship.[6] To be clear, it is not just that the role requirements of friendship *apply to* both Rena and Rob by virtue of their friendship. Rather, each is obligated in some sense to fulfill these requirements.

In what sense are they so obligated? To answer this question, it will be helpful to focus on loyalty dilemmas.

Loyalty dilemmas

Consider the following case, which I shall refer to as AFFAIR:

> Jane's friend Tanya tells her that she is having an affair with Phyllis's husband, Robert. Jane understands that this is told to her in confidence, and believes that, as Tanya's friend, she has an obligation to keep Tanya's confidences to herself. However, Jane and Phyllis are friends, and Jane believes that, as Phyllis's friend, she has an obligation to share with her any information that, she knows, would be of the greatest importance to Phyllis. In sum, Jane understands herself to have two loyalty obligations such that she cannot fulfill each one. In other words, she understands herself to face a loyalty dilemma.

Perhaps Jane is wrong about what her loyalty obligations are. For present purposes that need not concern us. The critical question is: what precisely do people understand when they understand themselves to face a loyalty dilemma? In particular, what

---

[6] "Absent special background understandings": some self-described friends may have side agreements that allow one or both of them to ignore some of the role requirements of friendship, or that add to these obligations. For present purposes I set such complications aside.

kind of obligations do they take to be in question, implicitly if not explicitly?

Loyalty dilemmas and moral requirements

Are loyalty obligations moral requirements—or, in other terms, moral obligations? As noted earlier, there are two familiar kinds of moral requirement: all-things-considered moral requirements, and moral requirements with a *ceteris paribus* clause.

The moral philosopher W. D. Ross labeled the latter *prima facie* duties.[7] Importantly, he did not regard them as duties *proper*.

Now, it is easy enough to imagine that, on certain grounds, I am morally required to do X, all else being equal, though, on certain other grounds, I am morally required to do something incompatible with X, all else being equal. To find out what, if anything, I am morally required to do *all things considered*, I need to know more.

If there is no final answer—if morality disdains, as it were, to make the choice for me—then, though I may face a difficult if not agonizing choice, I am not faced with a clash of obligations *proper* in the sense of moral requirements all things considered.

Might loyalty dilemmas involve a clash of all-things-considered moral requirements? I find the idea that such a clash is possible hard to accept.

Note that the situation envisaged here is not that, morally speaking, I am morally required, all things considered, *either* to do one thing *or* to do another thing with which it is incompatible and must choose which of these things to do. This may leave me with a difficult choice, but it does not present me with a clash of all-things-considered moral requirements. The situation envisaged here is,

---

[7] Ross 2002, Chapter 2. Nowadays theorists prefer to speak of "pro tanto" duties as opposed to "prima facie" duties, something I take to be a terminological matter, the current preference being based on the concern that "prima facie" means "apparent"—which is not the case in this context.

rather, that I am morally required, *all things considered*, to do one thing, *and* morally required, *all things considered*, to do another thing, when I cannot do both. I am, morally speaking, "damned if I do, and damned if I don't." Or, more poetically, "Which way I fly is Hell."[8]

This is not the place to delve more deeply into the possibility or otherwise of a clash of obligations in the sense of all-things-considered moral requirements. For, as I shall argue, there are reasons not to construe loyalty obligations as moral requirements of either of the kinds just mentioned. Relatedly, there is reason *to* construe loyalty dilemmas in a different way. My argument along these lines will show that one temptation to believe that there are conflicting *all-things-considered* moral requirements goes away.

Loyalty obligations and directed obligations

In AFFAIR, Jane may describe her situation in terms of obligations she has *to* Tanya, on the one hand, and *to* Phyllis, on the other. I call obligations to a person *directed* obligations.[9] I take it, indeed, that in AFFAIR Jane's dilemma involves a conflict of directed obligations. That leads us to the question: what is a directed obligation? And what relation, if any, does directed obligation bear to moral requirement?

Some may think that part of the answer, at least, is obvious. In particular, they may think that—to put it generally—to be subject to a directed obligation is to be subject to a moral requirement which bears a particular relation to the person to whom the

---

[8] Milton 2007, 387. Jollimore appears to envisage this possibility but goes on to envisage something weaker: "no matter what one does *one will have done something morally wrong*, or at the very least morally questionable—something one should feel uneasy if not downright bad about having done" (2013, 33, emphasis mine).

[9] Others have used the adjectives "relational" and "bipolar" in related contexts. "Directed" indicates that, as they would agree, the obligation in question is an obligation "to" the other party or parties.

requirement is directed. The requirement respects, for instance, significant interests of the person in question. Yet there is reason to doubt an "interest theory" account of directed obligations and for doubting, more generally, any account of directed obligations in terms of moral requirements.[10]

In saying this, I am operating with a relatively common understanding of directed obligations generally such that all of the following statements are equivalent to one another in the following sense: they all refer to one and the same relation between X and Y. Those beginning with "X" view the relationship from X's perspective; the others view it from Y's perspective. I italicize the key terms in each statement.

(1) X *is obligated to* Y to phi.
(2) X *owes* Y X's phi-ing.[11]
(3) X *wrongs* Y if X fails to phi.[12]
(4) Y *has a right against* X to X's phi-ing.[13]
(5) Y *has the standing (in the sense of authority) to demand* X's phi-ing.[14]

I take (5) to be the central statement here insofar as it is the least ambiguous of the five, if it is ambiguous at all. In any case I shall interpret the other four by reference to it.

---

[10] The phrase "interest theory" is the standard label for a particular theory of rights of which Raz 1984 offers an influential version. For discussion of the relation of Raz's theory to obligations of the sort on which I shall focus, see Gilbert 2018, Chapter 5.

[11] Jollimore writes: "Like contractual obligations, loyalty obligations are *owed* to particular persons" (2013, 32). Though, as is common, Jollimore writes that loyalty *obligations* are owed, I take it that what is owed, at the end of the day, is one or more *actions* of the obligated person.

[12] Cf. Jollimore, writing of two promises such that if I keep one, I will not be able to keep the other: "the inevitable result is that I wrong someone" (2013, 33). People differ as to what it is to wrong someone. For present purposes I understand it as indicated in the text.

[13] Hohfeld famously supposed that (1) and (4) were equivalent, if "a right" is interpreted in its "strictest sense" (1919/1964, 36).

[14] Cf., e.g., Thomson 1987: "To assert a right is to demand what one has a right to" (2).

Thus, I shall interpret "X is obligated to Y to phi" as referring to the relation that X stands in to Y when Y has the standing to demand X's phi-ing, and similarly for "X owes Y X's phi-ing," and "X wrongs Y if X fails to phi." "Y has a right against Y to X's phi-ing," in its turn, will be interpreted as referring to the relation that Y stands in to X when Y has the standing to demand X's phi-ing.[15]

There are other equivalents that could be listed. The following, in particular, should be noted here:

(6) Y has the standing (in the sense of authority) to rebuke X for not phi-ing if the time for X's phi-ing has passed.

I take it that, except potentially in institutional cases, to issue a rebuke, with the appropriate standing, to someone for not phi-ing is to indicate that the time has passed for an action one had the standing to demand to be performed.[16]

It is now time to return to the question: what kind of obligation is a loyalty obligation, such as the obligation one has as someone's friend to fulfill the role requirements of friendship? There are several reasons for understanding loyalty obligations as directed obligations understood as I have just characterized them.

Perhaps the most significant reason is the prevalence of demands and rebukes in the context of a potential or actual failure to fulfill one's loyalty obligations. If Phyllis somehow learns that Jane knew of her husband's affair with Tanya, and did not tell her of it, she may well confront her with a rebuke like this: "How could you not tell me something touching me so deeply?" She might add: "I thought you were my friend!" Similarly, if Jane tells Phyllis about the affair, and Tanya hears of this, she may well confront Jane in a similar way.

[15] For related discussion, see Gilbert 2018, Chapter 4.

[16] In institutional cases, one's standing to issue a rebuke may not be paired with the standing to issue the corresponding demand, and vice versa. I focus on noninstitutional cases in the text.

Beforehand, Tanya might have demanded of Jane that she keep her news confidential, understanding this as a matter of enforcing an obligation Jane already had. And, referring to her husband, Phyllis might have said to Jane, in a demanding tone, "You would tell me if you heard anything about Bob that I might not know, wouldn't you?"

Even if, in the event, neither Tanya nor Phyllis avails herself of the standing to demand fulfillment of the relevant loyalty obligation, or of the standing to rebuke for nonfulfillment, each will understand that she has these standings, an understanding that might express itself, internally, through a sense of potential or actual betrayal.[17]

Grounding directed obligations: joint commitment

It turns out that it is not easy to understand how any one person accrues the standing to demand an action of another person.[18] That said, there is a general ground of such standing, and hence of directed obligations, which answers well to the idea that there are such obligations in the context of personal relationships. Further, it fits well with the idea that such relationships involve an *association*, an associational *bond*, and so on.

The ground of directed obligation that I have in mind is what I call *joint commitment*. I have written about this at length elsewhere.[19] It must suffice, here, to outline some key points for present purposes.

A *commitment* of the kind at issue here is a *normative* condition directly engendered by the exercise *of one or more human*

---

[17] I take it that contexts for loyalty are also contexts for betrayal. For related discussion see Gilbert 2006, Chapter 8.

[18] The question of how one gains such standing is the central theme of Gilbert 2018.

[19] For longer discussions, see, e.g. Gilbert 2006, Chapter 7; Gilbert 2013; Gilbert 2018, Chapter 8, secs. 2 and 3.

wills. Such *commitments of the will* are of two kinds: personal and joint. In the discussion that follows, I should be understood to be referring to commitments of the will.

First, in my terminology, someone who is subject to a commitment to act in a particular way *has sufficient reason* to act in that way. In other terms, that person *ought* to act in that way, all else being equal. In other terms again: all else being equal, the person in question will make an *error in action* should they fail to act that way.

It is worth emphasizing that when I say that someone *has sufficient reason* to act in some way, I do not mean that they have one or more *reasons* so to act. Thus, I do not think that one can "bootstrap" *reasons* into being by an act of will.[20]

This may seem to leave it unclear how there can be any normativity in the offing—any practical "ought." Evidently, I believe that there can.

Consider the case of a personal decision, which I take to engender a personal commitment. I take it that if I decide to go to the beach tomorrow, I have changed my normative situation at least as follows: unless and until I change my mind, I ought to go to the beach tomorrow, all else being equal. In other terms, I will act in error, all else being equal, should I fail to go to the beach tomorrow.[21]

As with commitments of the will generally, the "ought" and the error in question here is not a specifically moral one: I don't think someone who acts contrary to a prior decision—perhaps having forgotten it—makes a moral mistake just for that reason.

Let me say something about the "all else being equal" clause. I take it that, given a commitment of the kind in question, certain

---

[20] Paragraph added in response to a query from Troy Jollimore.

[21] It has been argued that after I decide to do something, the normative upshot is that I ought to *either* change my mind *or* act on my decision, and that it does not follow from this that I ought to act on my decision, should I not have changed my mind (see Broome 2001). Broome may be right about what follows from what here. It seems to me, however, that the point made in the text holds.

factors that would otherwise argue against acting in the way in question—in particular, the person's inclinations, desires, and self-interest in a narrow sense of the term—are excluded from consideration. Moral considerations, meanwhile, are not so excluded.

Personal commitments are, by definition, commitments of one person by that one person. Let me turn now to *joint* commitments as I understand these.

I take it that one way for two or more people to create a joint commitment is for them to make an agreement.[22] To keep things relatively simple, I will focus on that case.

As I understand it, when two or more people have made an agreement, they are committed *as one*. In other terms, they are committed jointly. *As one*, then, the parties have sufficient reason to act appropriately. I take it that when this is so, each of the individual parties has sufficient reason to pursue, *in conjunction with the others*, fulfillment of the joint commitment. Each, we may say, is then *individually* committed, but the commitment is not a *personal* one in the sense explained earlier.

An important aspect of the parties' situation in this case is that, absent special background understandings between them, no one of them is in a position unilaterally to *rescind* the joint commitment: all of them need to be on board with its rescission. I say more on this point later.

Suppose that Nathan says to his colleague, Clare, "I'm going for a coffee. Want to join me?" and she responds with a confident "Yes." I take them now to be jointly committed to endorse as a body roughly the following plan: they will walk alongside each other to Nathan's intended coffee place, where each will get a coffee.

When I say that they are jointly committed to endorse the plan *as a body*, I mean, roughly, that they are jointly committed to emulate,

---

[22] For further discussion of agreements as joint commitment phenomena, see, e.g., Gilbert 2018, Chapter 9. It is argued there that promises, also, are joint-commitment phenomena.

by virtue of their several actions and utterances, a single endorser of the plan. In other words, they are to speak and act as if they are the representatives of such a single endorser.

By virtue of what are the parties to an agreement committed jointly? I take it that this came about, roughly, by virtue of each one openly expressing his or her readiness to be subject with the other, as one, to the commitment in question.[23]

In this case the open expressions were sufficiently explicit for an agreement between the parties to have been made. It is important to note that this need not always be the case in order that a joint commitment is created.

People can come to understand by processes other than explicit agreements that each has openly made the relevant expression of readiness—so they are jointly committed in the way in question. For instance, suppose that Nathan and Clare made their agreement to go for coffee around 10 a.m. one morning, and the same thing happened the next day. The day after that, as Nathan gets up from his desk at 10 a.m., Clare does likewise and, without explicitly agreeing to do so, they walk in the direction of the coffee place they have previously visited. This continues day after day.

Nathan and Clare have never explicitly agreed regularly to go for coffee at 10 a.m., but at some point they may be comfortable saying "We go for coffee at 10 every morning" to a newcomer, understanding themselves to be jointly committed to endorse as a body the practice of going for coffee then.

---

[23] Less roughly, the open expressions of readiness are *common knowledge* in something like the technical sense of Lewis 1969. I offer related accounts of "individual" and "population" common knowledge in Gilbert 1989, Chapter 4. Importantly, population common knowledge does not require that the parties involved know of each other as individuals as opposed to members of a given population, for example, as those who live on this island. For a review of the considerable literature on common knowledge, see Vanderschraaf and Sillari 2014.

In short, joint commitments can be formed explicitly, via an agreement or related exchange, or tacitly, as in the second example involving Nathan and Clare. They can also be formed through a single exchange, as in the case of Nathan and Clare's agreement, or gradually, as in the case of their gradually evolving practice.

One way in which people may indicate their understanding that a joint commitment is in place is by making related demands and rebukes. I say this because, as I have argued elsewhere, given any joint commitment, the parties have the standing to demand compliance of one another and to rebuke one another for noncompliance.[24]

This is, I think, intuitive, absent any argumentation. Let me elaborate briefly. Should any party to the joint commitment fail to conform to it, or appear to be in danger of doing so, any party is in a position to "call that party to order" qua one who together with the others has laid that particular "order" on each one. In other words, after a failure to conform, each has the standing to rebuke the nonconformist for noncompliance; before that failure, each has the standing to demand compliance.

Assuming, as I shall, that the parties to a joint commitment have the standing to demand compliance, and given the equivalences listed earlier, it follows that the parties to a joint commitment are *obligated to each other* to conform to it.[25]

As I have argued at length elsewhere, there is reason to think that joint commitment is the *only* ground of directed obligations as these have been characterized here.[26] Evidently, if that is right, and loyalty obligations are directed obligations as so characterized, then all loyalty obligations will be grounded in a joint commitment of the relevant parties.

---

[24] See Gilbert 2018, Chapter 8.
[25] See earlier discussion.
[26] See Gilbert 2018, esp. Chapters 5, 11–12.

The directed obligations of joint commitment are context, content, and consequence insensitive

I now focus on some central aspects of the directed obligations of joint commitment. Evidently, to say that the parties to a joint commitment are obligated to each other to conform to it is not to say that they are morally required to conform, all things considered. It is not even to say that they are morally required to conform, all else being equal. They may *be* morally required to conform, all else being equal, but that is not what is being said when it is said that the parties to a joint commitment are, as such, obligated to each other to conform to it.

What is being said is that the parties stand in a certain relation to one another. As we have seen, this relation can be described in different ways. One of these ways is that the parties are obligated to one another to conform to their joint commitment.[27]

Perhaps the most important thing about the directed obligations of joint commitment for present purposes is this. Any joint commitment, *whatever its content, context, or its consequences going forward*, obligates the parties to each other.

It is worth spelling this out. Joint commitments come into being as a result of expressions of (genuine) readiness to bring about a joint commitment in conjunction with the other parties. Such readiness may be present in a variety of contexts, including coercive pressure on one or more of the parties.

Think, for example, of Mack, who proposes marriage to Lily, his pregnant girlfriend, after receiving credible threats of harm

---

[27] Of course, in addition to being obligated to each other to conform to a joint commitment of which they are a party, each party has sufficient reason to promote its fulfillment, in the morally neutral sense that they ought to promote it, all else being equal. If one wants to say that *to have sufficient reason to do something* is, in itself, to have an obligation of sorts—as I am not inclined to do—one must be clear that the obligation in question is not a directed obligation.

from her father should he not propose and, in due course, marry his daughter. His readiness to make this proposal is genuine, given his strong preference to avoid the harm threatened by Lily's father. Given that this is so, if Lily accepts his proposal, Mack will be jointly committed with her to espouse as a body the plan that they will be married. He is then obligated to her through their joint commitment to do his part in carrying out their plan.[28]

Suppose that after a short while—and before the wedding—Mack's circumstances change. He is in no further danger from his prospective father-in-law. It may well be that it is morally permissible for him to refuse to marry Lily, given the coercive circumstances in which his proposal was made. If he does so refuse, however, he will be failing to fulfill his obligation to Lily through their joint commitment, assuming that she has not agreed to its rescission.

Similar things can be said for cases where conformity to a given joint commitment requires one or more of the parties to perform a dastardly deed, or where the consequences of fulfilling a joint commitment, however innocuous in its content, are likely to be dire. In many, if not all, such cases one will be morally required *not* to fulfill one's joint-commitment obligations. One's possession of these obligations, however, will not be affected. Those to whom the obligations are directed will understand that they have not received the actions to which they had a right, and that they have the standing, in the sense of authority, to rebuke one on account of this—though they may not be morally justified in exercising this authority.

Given the foregoing, it makes sense to suggest that the complex of ideas around joint commitment, including the idea of a directed

---

[28] Compare legal regimes in which a contract entered into under duress is not considered void *ab initio*, though it is considered voidable by the petition of the coerced party. I take the thought here to be that when coercion influences the coerced party's decision to enter the contract, that was indeed this party's (possibly quite wise) decision in the circumstances. He was not "rendered witless." See Gilbert 1993 and elsewhere.

obligation as characterized earlier, stands outside what Bernard Williams has referred to as "the morality system" or, more briefly, outside morality strictly speaking.[29] It may well be a more primitive set of ideas than those within morality proper, a precursor perhaps of the latter.[30] Whether or not that is so, it is a set of ideas that is, I believe, a fundamental part of our relations with one another to this day.[31]

Indeed, I find it plausible to propose that many of the situations that have been characterized as "moral dilemmas" in the literature, and in particular those characterized as involving a clash of moral obligations or requirements, are better characterized in other terms. In particular, they are better understood as clashes of obligations of joint commitment—obligations that lack a *ceteris paribus* clause. A standard case in point is the clash between one's promissory obligation to one person and one's conflicting promissory obligation to another.[32] The same is true, I shall argue, of loyalty dilemmas.

Loyalty dilemmas as involving directed obligations of joint commitment

Let me sum up my argument so far. I am assuming that, in a sense I have explained, loyalty is a matter of fulfilling one's *loyalty obligations* with respect to a relationship to which one is a party. *Loyalty dilemmas* occur when someone has two or more loyalty obligations such that she cannot fulfill each one.

The question arises: of what kind are these conflicting *obligations*? An important clue here is that loyalty obligations are

[29] Williams 1965, 175.

[30] For discussions of the relation of morality and joint commitment, see Gilbert 2018a.

[31] This has been a theme of my work since Gilbert 1989. For a recent collection of essays that illustrate this theme, see Gilbert 2013 and Gilbert 2023.

[32] For a joint commitment account of both promises and agreements, see Gilbert 2018b, Chapters 7–9.

directed obligations—obligations to the person to whom one will or will not be loyal.

Having clarified my understanding of such obligations, I invoked the idea of a joint commitment, understood in a way I explained. I briefly argued that any joint commitment grounds directed obligations. I noted, further, that—as I have argued elsewhere—it may well be their only ground.

I now propose that loyalty obligations are obligations of joint commitment. Relatedly, I propose that loyalty dilemmas are constituted by a clash of such obligations. The clashing obligations are obligations *tout court*—they lack a *ceteris paribus* clause.

Importantly, then, this proposal allows that loyalty dilemmas involve a clash of obligations *tout court*, without implying something that is puzzling at least to some: that in one and the same situation, morality can give conflicting *all-things-considered* judgments as to what it requires one to do, resulting in a clash of *all-things-considered* moral requirements.

My proposal does imply that if I choose one horn of a loyalty dilemma, I will default on at least one obligation, failing to give at least one person what I owed her. It supports, then, the idea that a loyalty *dilemma* is aptly so-called.

The case of friendship

Let me now make this proposal more concrete by returning to my focal example, AFFAIR.[33] This involves one person, Jane, and two of her friends, Tanya and Phyllis. Jane has a particular loyalty obligation to Tanya that conflicts with one of her loyalty obligations to Phyllis. These obligations are plausibly construed as obligations grounded in a joint commitment of Jane and Tanya, on the one hand, and a joint commitment of Jane and Phyllis, on the other.

---

[33] For details see the earlier discussion.

It is plausible, indeed, to think of a given friendship as constituted by a joint commitment of the people who are friends. In other words, something like the following *joint-commitment account* of friendship has some plausibility:

> Persons P1 and P2 *are friends* if and only if they are jointly committed to accept as a body that each of them is subject to the role requirements of friendship with respect to the other.

As I understand this account, friends need not employ the concept of friendship. To be friends, they need only to be jointly committed to accept as a body that each of them is subject to what are in fact the role requirements of friendship, not necessarily described by them as such.

Given the joint-commitment account, a particular friendship may arise more or less quickly—one person may even say "Let's be friends!" and the other concur. That said, the process by which people become friends may be both inexplicit and slow, as the necessary understandings are gradually established between them.

The forgoing joint-commitment account focuses on a case in which a given friendship is between two people. The account can easily be rephrased so as to cover cases in which a given friendship is between more than two people. In such cases, the people in question, however many they are, will be jointly committed, as one, in the relevant way.

It is important to emphasize that, as I understand them, one's joint-commitment *obligations* to a particular friend are dependent only on the content of the joint commitment, *without reference to the moral quality of the actions* one is obligated to perform. One may therefore be obligated through a joint commitment to perform an action that would otherwise be morally prohibited.

One can expect, therefore, that on occasion morality will forbid one from fulfilling particular obligations of joint commitment, even when the fact that one has the obligations in question are factored in. I return to this point later.[34]

I should make one final remark about the joint-commitment account of friendship just presented. A significant aspect of joint commitments—as I have noted—is that they are not unilaterally rescindable by a given party, absent special background understandings. This means that for a friendship *properly* to end, the parties must be "on the same page" with respect to its ending. That said, it is not necessary for them to get together and agree to rescind their commitment. Each one's readiness to rescind it can be expressed gradually by virtue of small indications, verbal and otherwise.[35]

Another case: citizenship

Friendship is not the only paradigmatic site of loyalty. Another is citizenship. Can the loyalty of a citizen be understood in terms of the directed obligations of joint commitment? Here is one way of arguing—briefly—that it can.[36]

I start with the general idea of an association or, in other terms, a social group.[37] I take it that social groups come in a variety of types and sizes. Jane and Phyllis may form a two-person group of friends. This is the smallest possible social group, the sociologists' "dyad." At the other end of the spectrum lie political societies. These are likely to include myriad smaller social groups: groups of friends, families, discussion groups, sports teams, labor unions, and so on. Evidently, the members of the larger society—its *citizens*—may not

---

[34] In the section "Loyalty as a virtue," which follows.

[35] For a relatively nuanced discussion of how joint commitments may come to an end, see Gilbert 2006, Chapter 7.

[36] See Gilbert 2006 for related discussion.

[37] The phrase "social group" has been used in broader or at least different senses to the one I use here. In the text I focus on social groups on my understanding of these.

know each other personally or even know of one another as particular individuals.

I have argued elsewhere that social groups, both large and small, are *plural subjects*. A plural subject in my sense is constituted, by definition, by one or more joint commitments of its members.[38] My use of the phrase "plural subject" in this context was intended to allude to the first-person plural pronoun, "we," which I take to refer, in its collective sense, to a number of jointly committed persons of which the speaker is a member.[39]

Evidently, members of any plural subject will have associated obligations of joint commitment to one another. If political societies are plural subjects, then, their citizens, as such, will be obligated to one another in relevant ways.

That people often think of themselves as members of political societies construed as plural subjects is indicated by the use of such phrases as "We, the people of the United States" followed by a verb of action, broadly speaking. Such utterances are generally accepted by those addressed without demur. It is possible, indeed, that it is in large part by engaging in plural subject talk freely and openly that, over time, a number of individuals come together to constitute a plural subject with associated obligations to one another.

Suppose, then, that the members of a political society are jointly committed at least to uphold as a body the political institutions of that society, and hence obligated to one another to do so. These will be their primary loyalty obligations as citizens.

Sometimes fulfillment of a citizen's loyalty obligations, such as the obligation to pay one's taxes, will be easy enough—though there may be self-interested reasons not to fulfill them. Sometimes fulfillment will require great courage, as when one is ordered by the

---

[38] Gilbert 1989, Chapter 4; 1990; 2006; and elsewhere.

[39] Contrary to what some have assumed, my use of the phrase "plural subject" is not intended to imply a center of consciousness distinct from the consciousnesses of the individuals who comprise it. It is intended to indicate that it is a fit referent for the collective "we."

powers-that-be to fight in a war, and following this order means risking one's life.

Sometimes, I take it, citizens will be morally required *not* to fulfill a particular loyalty obligation. For instance, one may have been ordered to fight in an unjust war, and be morally required to resist the draft in morally appropriate ways, irrespective of one's obligations to one's fellow citizens as such.

Loyalty as a virtue

How, if at all, do the considerations herein help one to understand loyalty as a virtue? Clearly, it is important to consider the virtuous way to handle one's loyalty obligations as those have been characterized. Here I make a start on that question.

Conformity to one's loyalty obligations, construed as obligations of joint commitment, is reasonably considered to be virtuous, *all else being equal.* Those who fail to conform to their joint commitments default on their obligations to others and lay themselves open to those others' authoritative rebukes. To that extent they fail to respect those with whom they are jointly committed. To respect those with whom one is jointly committed is not quite to respect them as *persons*, or, to use a phrase from John Rawls, as "free and equal" persons. It is rather to respect them as *associates* or, depending on the case, as *friends, fellow citizens*, or other relationship partners.[40] This is, surely, an important form of respect. One might call it *associational respect.*

At the same time, I take it that if I am morally required, all things considered, not to conform to a given joint commitment, thereby

---

[40] The meaning of "person" may take on different meanings in different discussions, but insofar as, in some context, it relates to relationships, I expect it would have to do with one's capacity to enter them.

defaulting on the associated obligations, then that is what I, as a virtuous person, should do.

It is plausible to think of "blind loyalty" as a matter of not respecting this point. One might, indeed, say that people are *blindly loyal* just in case they choose to fulfill their loyalty obligations even in circumstances in which morality requires them not to do so, all things—including the joint commitment in question—considered. Acting in this way is not, I take it, virtuous—though it may be a great convenience for those to whom one is blindly loyal. These people are, if you like, loyal *to a fault*.

Something similar may be said of those who, while not blindly loyal, only fulfill their morally sanctioned loyalty obligations when these fail to conflict with their inclinations, desires, or self-interest narrowly construed. Such people are mindful of, and to some extent care about, their loyalty obligations. They are loyal "in their fashion" but not in a way that, overall, exemplifies the virtue of loyalty.

Though aware of their loyalty obligations, some people may simply ignore them. If and when they fulfill their loyalty obligations, they do not do so out of regard for them, but coincidentally— because they are naturally discreet, for instance. Even if such people regularly fulfill their loyalty obligations, they have no claim to the virtue of loyalty.

The foregoing considerations suggest something like this: one *exemplifies* the virtue of loyalty if one gives one's loyalty obligations their proper place in one's practical reasoning. In particular, one fulfils one's loyalty obligations even when they conflict with one's personal inclinations, desires, and narrow self-interest, as such, but only when morality does not dictate that one act otherwise, all things considered. To say this is not, of course, to characterize the virtue of loyalty in the sense of enumerating the qualities of judgment, perception, emotional and moral intelligence, and so on that are required for its possession. It is not, in other words, to say what it is to *possess* the virtue of loyalty. It is, rather, to characterize, in part, the predictable results of that possession, from which a full under-standing of the virtue of loyalty may at least partially be derived.

As to loyalty dilemmas, some may properly be dealt with, in our practical reasoning, by reference to moral considerations. It may be clear, for instance, that defaulting on a particular loyalty obliga-tion will cause more harm to others than defaulting on one or more others, which may reasonably be taken to settle the question in this case. In other cases, the moral considerations on the different sides may leave one at liberty, morally speaking, to make a choice.

In any case, one's opting to fulfill one of two or more conflicting loyalty obligations will give one reason for regret. True, one will have fulfilled one loyalty obligation, giving one person what one owes them. At the same time, one will have defaulted on an obliga-tion to one or more others, failing to give them what you owe them, and giving them grounds for rebuke. All else being equal, some re-parative action will be necessary, such as expressing regret to the injured parties, apologizing to them, and explaining the loyalty di-lemma with which one was faced.[41]

Concluding note

My main aim in this paper has been to suggest that any investiga-tion of loyalty, and the extent to which it is a virtue, will do well to consider the potential role of joint commitment, and the directed obligations that flow from it, in the life of the loyal person. That loy-alty concerns at least in part in respecting the directed obligations

---

[41] This reference to regret in the situation with respect to loyalty dilemmas may remind some readers of Bernard Williams's idea (referring to moral conflicts) that the phenom-enon of regret shows it is a mistake to think that "one *ought* must be totally rejected in the sense that one becomes convinced that it did not actually apply" (Williams 1965: 122). In the case of loyalty dilemmas, construed in terms of the directed obligations of joint com-mitment, there are two *directed obligations* neither of which need be "totally rejected" in Williams's sense. Indeed, they must be totally accepted, and they must be reckoned with one way or the other. Meanwhile the usual *ought* of joint commitment—an *ought* that is both exclusionary, and pro tanto, clearly applies.

associated with particular forms of relationship is a common theme in discussions of loyalty. The nature of directed obligations, however, is a debated matter, reaching from relationship theory to rights theory.[42] That loyalty obligations are at least in part obligations of joint commitment is worth serious consideration by theorists of loyalty generally.[43]

Bibliography

Broome, John. "Are Intentions Reasons? And How Should We Cope with Incommensurable Values?" In *Practical Rationality and Preference: Essays for David Gauthier*, edited by Christopher Morris and Arthur Ripstein, 98–120. Cambridge: Cambridge University Press, 2001.

Fletcher, George P. *Loyalty: An Essay on The Morality of Relationships*. New York: Oxford University Press, 1993.

Gilbert, Margaret. "Agreements, Coercion, and Obligation." *Ethics* 103 (1993): 679–706.

Gilbert, Margaret. *Joint Commitment: How We Make the Social World*. New York: Oxford University Press, 2013.

Gilbert, Margaret. *Life in Groups: How We Think, Feel, and Act Together*. Oxford: Oxford University Press, 2023.

Gilbert, Margaret. *On Social Facts*. London: Routledge and Kegan Paul, 1989; Princeton, NJ: Princeton University Press, 1992.

Gilbert, Margaret. "Remarks on Joint Commitment and Its Relation to Moral Thinking." *Philosophical Psychology* 31 (2018a): 755–766. https://doi.org/10.1080/09515089.2018.1486611

Gilbert, Margaret. *Rights and Demands: A Foundational Inquiry*. Oxford: Oxford University Press, 2018b.

Gilbert, Margaret. *A Theory of Political Obligation: Membership, Commitment, and the Bonds of Society*. Oxford: Oxford University Press, 2006.

Gilbert, Margaret. "Walking Together: A Paradigmatic Social Phenomenon." In *Midwest Studies in Philosophy XV, The Philosophy of the Human Sciences*,

---

[42] For a review of some central positions in rights theory, see Gilbert 2018, esp. Chapter 5.

[43] Warm thanks to Matthew Dean, John Kleinig, and, in particular, Troy Jollimore for comments on a draft of this essay. Thanks also to the discussants at the *Loyalty* conference held in Norman, Oklahoma on June 14–15, 2019, where the first version of this essay was presented.

edited by P. A. French, T. E. Uehling, Jr., and H. K. Wettstein, 1–14. Notre Dame, IN: University of Notre Dame Press, 1990.

Hohfeld, Wesley. *Fundamental Legal Conceptions as Applied in Judicial Reasoning*. Edited by Walter W. Cook. New Haven, CT: Yale University Press, (1919) 1964.

Jollimore, Troy. *On Loyalty*. New York: Routledge, 2013.

Kleinig, John. *On Loyalty and Loyalties*. New York: Oxford University Press, 2014.

Lewis, David. *Convention: A Philosophical Study*. Cambridge, MA: Cambridge University Press, 1969.

Milton, John. *Paradise Lost*. In *The Complete Poetry and Essential Prose of John Milton*, edited by William Kerrigan, John Rumrich, and Stephen M. Fallon. New York: Random House, 2007.

Raz, Joseph. "On the Nature of Rights." *Mind* 3 (1984): 194–214.

Ross, W. D. *The Right and the Good*. Oxford: Clarendon Press, (1930) 2002.

Thomson, Judith Jarvis. *The Realm of Rights*. Cambridge, MA: Harvard University Press, 1990.

Vandershraaf, Peter, and Giacomo Sillari. "Common Knowledge." In *Stanford Encyclopedia of Philosophy*, edited by Edward Zalta (2014). http://plato.stanford.edu/archives/spr2014/entries/common-knowledge

Williams, Bernard. "Ethical Consistency." *Proceedings of the Aristotelian Society Supplementary Volumes* 39 (1965): 103–124.

4

Betrayal

John Kleinig

It is easier to forgive an Enemy than to forgive a Friend.
—William Blake[1]

Introduction

It is an intriguing fact that attitudes to loyalty tend to be spread more evenly across the normative spectrum than attitudes to betrayal. That is, there is usually less moral ambivalence about the vice of betrayal than there is about the virtue of loyalty.[2]

At one end of the spectrum, loyalty is seen as a "sham virtue," one that is invoked to cover up wrongdoing.[3] At the other end of the spectrum, loyalty is heralded as the ultimate and almost absolute relational virtue.[4] Somewhere in the middle, more Janus-faced, loyalty is seen as having a valuable—even important—but limited place in relational life, albeit one that is prone to misuse or corruption. Betrayal, on the other hand, is generally seen as an

---

[1] Blake 1904, 113.

[2] As Ewin 1993 puts it: "Disloyalty is always a vice, but loyalty is not always a virtue" (387). (I suggest later, however, that disloyalty is usually considered worse than (mere) betrayal. Nevertheless, in each case an asymmetry is often claimed.) It may be no accident that in *The Republic* (1891b, 442e–443a) Plato suggests that betrayal/treachery is the paradigmatic form of injustice.

[3] Blamires 1963, 24.

[4] In some cases the absoluteness applies only to particular objects of loyalty (say, the Party or God); in other cases loyalty as such is seen as a value "above all else" (Reddington 2014).

John Kleinig, *Betrayal* In: *The Virtue of Loyalty*. Edited by: Troy Jollimore, Oxford University Press.
© Oxford University Press 2024. DOI: 10.1093/oso/9780197612644.003.0005

unmitigated vice—a generalized characterization of sphere-of-activity-related normative breaches such as infidelity, treason, perfidy, and apostasy—manifestations not simply of a lack of loyalty but of outright *dis*loyalty. Not only is betrayal seen as bad, but as among the worst of vices.[5] The most likely reason for this severe judgment is found in the personal importance we accord to certain relationships and collectivities, the *kind* of trust that betrayal violates, and the reasons for the violation of that trust.

It is, of course, more complicated than that, with respect to both loyalty and betrayal. There is a lot to be said for the importance of loyalty as a form of relational and associational "glue," although many associative connections do not and do not need to develop to the point that loyalty between or among the parties is involved. And, even when loyal bonds do develop between associates, such loyalty is not usually unconstrained but would often be acknowledged as having normative, albeit implicit, limits. As a virtue, loyalty is most fruitfully seen as an executive virtue or virtue of the will (as is conscientiousness or sincerity or courage), rather than as a substantive virtue (as is kindness or compassion or generosity). The virtuousness of executive virtues can be counteracted (or undermined) by their objects—the sincere racist or loyal Nazi—though they retain their virtuousness because a person devoid of sincerity or loyalty would be diminished as a person.[6]

Betrayal, too, is subject to a number of ambiguities.[7] The child whose cry betrays the presence of hidden refugees does not betray in the way that Judas reputedly does when he kisses Jesus.[8] Nor does the bead of sweat that betrays my anxiety or guilt during an interrogation constitute a normative failing.

---

[5] Whether these commonalities vary depending on their background in a particular moral theory is an interesting but complex question that I leave to one side.

[6] Although substantive virtues can go wrong, they are less likely to do so. (See Kleinig 2022, sect. 4). I think this distinction brings some theoretical order into Milligan and Cobham's discussion of "a dubious virtue" in Chapter 10 of this volume.

[7] In a rich and suggestive discussion, Shklar 1984 allows for much greater ambiguity, though I think she takes some unwarranted liberties with the concept.

[8] Matt. 26:47–50; Mk. 14:43–45; Lk. 22:47–48.

Indeed, some of what are often treated as betrayals may even be thought of as commendable. The term "whistleblower" was introduced to provide a normatively neutral description of someone who—so it was believed of those persons whose acts of disparaging disclosure were oriented to or motivated by a notion of the public good—violated expected loyalties to the institutional or organizational collective to which the whistleblower belonged. It can, of course, be debated whether a whistleblower violated a legitimate expectation of loyalty and thus engaged in an act of betrayal, or whether the behavior that prompted the whistleblower's disclosure was directed at a collective that had—by its actions—forfeited its claim to the whistleblower's loyalty.[9] The salient point is that "traitor" ordinarily carries a lot of negative normative baggage.

Even more extreme have been those moral provocateurs—such as Jean Genet and perhaps Graham Greene—who have extolled the virtues, or at least the pleasures, of betrayal or disloyalty.[10] Although there is a place for the discussion of such outliers, it would take this essay too far afield to do justice to their views. In any case, their views piggyback on the more standard understandings.

---

[9] This is a point of difference with Diane Jeske, who is more willing to speak of justified betrayals (Chapter 2, this volume), perhaps reflecting my greater concern with the evil associated with betrayal (and characterization as a traitor). To some extent, as Jeske recognizes, our differences may be semantic—I, suggesting that forfeited obligations of loyalty undercut the characterization of what one does as betrayal, and she, suggesting that the forfeited obligations of loyalty justify the betrayal. In some ways I am reminded of the debate between those who see promising evil as nonobligatory promising and those who, seeing promises as inherently obligation-creating, do not view evil promises as promises.

[10] Genet is uncompromisingly perverse, almost sociopathic, in his attitudes: "Betrayal is beautiful" (1965, 219); "Anyone who hasn't experienced the ecstasy of betrayal knows nothing about ecstasy at all" (2003, 70). Greene almost certainly makes a distinction between disloyalty (which he considers virtuous) and betrayal—about which he often writes. He famously titled a speech, "The Virtue of Disloyalty" (1972) and was coy about whether his friend Kim Philby had "betrayed" his country (1968, xvii). He is sensitive to the less savory associations of betrayal but thought there was much to be said for challenging (i.e., being disloyal to) conventional thinking. There is some reason to think that Greene's unconventional views on betrayal and disloyalty might be tied to problems he appears to have had with conventional relationships (see Greene 2021).

Is there a central or paradigmatic core to betrayal that helps us to understand why it is so often deemed a terrible vice? Judith Shklar opines that betrayals are too diverse to be put into any "coherent order," yet she is struck by the "sharp and intense" reaction we have to its experience,[11] and it is this that I seek to capture in much of the remainder of this essay. First, however, I outline and comment on several cases and contexts that will help to center the discussion. Although they overlap in various ways, they enable us to perceive more clearly the fabric of betrayal.

Five cases and contexts

(1) Persuading a gang or organized crime member to snitch on other members. Let us reflect on two scenarios. One involves a government agent who convinces a detained group member that she has hitched her wagon to the wrong star; that is, the agent has convinced her that, for all their cohesiveness, crime groups of the kind with which she has associated herself are antisocial and violative of the rights of others, and for this reason they have no general moral claim on the allegiance of their members, including herself.[12] Thus persuaded, the member may now consider that the allegiance she has owed to others in the group lacks a moral undergirding that she recognizes *qua* human, and that she has been—morally, if not psychologically—mistakenly bound to the crime community more deeply than to the wider human community of which she is also a part.

---

[11] Shklar 1984, 138.
[12] This suggests that, to a significant degree, particularistic obligations should not violate universalistic ones: a particularistic obligation that requires the violation of a universalistic one loses its normative claim. I am generally sympathetic to that position. However, this doesn't rule out the possibility that, say, one might lie to protect an intimate other. However, I would suggest that the scope of permissible lying is limited by considerations that would be upheld when viewed from a universalistic standpoint.

A second scenario arises when the government agent convinces the member that she faces a long period of incarceration (along with its consequences) if she does not assist the government's investigation, whereas her assistance with that investigation is likely to greatly reduce the incarcerative consequences. She decides that the trade-off is worth it and "spills the beans" on her erstwhile group colleagues.

There is little doubt that the detained person's (former) partners—and perhaps others as well—will view the disclosures as a betrayal, whether or not the disclosures have been motivated by a change of heart. Whether or not the other crime members see the loyalty they believed they were owed as morally questionable and so perhaps properly forfeited, it is likely that they will consider the obligations of their particularistic commitment as taking precedence over universalistic obligations.

Indeed, they may even deny the validity of such universalistic obligations. If, as Andrew Oldenquist and Alasdair MacIntyre appear to argue,[13] all morality is group morality, then even what purports to be a universalistic standpoint, or perhaps the standpoint of an "ideal observer,"[14] will ultimately reduce to some particularistic or partial position, and there will be no position *sub species aeternitatis* or even *humanitatis* for objectivity in moral judgments. My own inclination is to recognize partialities as a reason for open-mindedness, without sacrificing the aspirational value of objectivity and universality.

Our vacillations here, though, may leave us with alternative ways of stating the difference between the two scenarios. On the one hand, we might argue that the moral convert is not bound by a loyalty focused on an illegitimate enterprise: any apparent loyalty obligations have been forfeited by virtue of the criminal

---

[13] Oldenquist 1982; MacIntyre 1984.
[14] Cf. Firth 1952.

undertaking[15]; on the other hand, we may recognize that betrayal occurred but argue that it was legitimate. On the part of the person whose betrayal was purely instrumental, however, we may not choose to qualify the betrayal, even if we think the loyalty was illegitimate: only certain kinds of reasons legitimize betrayals (or, if you will, sanction them as non-betrayals).

Unless one can make the argument that the obligations of loyalty take precedence over all other considerations, moral and otherwise, it is doubtful whether both scenarios should be seen as morally equivalent. No doubt the self-regarding reasons for disclosure qualify the person as a traitor of some kind—a rat or snitch—though it is something of an open question how strongly we should condemn a person who betrays those who rely on what may well be a morally illegitimate loyalty. We might, nevertheless, all be inclined to view with suspicion the instrumental turncoat, *even if* she does what we think is right—all things considered—for this is a person whose eye is fairly firmly trained on the bottom line, one who might well sacrifice principle to advantage.[16] That person may betray us for the same kind of reason. This is not to deny that there may be a rationality to cost-benefit calculations of the kind this person has undertaken, but it is not the kind of virtuous rationality that serves a flourishing social life. As for the person who has a change of heart about her previous life—provided of course that we can be assured that the change was genuine—we might be reluctant to use the language of unqualified betrayal (rather than, say, that of repentance or conversion), and we may choose to advance the transformation in mitigation of acts committed as a gang member. Although not a change of identity of a Parfitian kind, the convert has been restored to the moral world of the community

---

[15] Or, to put it another way, recognizing that loyalty was misplaced would not amount to a rejection of the virtuousness of loyalty so much as a rejection of the virtuousness of *this manifestation* of it.

[16] Jeske makes much the same point, when she discusses Benedict Arnold. Cf. also Aristotle 1925, 1105a–b.

that one might identify as that of common humanity, and should be welcomed into it. This does not negate responsibility for what may previously have been done, but it probably warrants some moral and legal acknowledgment.

There is, however, a further dimension to such scenarios—and that is whether police, who often carry to extremes their loyalty to each other, should seek to persuade a gang member to snitch on other members and/or to work undercover. In some cases, police have sought to persuade witnesses to violate local or ethnic loyalties. Might there be something unseemly about trying to undermine one of our most important group values?[17] True, some of the resistance to providing such assistance is likely to be generated by fear of the consequences of informing on others. Nevertheless, it is also likely that bonds of loyalty will be involved, and police will need to be careful that their tactics are implemented in a way that does not erode the capacity for important social trust and other values. That is so with other police prerogatives—such as deception, invasions of privacy, and the use of force. Justified or not, strategic practices may have unintended consequences that are morally corrosive.

(2) A police officer is questioned following the occurrence of a botched arrest and the shooting of an unarmed black man. The officer was a witness to the event and although he has significant doubts about the way in which the situation was handled, he is deeply conscious of both the risks involved in police work and the need for police to "have each other's back," something that is believed to involve mutual support through thick and thin. He is equally conscious of the fact that things can easily go wrong and that in the past other officers have had his back when he himself screwed up: we are limited and flawed beings. He now has the choice of describing the situation as he believed he saw it or in a way that will not reflect badly on the officer responsible for the shooting. With

---

[17] Mehler 1997.

respect to the officer in question, at least two motivating reasons weigh heavily on him. One is that he is genuinely troubled about the way in which the original arrest was handled, and believes that, as an agent of public authority, his ultimate responsibility is to the larger community. The other is that if he refuses to be a snitch and joins in a cover-up that may unravel, he will be implicated in any scandal that subsequently occurs.

Police work is complicated by the fact that, although it is socially important, loyalty among police officers is critical to the performance of their work.[18] An officer who violates the so-called blue wall of silence is believed to create a hazard for work that relies on the kind of team effort and support that loyalty helps to guarantee. As police officers sometimes see it, they have only each other to rely on, and if they can't do that, the sacrifices they make to ensure a larger social good may be reduced (what has recently come to be referred to as the Ferguson Effect[19]).

As already noted, police work is not a world unto itself, but is structured to achieve socially important ends (in broad terms, social peace through public safety, order maintenance, and law enforcement), and if police exploit the "code" of silence in a way that undermines the confidence a public has or should have in the legitimacy of their authority, then the capacity of police to achieve their ends will also be diminished. So there is likely to be something of a tradeoff here, if police are to achieve the social ends for which their organizations have been instituted. If they are held accountable in a way that weakens their needed bonds, their social effectiveness will be diminished; but if they are not held accountable for their failures, their social effectiveness will also be diminished.

It is not an impossible tradeoff, though it is often handled badly.[20] One reason for this is that oversight bodies within police

[18] Wren 1985.
[19] Wolfe and Nix 2016.
[20] Kleinig 2001.

organizations tend to be punitive when they might instead be corrective and educative, and mistakes made as a result of the difficult conditions under which police often operate are not seen as opportunities for improving competence but occasions for retribution (albeit sometimes as a sop to populist outcry).[21] The blue wall of silence then becomes a means of avoiding accountability. Of course, this is not an argument for sloppy or vindictive work on the part of police. It is important to the social legitimacy of police organizations that their members act with professionalism, and the latter requires a high level of competence along with goodwill. An organization that fails to foster that kind of competence or that breeds a toxic culture (whether of corruption or of "us-them" differentiations) should be as answerable for its failures as are its individual members.[22]

(3) People commonly break preexisting bonds because it advantages them in some way to do so. Consider a married couple who experience the usual ups and downs of marital life, but generally work through their problems satisfactorily. Suppose, now, that a new person joins the husband's office, the two "click," and, over time, an intimate romantic bond forms and they begin an affair. Eventually the husband leaves his wife and children and partners with his new love. Although the original marriage was sealed with a commitment to be faithful in good times and bad, the new relationship promises a level of excitement and fulfillment that he feels he cannot resist.

Everyday cases of betrayal (such as marital infidelity) vary a fair bit in their characteristics and in the kind of condemnation, if any, that they garner. There are those who believe that the marital bond is clear-cut and indissoluble, and that no circumstances excuse, let alone justify, breaches: the pledge of loyalty is seen as absolute.

---

[21] Of course, as we also know too well, police unions, and sometimes administrations cover up acts for which individual police ought to be held accountable.

[22] For the most part, individual accountability is avoided via the doctrine of qualified immunity, currently under scrutiny (see Schwarz 2018).

In some religious circles, even if divorce is occasionally sanctioned, remarriage is seen as a form of adultery. Other couples, however, may recognize or agree to lesser constraints or, if (sexual) betrayals occur, may be more willing to allow for repair. In a so-called open marriage, sexual fidelity may be replaced by emotional fidelity, with one-night stands or wife-swapping being countenanced so long as marital affections are sustained. Nevertheless, depending on the understanding that exists on the part of the partners, sexual betrayal will often be seen as either testing the parameters of their relationship or destroying it.[23]

A particularly fraught kind of betrayal is involved when a parent sexually abuses a child and then demands secrecy as a manifestation of loyalty. Given the strong bonds of loyalty that a (vulnerable) child is likely to develop toward a parent, such exploitations of loyalty are particularly egregious and psychologically burdening. Indeed, even what we might view as a "justified betrayal" (by the child) can be psychologically damaging to the child victim. In this situation, it may be claimed, the betrayal came with the abuse, not with its reporting.

(4) Albert has been brought up in country Q. By his later teens he has become unsympathetic to—indeed, alienated from—the politics of Q, and his developing ideological leanings incline him to favor the policies of country R, a rival to Q. Albert believes that the capitalist economy of Q has resulted not simply in enormous inequalities in Q, but in the formation of a large and mostly powerless underclass. Albert later becomes a public servant whose work role gives him access to classified information that would be of considerable interest to country R in its rivalry with Q. A chance meeting with an official of R provides Albert with the opportunity to furnish R's authorities with such information, and he clandestinely

---

[23] There is a fascinating discussion of the complexities and corruptions of marital (dis) loyalty in Milligan and Cobham's analysis (Chapter 10, this volume) of Iris Murdoch's novel, *The Bell* (1962).

passes on that information. Betrayal? Justifiable betrayal? Or does the fact that Albert no longer feels any patriotic connection with Q make what he does no longer an act of betrayal? And what if we change the terms of the story to one in which Albert's disenchantment is not with the Q's capitalism, but Q's National Socialism and its anti-Semitic policies? How dependent, if at all, is our reaction on the substantive details of Albert's disenchantment?[24] And how dependent, if at all, does our judgment depend on our assessment of the reasons that Albert appealed to in support of his shifting allegiance to R? Even if there is some basis for Albert's disenchantment with capitalism, suppose Albert falsely believes that R is a socialist paradise: how, and how much, do questionable beliefs or values count in how we assess Albert's behavior?

Consider the possibility that Albert's disenchantment has arisen because he has come under the sway of a potent online conspiracy theory, Z-Anon, which claims that the ruling politicians of Q have been seduced by an extra-terrestrial power preparing for world conquest, and that only the politicians of R are capable of seeing through and counteracting its schemes. How will this affect our judgments?[25]

If Albert is caught or at least exposed, there is little doubt that he will be viewed and treated as a traitor. He will be seen as a traitor not only by the authorities of Q but also, most likely, by a substantial number of Q's citizens. Why should this be, if he no longer feels any loyalty to Q? Whether or not he now professes some allegiance to R, his behavior is likely to be seen as treasonous, and an important reason for this will probably be that he has acted *as if* he maintained his loyalty to Q, while providing aid to R. Sedition, in which a person seeks to foment opposition to the government, does not constitute betrayal, even if it is considered politically unacceptable. It is the

---

[24] See, for example, Case 5.

[25] How large a burden does a person have, when taking consequential steps, to verify their beliefs? One might argue that the greater the potential consequences, the greater the burden. Some of these examples connect with those considered by Jeske in Chapter 2.

deceptiveness of what Albert does that contributes most to the charge of betrayal.[26] Q has some expectation of loyalty from Albert, providing as it does a social and institutional context within which its citizens—including Albert—are presumed able to flourish, as well as entrusting Albert with certain responsibilities. If Albert disputes the official story about flourishing, he may express his opposition (perhaps at some cost), without being so much a traitor as a dissident.[27] One might also expect that Albert could move from Q to R, a reasonable possibility given Albert's position.[28] But, as a beneficiary of Q, Albert has chosen instead to surreptitiously undermine Q from within. That will be seen to constitute betrayal.[29]

(5) After joining the administration of a large pharmaceutical company, George becomes aware that some of its most successful products are less safe than they are claimed to be. Documentation that he sees—in reports from research chemists to managers to marketers—gives him reason to think that some public claims by the company (especially that an enhanced version of a painkiller is "less addictive" than an earlier form) are false, and that the company is making these claims in an aggressive marketing program, without presenting appropriate additional cautions. George's discomfort with what he has learned leads to discussions with company officials, and it becomes clear to him that although the data on addiction can indeed be read in the way that the company suggests, any benefits in this regard are fairly easily circumvented (slow-release tablets can be crushed). The company's promotion of the

[26] One might, of course, tell a different story, in which, Albert has gained the classified information prior to his change of political views (about which he has become vocal). Here there is no deception, but there is an assumption that classified information remains "confidential," and Albert's passing it along violated a continuing expectation. (Compare this with the person who passes along to a later lover confidential information concerning an earlier one.)

[27] Contrary to the judgment of the Athenian court, dissidents such as Socrates aren't ipso facto traitors. See Plato 1891a.

[28] Maybe, given his beliefs, Albert should do more. But moving from Q to R may make a point without being excessively disruptive.

[29] Cf. Shklar 1984, 142.

painkiller is enormously successful and the generated profits are used, in part, to bankroll other R&D initiatives undertaken by the company. The strong message conveyed to George is that he should not rock the boat. They rest their case with the claim that it is *doctors* who overprescribe and their failures should not be held against the company. Eventually, George decides to send copies of some internal documents to a reputable newspaper, which then publishes a damaging exposé of the company's marketing practices. Although George claims that he is being a responsible whistleblower, his actions—clearly against company policy—are seen as traitorous. He is fired and the company makes a concerted effort to prevent his obtaining comparable employment elsewhere.

George's whistleblowing situation and experience is not uncommon.[30] Although, at least from the perspective of those who manage the pharmaceutical company, what George has done has some of the elements of betrayal—that is, he has a position of trust and the information he provides to critical others is both damaging to the company and the trust that it has placed in him—George's motivation does not easily fit with the claim that he is a *traitor*. His concern about the impact of the company's deceptive practices does not constitute a self-righteous concern with his own opinions or payback for failure. Spokespeople for the company may claim that he acted out of some disreputable motive (such as failure to be considered for a higher position—a not uncommon response to whistleblowing). Or, they might claim, if George's motivation was truly moral, that he should first have left the company ("he bit the hand that fed him"). Attributing a sleazy or less than high-minded motive is a familiar enough tactic intended to knock whistleblowers off their moral perch—though even if George's motives had been less than high-minded (unlikely in the present case), this would not constitute an argument against the disclosure, *only* against seeing

---

[30] See Glazer and Glazer 1991.

what George had done as exemplifying moral probity. Defects in process do not always impugn substance.

This is not to deny that whistleblowing can get out of hand in a number of ways, but only to note that its getting out of hand does not ipso facto make the act one of betrayal. Betrayal or not, whistleblowing should not be embarked upon lightly. An exposé of the pharmaceutical company's failures could be very damaging, and not just economically. Or it could be ineffective—disruptive without changing anything for the better. If the whistleblowing leads to public censure, innocent people employed by the company may have to be laid off; good research may be curtailed; the company may lose critical control over some of the good it does; and (in the particular case we are looking at) some beneficiaries of the problematic painkiller may find their access made more difficult, with serious implications for their quality of life. For these reasons— quite apart from the possible characterization of whistleblowing as betrayal—it is expected that whistleblowers will have made reasonable efforts to have their concerns appropriately dealt with internally, that they have solid grounds for the conclusions they have come to, and that they will have taken into account issues of proportionality (such as whether the company's wrongdoing is serious enough to risk the consequences of revealing it).[31]

Some central themes

Despite their potential for further complexity, the five cases we have looked at enable us to pinpoint certain central themes in betrayal.

---

[31] Some of these requirements might also be relevant to earlier cases I have considered. I have a longer discussion of whistleblowing in Kleinig 2014, 206–211. Troy Jollimore has suggested to me that most cases of betrayal involve exposure of private information or secrets to others. There is some paradigmatic truth in that insofar as, if A betrays B to C, something that was intended to be hidden is exposed to another. I think, however, we may betray another's trust without betraying them to others.

The relational dimension to betrayal

In previous work on loyalty, I have argued that loyalty is centrally a relational virtue, one that is critical to many relationships—and in some contexts not merely contingently but almost conceptually so. Many of those relationships are or have become central to us as the persons we are: they are crucial elements in our identity and constitute aspects of who we are. Perhaps the most deeply implicated of those relationships is friendship, a particularistic connection with one or more others, that would hardly make sense were it not also expressive of some sort of loyal bond.[32] Of course, as even Aristotle saw, there are various kinds of friendship.[33] There is the sort of which Dale Carnegie spoke when he set out to give advice on "how to make friends and influence people,"[34] and there are also Facebook friends[35] who are expected to be instrumentally rather than intrinsically valuable. In contrast, the paradigm of friendship—that which gives friendship such a critical role in human experience—is the relational bond it exemplifies.

At one level, that relational bond gives substance to the idea that human life and experience is not solitary—as is often the case with a stand of trees, each fending for itself—but a joint endeavor characterized by many connections of varying degrees of intimacy. Some of those connections are more central than others. Family—that cradle-to-grave bio-social connection—is often seen as a central locus for friendship, though the vicissitudes of human relationships are sometimes transferred to the consensual intimacies of a spousal connection and may even become detached from family. At its more intimate level, the relational bond of friends

---

[32] Kleinig 2014, especially Chapter 8. I am therefore contingently sympathetic to the special place that Jeske (and Aristotle before her) gives to the importance of friendship not only in a good life but also in our sense of who we are.

[33] Cf. Gilbert, Chapter 3, this volume.

[34] Carnegie 1936.

[35] Cocking and Mathews 2000; Jeske 2019. Not to mention the many charitable solicitations I receive that commence: "Dear Friend."

includes the self-sacrificial willingness of one to protect or advance the interests of the other.[36] Shklar sees *desertion* as betrayal's central feature, though I am less confident about her attempt to link this with the childhood fear of abandonment.[37]

In some other cases—where the relational partner is a team or organizational associate, a professional colleague, an ethnic or patrial member, the relationship is still to some degree considered integral to the self, and betrayal will involve acts that threaten to undermine the relevant associative bond. Betrayal can wound profoundly, because what it injures has (rightly or wrongly) become deeply integrated into the person betrayed. Betrayals, especially those that display disloyalty,[38] violate who we are or have become: they involve an attack on our identity—whether it is our identity as friends, family members, citizens, or members of an ethnic or religious group.

True, sometimes loyalties are associated with principles and values and abstract institutions. But I believe that this involves a shift created by disappointed relational expectations.[39] Having lost faith in role incumbents or relational intimates, we ascribe loyalty to the role or relation in question—to kingship rather than kings, friendship rather than to particular friends.[40]

[36] Leaving aside whether these interests are to be conceived subjectively or objectively. Aristotle, recognizing the depth and demands of friendship, suggests that one should not have too many friends (1925, book IX, ch. 10).

[37] Shklar 1984: 139–140. Elsewhere Shklar speaks of "having an expectation disappointed" as the "one irreducible experience" of betrayal (Shklar 1984, 140–141, though cf. 151–152), but this is too broad to be helpful, conflating the disappointment of misplaced reliance with that of misplaced trust (Kleinig 2017, 134).

[38] The child's crying, which betrays the presence of the hidden refugees, does not constitute disloyalty.

[39] See Kleinig 2014: 27–31; 2019: 638–641.

[40] Leah Kalmanson notes a similar shift in her essay (see Chapter 6, this volume). Even Josiah Royce, the preeminent philosopher of loyalty, articulates his idea of loyalty as "devotion to a cause" in relational terms (see Foust's essay in Chapter 7, this volume; Kleinig 2014, 28). In my view, Sanford Levinson's essay on "Loyalty to the Constitution" exemplifies this shift in its distinctively American form (see Chapter 8, this volume). A capricious monarchy (exemplified by George III) has been "superseded" by a constitutional document—the rule of men replaced by the rule of law. But, as Levinson sees too well, not only is the document problematic, but so are the interpretations of its clauses. Perhaps, in the end, what seemed to be stable has been beholden to movements and

In *On Betrayal*, Avishai Margalit uses the language of "thick" and "thin" relations to portray what I am more inclined to characterize as particularistic and universalistic relations. Although they are not matching contrasts,[41] universalistic/thin relations are those that normatively inform our relations with others as fellow human beings—whether strangers or intimates. Particularistic/thick relations are those that concern our normative connections with others or groups that help to constitute what we individually are—what, as Margalit puts it, constitutes our *belonging*. Betrayal threatens to drive inside connections outside, not necessarily leaving us outside the domain of normative connection, but outside (some of) the more intense personal and identity-conferring connections that are so critical to our lives.

Betrayal and harm

It should be evident from what has already been said that betrayal does not merely strike at the foundation of a relationship; it does so in a way that is likely to be harmful to the betrayed. If loyalty expresses costly perseverance in maintaining the terms of a significant relationship that inter alia seeks to protect or advance the interests of the relational object, betrayal jeopardizes those interests.

Because the relational bond that is threatened or lost by betrayal is one that is valued by the betrayed party, the betrayal is harmful. Where the betrayed party is another person, it constitutes an assault on the personhood or dignity of the other. That is bad

cliques, to whom our loyalty is only problematically given. There is room here for a revival of the idea of a loyal opposition.

[41] Margalit 2017. The language of thick and thin was popularized by Bernard Williams 1985, though the contrast that Williams had in mind was between general normative characterizations such as good, bad, right, and wrong, and more textured ones such as courageous, cruel, kind, and traitorous. See Väyrynen 2019.

enough. But the harm that is caused by betrayal may also include additional damage. The political traitor may place a country at risk. Unauthorized disclosure of information about an intimate other may not only undermine the relationship with that other but also lead to reputational, social, financial, and/or other sorts of harm. It's an interesting question, of course, whether Albert, unlike the Mafia member, has jeopardized a legitimate way of life when he works for R against Q. We have become familiar with debates about whether the difference between freedom fighters and terrorists is just one of perspective.[42] History, as they say, is written by the victors, and we can conceive of a situation in which, if the values of R were to supplant the values of Q, Albert would no longer be labelled a traitor but hailed as a liberator.

Of course, not everything harmful that an intimate or identity-conferring other does constitutes betrayal. If a marital disagreement gets out of hand and one party assaults the other, that is not obviously a betrayal. It may contribute to the breakdown of an intimate relationship, but no loyalty is violated.[43] However, if a confidant intentionally conveys private information about me to our common enemy, then betrayal is likely involved.[44] Betrayal is not simply activity that threatens my interests; in addition, it must be targeted (even if reluctantly or negligently) at the bond that exists between us. It is an attack on the trust that sustains our bond. This bond, as I suggested, is important to our sense of self and to our flourishing as the individuals and particular persons that we are.

[42] Cf. Ganor 2002.

[43] This may require some fine-tuning. There is a case for arguing that marital vows include a commitment to care, assault falling short of being an expression thereof. But we may need to distinguish a provoked (but quickly apologized for) slap from a pattern of domestic violence—both wrong, but the latter more obviously violative of marital loyalties. Perhaps a different example would work better (fibbing, though here, too, there are cases and cases). I thank Nancy Snow for pressing me on this point.

[44] Although I do not entirely agree with her analysis, Gilbert's example (Chapter 3, this volume) of Jane, Tanya, and Phyllis captures something of the conceptual and moral issues involved when loyalties clash.

Although all betrayals are harmful in the sense of undermining the terms of a relationship, how much additional harm is caused (if any) will depend on the substance of the betrayal. Some betrayals may amount to little beyond the threat to a trusted relationship; others might result in the loss of a war. Sometimes, all things considered, a betrayal may be thought to have accomplished some social good, as is the case, perhaps, with cooperating witnesses. The harm that is brought upon gang or crime members by their betrayal to police authorities provides respite or justice for innocent others.[45]

Motivations that betray

As I indicated earlier, not all unwanted disclosures constitute betrayals in the paradigm sense of the term. An act of betrayal may be accidental, and though the betrayer is likely to be aggrieved by the resulting damage to the other's interests, we may not condemn the person for it. The situation is different, however, if the betrayer's act has involved negligence. A failure to show due diligence might constitute a condemnable breach of relational expectations. But the kinds of betrayals that constitute disloyalty display corrupted motivations. Of considerable importance to the normative weight we give to betrayals we hold in most contempt will be the kind of corrupt motivation behind the actions or disclosures that jeopardize the bond that exists between the parties in question.

What is a corrupt motivation? Perhaps nothing that can be simply characterized, though I am inclined to think that the motivation behind betrayal in the worst sense—the sense in which it is characterized as disloyalty and seen as a terrible vice—is a kind of *self-servingness*: if not of the simple self-advantaging (greener pastures elsewhere) kind, or akratic self-protection (think of Jesus's

---

[45] Cf. various instantiations of the religious doctrine of *felix culpa*.

disciple, Peter[46]) at another's expense, then of an endangering elevation of self-certitude (the lack of humility by the person who "knows" he's right and sacrifices the relationship to that certitude). The first account is probably the most common, though weakness of will and arrogance are not uncommon (and may not exhaust the possibilities).

Although a problematic self-servingness tends to infect the worst of betrayals, the situation is sometimes complicated by other factors—when, for example, the self-servingness takes the form of self-preservation. Despite his social concerns, George may well have wondered whether the costs of whistleblowing relieved his obligations to do something about the situation in which he found himself. Rather than the company, might he have betrayed the wider community of which he was a part had he not reported on the pharmaceutical company's actions? At what point does the personal (or familial) cost excuse?[47] The issue is even more acute during wartime situations in which erstwhile friends betray as an act of self-preservation—the Jewish or Muslim friend whose pleas for help are turned down, lest discovery lead to the neighbor's death as well. Sometimes we may be inclined to excuse, but in other cases we expect more of a friend.[48]

Margalit argues at some length that treason is an act of ingratitude, and that political betrayal is constituted by ingratitude.[49] The background to his contention is feudal allegiance, in which the lord is a benefactor to the vassals who serve him. Their relationship, though personal, is vertical rather than horizontal. The lord provides security and favors, and those who loyally give him their fealty owe him a debt of gratitude: "At the basis of feudal ethics is

---

[46] Matt. 26:69–74; Mk. 14:66–72; Lk. 22:55–62; Jn 18:15–18, 25–27.
[47] Martin 1992.
[48] Shklar 1984, 196.
[49] This, essentially, is Socrates's argument in Plato's *Crito* (1891c, 48b–52d), where an analogy is drawn with gratitude owed to parents.

the idea that betrayal in general and treason in particular are extreme acts of ingratitude."[50]

That there is often—perhaps mostly—some form of ingratitude in treason I can concede. One of the benefits of a country is the way in which it enables, through its combination of culture and institutions, a way of life for which—for the most part—we can and ought to be grateful.[51] I am less convinced, however, that treason is *constituted by* a form of ingratitude. Although the vassal who betrays his lord may display ingratitude, what about a lord who betrays a vassal? Ingratitude? Assuming some reciprocity in loyalty, lords owe loyalty to those who display appropriate fealty. Absent a reciprocal loyalty on the lord's part, the vassal shows obedience or subservience. Absent loyalty on the lord's part, a failure of deference is not obviously a display of ingratitude.

Take the case of Albert: his betrayal of Q is not easily characterized as ingratitude. Rather, Albert has come to adopt an ideology that leads him to believe that the country of which he is a citizen either is or has become exploitative of many of his fellow citizens, whether or not they appreciate the extent of their exploitation. Even if Albert has personally benefited from the social practices of his country, and has something to be grateful for in that respect, he is not grateful for what his benefit has cost others. Any loyalty (and gratitude) that he may have felt has now been extinguished, and he has determined to act in ways that will undermine and help change the status quo. Even if Albert should be grateful, his betrayal is more than an act of ingratitude. Its deeper motivation— shown by his treasonous deception—lies in other factors, a willful self-assertion, in which, even if altruistically motivated, he has arrogantly prioritized his own perspective and often deceptively engaged in self-advantaging behavior.

---

[50] Margalit 2017, 163.
[51] Cf. Walker 1988.

Many of those who betray their country do not do so from idealistic motives but (perhaps inter alia) for some form of personal gain. Benedict Arnold, Aldrich Ames, Robert Hanssen, and John Walker, Jr. all had self-advantaging motives for betraying the United States, whatever personal and political alienation they may also have felt. In some other cases, such as those of Julius and Ethel Rosenberg, Klaus Fuchs, and the Cambridge Five, ideological considerations appear to have been primary. Arrogating to themselves a certitude in their political beliefs that motivated them to place their countries at risk, they then betrayed them. They did not become public dissidents, critics of the status quo. It is not, I believe, a failure of gratitude but a deceptive placing of their ideological vision above the well-being of others to whom they are supposedly bound that makes their activity one of betrayal. In contrast, suppose an escaped slave, by virtue of deviously obtained access to documents, betrayed the troop movements of the Continental Army to the British, and therefore jeopardized its success. Would this be an act of ingratitude? For what?

That said, I think ideological betrayals are a mixed bag, and some we may even consider justified. Our reactions to the Cambridge Five are likely to be different from our reactions to Wilhelm Canaris, the head of Hitler's *Abwehr*,[52] and Claus von Stauffenberg, a leader of the plot to assassinate Hitler. Some involve self-serving arrogance, others a more measured appraisal of a situation—of forfeited loyalty, if you like.

In taking issue with Margalit, my purpose is not to deny that gratitude is an appropriate response to a benefactor. Margalit uses the example of a surgeon who has saved my life.[53] Even though it was her job to do what she did, insofar as she gave me something of great value that I was unable to provide for myself, I have every reason to be grateful. And I may express my

---

[52] Mueller 2017.
[53] Margalit 2017, 167–168.

gratitude in a number of ways: a thank-you note, a bottle of wine, or a donation to the hospital in which she works. I may do less without being ungrateful, though if I go online and write a mis-leading and critical anonymous review of her work, that would certainly count as ingratitude. But what if my work as a tax in-spector gives me access to her tax returns and I am reasonably led to believe that she is cheating on her taxes? Would it count as either ingratitude or—more saliently—betrayal, if I begin pro-ceedings against her? I do not think so. I can imagine that, as a result of her saving my life, I might find some way to suggest to her that she should revisit her returns—that would be an ex-pression of gratitude on my part—but if I institute proceedings, it could hardly constitute betrayal. I owed her no loyalty, even if I owed her gratitude. Had she not attended my surgical needs, another physician would have, and to that person I would have owed gratitude, albeit not loyalty.

I can accept a good deal of what Margalit says about gratitude and to whom we owe it. But even in some of the cases that he thinks central to gratitude—child–parent relations—it is quite possible to separate both gratitude from loyalty and ingratitude from betrayal. Consider exceedingly wealthy but emotionally and often physically distant parents. Suppose the parents provide nannies, resources, and opportunities, but there is scant "connection" to the children. Suppose also that at least one of the children turns out well and ex-ceedingly successful. That child may be grateful to its parents but have developed no great love or loyalty to them. Eventually she publishes a memoir of the children's early years, and the parents are revealed more by their personal absence than presence, their glittering lifestyle rather than their parenting skills. Have they been betrayed? Some may claim so, and may also complain of the suc-cessful child's ingratitude, but I think it a stretch to claim that the parents have been betrayed. What is more, gratitude may be shown for what they have provided, even if others may have had more to do with the memoirist's success.

Responding to betrayal

Insofar as betrayal targets the relational bonds between people and/ or collectivities, we might expect some permanent enmity or at least relational rupture to be the outcome of acts of betrayal. Intentional or negligent betrayal is a serious wrong, and its occurrence a legitimate cause for ongoing resentment. That is often the case. People divorce because of infidelity, are excommunicated because of apostasy, and are executed for treason. Is permanent rupture the proper or only response to betrayal? Practically, it may be the only viable option, for it is at least conceivable that a relationship has been so damaged by betrayal that there remain no feasible or practicable alternatives.

Some who have been left bereft by betrayal see suicide as their only reasonable option. If they have viewed a particular relational connection as central to their raison d'être for continued living, then betrayal may crush the chief reason they have for continuing their lives, and suicide may appear to be a rational if despairing option. Collectives that have been betrayed often adopt measures—permanent isolation or enmity (deportation, deprivation of citizenship, etc.)—that may allow for no significant redemption of the betrayer. Indeed, isolation of and hostility toward the betrayer sometime becomes part of the impelling identity of the betrayed collective. Serbian–Croatian and Hamas–Israeli relations have sometimes been so characterized. And some of the Catholic Church's most bitter antagonists have become so after betrayal by predatory priests and an unresponsive institution.

Yet permanent rupture has not always been or been seen as the only option. At the level of collective action, pardons have been given and clemency shown, actions which, if not exactly a form of "welcoming someone back into the fold," at least remove a formal punitive burden incurred by the person's betrayal. Whether pardons or clemency are morally justified is a more complicated matter—especially when administered as part of an unconstrained formal power; but pardons that are seen as ethically justified may also be restorative of breached associations.[54]

On the individual front, more nuanced responses are available. Within moral traditions that give a role to forgiveness and redemption, some forms of relational restoration are at times provided for. The possibility of forgiveness, of course, is not limited to betrayals. Any wrong done to another may be a candidate for forgiveness. Nevertheless, on one account of forgiveness, the (or at least a) point of forgiveness is the restoration of a breach in human relationships. Although I do not see forgiveness quite so narrowly—it may be seen as the overcoming of resentment along with a determination not to be bound by the past—there are certainly occasions for which seeking and bestowing forgiveness may presage restoration after relational betrayal. Whether such forgiveness also involves a forgoing of punishment, insofar as punishment might be anticipated, is a matter of contention. Where the betrayal is of an individual, forgiveness might be partially expressed as choice to withhold punishment; where the betrayal has had social repercussions, a victim's forgiveness might nevertheless be compatible with a socially sanctioned punishment.

There has been considerable discussion about how forgiveness works and whether merited or justifiable forgiveness requires some apology or repentance or other gesture of contriteness on the part of the betraying party. Most would agree that on the part of the forgiver there must be an appropriate sense of the wrong that was done in betrayal and—in many cases—a recognition that the person who betrayed is a fellow human being, possessing the same frailties as oneself. Forgiveness is not an act that expresses a lack of self-respect or servility. Even if, as will sometimes be the case, the person who betrayed is not restored to relational intimacy, there is normally an acknowledgment of the other's fellow humanity and restoration

[54] Alschuler 2020.

to the basic moral regard one owes to another human being qua human being.

Some would advocate unconditional forgiveness, at least in some circumstances. But in most cases that involve betrayal, it would be problematic for a restoration of the relation that has been undermined were there not some conditionality involved.[55] The mutuality that usually characterizes relationships generally calls for some acknowledgment of violation, remorse, and repentance on the part of the betrayer. Although it is not impossible to rebuild the trust that has been undermined by betrayal, rebuilding may take some doing (as well as time).[56]

Sometimes, though, a case might be made for proleptic forgiveness—an act of forgiveness that may itself evoke contrition on the part of the betrayer—an "interpersonal moral social construction" that treats the forgiven person as though he or she recognizes the wrong that was done.[57] Although such forgiveness may easily degenerate into instrumentalism, it may have a legitimate role in the recovery of relational trust, especially where the undermined relation was important to both parties and there is also a strong desire to express a common humanity with the wrongdoer.

Thus, although it may be—and certainly provides a basis for—the termination of a relational connection, betrayal need not—though it may—signal a permanent rupture. Relations broken may sometimes be repaired, and forgiveness is our most morally effective means of achieving it. Not always. There may be unforgiveable relational breaches and even with respect to those that are not, there will be a discretionary dimension. Forgivingness itself is a

---

[55] We might envisage unconditional forgiveness in cases that involve ignorance (cf. Lk. 23:34); but where some relational intimacy is involved, ignorance is more likely to be culpable, thus requiring some condition to be satisfied by the wrongdoer.

[56] Sometimes it may be a matter of rebuilding a more realistic trust. Shklar 1984 points to cases in which betrayals result from the excessive trust that a subject of trust places in its object (143–145, 153–155).

[57] Fricker 2018, 166.

nuanced virtue,[58] always requiring certain normatively important conditions of the forgiver, and most often (especially in betrayals) on the part of the wrongdoer. It cannot be demanded as a right. To be acceptable, our relations with others must always be grounded in choice.

Conclusion

I have argued that, in paradigm cases, betrayal is seen as a particularly egregious vice—a worse vice than loyalty is a virtue. If loyalty binds, betrayal (especially in the form of disloyalty) undermines identity-constituting social connections. Even though social connections are important to human flourishing, not all involve loyalty, and even some that do involve loyalty may be problematic. Betrayal as disloyalty, however, is threatening to deep social connections and, in addition, may wreak a variety of harms beyond that of a severed connection. Moreover, because betrayal/disloyalty is generally motivated by forms of self-servingness, it aggravates the wrongness of betrayed relationships. It may be, as J. L. Austin memorably phrased it, that betrayal/disloyalty, rather than loyalty, "wears the trousers."[59,60]

Bibliography

Alschuler, Albert W. "The Corruption of the Pardon Power: What Are the Limits?" *SSRN: University of Chicago, Public Law Working Paper No. 756* (2020): 446–482. https://papers.ssrn.com/sol3/papers.cfm?abstract_id=3734588.

---

[58] I make that assumption, realizing that there is a strand of thought that sees no virtue in forgiveness (e.g., Kekes 2009, 488).

[59] Austin 1964, 70 (but cf. Coval and Forrest 1967).

[60] I am grateful to Troy Jollimore, Tziporah Kasachkoff, and Nancy Snow for many valuable criticisms and suggestions.

Aristotle. *Nicomachean Ethics*. Translated by W. D. Ross. Internet Classics Archive, 1925. http://classics.mit.edu/Aristotle/nicomachaen.html.

Austin, J. L. *Sense and Sensibilia*. Oxford: Oxford University Press, 1964.

Blake, William. *The Prophetic Books of William Blake: Jerusalem*. Edited by E. R. D. Maclagan and A. G. B. Russell. London: A.H. Bullen., 1904.

Blamires, Harry. *The Christian Mind*. London: S.P.C.K., 1963.

Carnegie, Dale. *How to Win Friends and Influence People*. New York: Simon and Schuster, 1936.

Cocking, Dean, and Steve Matthews. "Unreal Friends." *Ethics and Information Technology* 2 (2000): 223–231.

Coval, S., and Forrest, Terry. "Which Word Wears the Trousers?" *Mind*, N.S., 76 (1967): 73–82.

Ewin, R. E. "Corporate Loyalty: Its Objects and Its Grounds." *Journal of Business Ethics* 12 (1993): 387–396.

Firth, Roderick. "Ethical Absolutism and the Ideal Observer." *Philosophy and Phenomenological Research* 12 (1952): 317–345.

Fricker, Miranda. "Ambivalence About Forgiveness." *Royal Institute of Philosophy Supplement* 84 (2018): 161–185.

Ganor, Boaz. "Defining Terrorism: Is One Man's Terrorist Another Man's Freedom Fighter?" *Police Practice and Research* 3 (2002): 287–304.

Genet, Jean. *Prisoner of Love*. Trans. Barbara Bray. New York: New York Review of Books, (1986) 2003.

Genet, Jean. *Thief's Journal*. New York: Bantam, (1949) 1965.

Glazer, Myron P., and Penina M. Glazer. *The Whistleblowers: Exposing Corruption in Government and Industry*. New York: Basic Books, 1991.

Greene, Graham. "Foreword" to Kim Philby, *My Silent War: The Soviet Master Spy's Own Story*. New York: Grove Press, 1968.

Greene, Graham. *The Virtue of Disloyalty*. London: Bodley Head, 1972.

Greene, Richard. *The Unquiet Englishman: A Life of Graham Greene*. New York: W.W. Norton, 2021.

Jeske, Diane. *Friendship and Social Media: A Philosophical Exploration*. Abingdon, England: Routledge, 2019.

Kekes, John. "Blame versus Forgiveness." *The Monist* 92:4 (2009): 488–506.

Kleinig, John. "The Blue Wall of Silence: An Ethical Analysis." *International Journal of Applied Philosophy* 15 (2001): 1–23.

Kleinig, John. "Loyalty." In *The Stanford Encyclopedia of Philosophy* (Summer 2022 edition), edited by Edward N. Zalta. https://plato.stanford.edu/archives/sum2022/entries/loyalty/

Kleinig, John. "Loyalty Betrayed." *Social Research* 86:3 (2019): 633–649.

Kleinig, John. *Loyalty and Loyalties: The Contours of a Problematic Virtue*. New York: Oxford University Press, 2014.

Kleinig, John. "Trust and Critical Thinking." *Educational Philosophy and Theory* 50:2 (2017): 133–143.

MacIntyre, Alasdair. *Is Patriotism a Virtue?* Lawrence: University of Kansas Press, 1984.

Margalit, Avishai. *On Betrayal.* Cambridge, MA: Harvard University Press, 2017.

Martin, Mike W. "Whistleblowing: Professionalism, Personal Life, and Shared Responsibility for Safety in Engineering." *Business and Professional Ethics Journal* 11 (1992): 21–40.

Mehler, Gordon. "Informants, Rats, and Tattletales: Loyalty, Fear, and the Constitution." *Criminal Justice Ethics* 2 (1997): 57–58.

Mueller, Michael. *Nazi Spymaster: The Life and Death of Admiral Wilhelm Canaris.* New York: Skyhorse, 2017.

Murdoch, Iris. *The Bell.* London: Penguin, 1962.

Oldenquist, Andrew. "Loyalties." *Journal of Philosophy* 79 (1982): 173–193.

Plato. *Apology.* Translated by Benjamin Jowett, 1891a. http://classics.mit.edu/Plato/apology.html

Plato. *Crito.* Translated by Benjamin Jowett, 1891c. http://classics.mit.edu/Plato/crito.html

Plato. *The Republic.* Translated by Benjamin Jowett, 1891b. http://classics.mit.edu/Plato/republic.html

Reddington, Raymond [James Pader]. *The Blacklist.* NBC TV series (dir. Andrew McCarthy) (2014) Season 2, Episode 3. https://www.youtube.com/watch?v=pNXB7SJdZso

Schwarz, Joanna C. "The Case Against Qualified Immunity." *Notre Dame Law Review* 93 (2018): 1797–1851.

Shklar, Judith N. "The Ambiguities of Betrayal." In *Ordinary Vices*, 138–191. Cambridge, MA: Belknap Press, 1984.

Väyrynen, Pekka. "Thick Ethical Concepts." In *The Stanford Encyclopedia of Philosophy* (Spring 2021 edition), Edward N. Zalta, ed. https://plato.stanford.edu/archives/spr2021/entries/thick-ethical-concepts/>.

Walker, A. D. M. "Political Obligation and the Argument from Gratitude." *Philosophy & Public Affairs* 17:3 (1988): 191–211.

Wolfe, S. E., and J. Nix. "The Alleged 'Ferguson Effect' and Police Willingness to Engage in Community Partnership." *Law and Human Behavior* 40 (2016): 1–10.

Wren, Thomas E. "Whistle-Blowing and Loyalty to One's Friends." In *Police Ethics: Hard Choices in Law Enforcement*, edited by William C. Heffernan and Timothy Stroup, 25–43. New York: John Jay Press, 1985.

5

Is Loyalty Redundant?

Troy Jollimore

> When an organization wants you to do right, it asks for
> your integrity; when it wants you to do wrong, it demands
> your loyalty.
>
> —Aaron Rosenthal, former Deputy Chief of
> the New York City Police Department
> (quoted in Kleinig 2014, 189)

The redundancy argument

To some, it is obvious that loyalty is a virtue. To others it is equally obvious that it is not. There is no denying that, as Aaron Rosenthal's remark implies, appeals to loyalty have been used to motivate people to perform immoral, even evil actions. Still, it seems difficult to deny that some particular loyal actions are morally admirable. How resistant to exploitation must a character trait be in order to count as a virtue? The question is very difficult to answer. How, then, might it be determined whether loyalty is a genuine virtue, and what is at stake in this question?

One way to proceed is to focus on the question of whether the fact that an act is loyal, in itself, gives a virtuous agent reason to perform it. The following principle seems plausible:

Troy Jollimore, *Is Loyalty Redundant?* In: *The Virtue of Loyalty.* Edited by: Troy Jollimore,
Oxford University Press. © Oxford University Press 2024. DOI: 10.1093/oso/9780197612644.003.0006

Virtues give Reasons (VR): The fact that an action would express some virtue constitutes a (defeasible) reason for a virtuous agent to perform that action.

The fact that an action is an *honest* action, for instance, or a just action, clearly seems to constitute a reason for a virtuous agent to perform it.

(VR) suggests a possible argument for showing that loyalty is not a virtue. If we could show that (VR) does not hold with respect to actions that express loyalty—if we could show, say, that the fact that an action expresses loyalty is irrelevant to a virtuous agent's reasons for action, and thus should play no role in such an agent's deliberations—this would be evidence that loyalty is no virtue. Conversely, if we can show that such facts *are* relevant, and *do* reliably generate reasons for action, that would be at least some evidence that it *is* a virtue.

Why might we doubt that (VR) holds of loyalty? First, cases in which appeals to loyalty are used to motivate immoral actions, to persuade people to act against their conscience, and to overlook moral scruples are not too hard to find, and the fact that loyalty is liable to be exploited in this way might seem to derive from its very nature. Many would agree with R. E. Ewin that loyalty "appears to involve as part of itself a setting aside of good judgement, at least to some extent."[1] The true test of loyalty, it might be said, will not be found in situations in which the object of loyalty is objectively worthy of one's devotion, or where a "loyal" action is good for independent reasons. For in those situations *anyone* would have reason to protect and support the loyalty object, or to perform the action; ties of loyalty will not be required. It is where an object of loyalty cannot claim to be entitled to one's efforts on grounds of objective merit that the appeal to loyalty will be necessary. But it seems likely

---

[1] Ewin 1992, 411.

that in many of those cases the balance of reasons will oppose doing the thing that loyalty supposedly recommends.

Of course, loyalty is not always directed toward unworthy objects, and many of the actions loyalty would have us perform are morally admirable. But in such cases, it might be claimed, the appeal to loyalty is unnecessary: if an action is morally laudable for other reasons, then appeals to loyalty will be superfluous. Consider the following pair of cases regarding X, a hypothetical soldier:

> *Flood.* X's platoon is ordered to save a group of endangered children in a flooded village.
>
> *My Lai.* X is ordered to take part in an evil action: a massacre of innocent civilians. X protests that this would be morally wrong. His commanding officer responds by appealing to X's patriotism: X will be a traitor if he refuses to take part.

A soldier being ordered to save children from drowning should hardly need to be told that doing so is a patriotic act: the fact that there are children whose lives are in danger is clearly reason enough. By contrast, in *My Lai* it is apparent why an appeal to loyalty or patriotic sentiment would be required: X's moral beliefs, and conscience, must be overcome to get X to perform the action. But here, of course, X should not perform the action. If this is the sort of work loyalty is well suited to do, then loyalty is likely a character trait we are better off without.

We might sympathize, then, with Joseph Agassi's claim that "When an appeal is made for patriotism, for any loyalty, it is because reasonable arguments have been tried and failed. This is so because loyalty at times when it is supportable by other considerations is simply redundant and is thus usually not evoked."[2] Harry Blamires argues similarly:

---

[2] Agassi 1974, 315.

Loyalty may be said to be evil in the sense that if any action is defended on the grounds of loyalty alone, it is defended on no rational grounds at all. [. . .] Loyalty to a good man, a good government, a good cause, is of course a different matter. But in these cases, where one stands by a man, or a government, or a cause, because it is good, one is standing by the good. The basis of action in these cases is moral in that one is serving the good; and thus the concept of loyalty is redundant.[3]

I will refer to the argument expressed in these various passages as the Redundancy Argument. It claims, in essence, that (VR) fails to obtain in cases where the putative virtue is loyalty, for the fact that an action would express loyalty in itself provides no reason for action. If there are reasons for performing that action, loyalty is not their source. The fact that an action would be a *loyal* action, then, is not a relevant fact that ought to figure in the deliberations or motivations of virtuous agents; and loyalty, being incapable of generating legitimate reasons for action, turns out not to be a virtue.

We might observe that in certain trivial cases, where there is very little at stake, the Redundancy Argument seems to fail. Suppose that Moira is her softball team's best hitter, and that her team has reached the playoffs. On the morning of the first playoff game, she finds herself not in the mood to show up to play softball. Surely, one might say, she owes it to her teammates to show up anyway. Surely, too, this obligation *is* a matter of loyalty and cannot be traced back to some impartial source. (Impartially speaking, it really doesn't matter which team ultimately wins the championship.) I myself find these claims fairly plausible. They do not, however, ground a very powerful case against the Redundancy Argument, as there just isn't enough at stake. As Simon Keller observes, one sign that a particular loyalty is "serious" is that "you allow that loyalty to

[3] Blamires 1963, 24.

have some force when making some morally weighty decisions."[4] The decision whether to skip a softball game is *not* morally weighty, and this lack of moral weight seems to be part of what accounts for why, in such cases, loyalty is able to exert an influence. That the Redundancy Argument fails in trivial cases does not offer strong support for the claim that loyalty is a virtue. If loyalty is a virtue, it must be capable of making a difference in cases that matter.

The accused friend

The Redundancy Argument focuses our attention on the relation between loyalty and the broader framework of morality: general principles, universal values, impartial requirements, and so on. Its charge is that when loyalty conflicts with impartial morality, impartial morality wins; and that in cases in which it is not so defeated, and in which it might at first look like loyalty is playing a role, that appearance is an illusion, as the reasons that matter are those, again, that arise from impartial morality. If this argument is correct, then loyalty is morally insignificant (and hence, presumably not a virtue).

We noted earlier that trivial cases are of little use in showing that this is not so. What about cases in which there is more at stake? Again, some such cases—*My Lai* and *Flood*, for starters—seem to fit the Redundancy Argument quite well. And there might seem to be reason to expect this fit to hold generally. Consider E. M. Forster's famous statement, "If I had to choose between betraying my country and betraying my friend, I hope I should have the guts to betray my country." Many tend to approve of the sentiment when they first hear it. But as Diane Jeske observes in her contribution to this volume, we should be cautious: surely the question of what we hope we would do cannot be determined without knowing the

---

[4] Keller 2007, 60.

details of the case.[5] If, as per Jeske's example, my friend turns out to be a participant in the January 2021 assault on the US Capitol, then I hope that I would have the guts *not* to take his side. Here we have one loyalty in competition with another; and in the end, what we have reason to do is determined not by considerations of loyalty but by those of impartial justice. It would be easy to conclude that the Redundancy Argument has once again been vindicated.

Perhaps not everyone will share Jeske's intuition that one ought not to protect one's Capitol rioter friend (though I do). Richard Rorty, in presenting a similar case—one in which "you know that one of your parents or one of your children is guilty of a sordid crime"—claims that "Many of us would be willing to perjure ourselves in order to supply such a child or parent with a false alibi."[6] Maybe, when push comes to shove, many of us will decide that loyalty's moral claims bear more weight than we had thought; or maybe we will decide that morality is not as important to us as we had presumed. Fortunately, I do not think we need to reach general agreement regarding all such cases in order to show that the Redundancy Argument, though it captures an important truth in cases such as *My Lai*, cannot succeed in showing what it intends to show.

Let's put aside, for now, cases in which we know that the accused person is guilty; we will work our way back to those. Consider, then, cases in which a friend of yours is accused of some serious crime, and pursued by the authorities, but is nonetheless innocent. We might be tempted to say that here it is clear that we should protect the accused person, but that since it is the fact of their innocence that grounds our obligation to act, the Redundancy Argument holds: we might have reason to do the thing that is picked out by the virtue of loyalty as the thing to do, but our reasons for doing so are grounded in impartial justice, not

[5] See Jeske, Chapter 2, this volume.
[6] Rorty 1997, 139.

loyalty. We ought to protect the accused when they are innocent, and refuse to do so when they are guilty. Either way, loyalty has nothing to do with it.

But this position oversimplifies matters. First, protecting an innocent person might be a costly thing to do. It might require an investment of resources; it might be unpleasant; and one might well risk legal penalties oneself. Suppose the case is one of persecution rather than simple error: we are in a dictatorship, and the charges against the accused are purely political and entirely bogus. Anyone who tried to help them evade punishment might themselves become a target. Even in non-dictatorships, and even where honest error rather than persecution lies behind the accusation, a person who knows the accused to be innocent but has no way of proving it to the satisfaction of the courts, and who chooses to hide that person in their house, perjures themselves to provide an alibi, or performs some similar action, is putting themselves at risk. Where substantial costs and risks are involved, it is far too simple to say that everyone is under an obligation, let alone an equal obligation, to protect the innocent. Impartial justice, then, presumably does not always place us under such an obligation. But when the accused is someone close to you, such an obligation—or, if not an out and out obligation, then a stronger, more compelling *reason*—might be generated by loyalty.

Something similar can be said regarding moral costs. I might save my innocent friend by providing a false alibi, and hence perjuring myself; but many would hold that perjury always has a serious moral cost, even when it serves the greater justice of reaching the objectively correct verdict. I do not defend any particular claim here about when protecting innocents outweighs the moral cost of perjury. For in order to show that loyalty may play a substantial role here, it is enough to claim that that answer may be affected by ties of loyalty: that, for instance, my loyalty to my friend, combined with the value of protecting an innocent person, may together override the moral cost of committing perjury in cases where the latter consideration would not itself have been sufficient. This claim is highly plausible.

What if you are not certain that your friend is innocent? Many of the same considerations will still apply, depending on just how much uncertainty attaches to your belief (or hope) that your friend is indeed innocent. Uncertainty, after all, is not an all-or-nothing matter. Cases in which it is very likely that your friend is innocent, though you cannot be certain, will resemble those we discussed earlier; here, however, given the fact that there is a chance your friend is in fact guilty, loyalty might have a bit more work to do in overcoming the various reasons, both moral and prudential, that speak against protecting her. Moreover, loyalty-generated reasons are in play in another and subtler manner as well. I have been speaking of the guilt or innocence of the accused person as a straightforward matter of fact, and as if our knowledge of it were entirely independent of our loyalty ties. But a person's loyalties can themselves be expected to exert an influence both over the verdict she arrives at—that is, whether she believes her friend is innocent or guilty—and also over the ultimate import that verdict holds for her.

The point I am developing involves what has come to be known as *epistemic partiality*. We tend to favor our friends not only in actions but also in beliefs, thinking more highly of them than we would of others on the basis of similar evidence. Friendship and other loyalty-involving relationships seem to require such partiality. One's natural first thought at hearing that a friend has been accused of some terrible crime will likely be, "But she would never do such a thing!" As Sarah Stroud (who first introduced the term 'epistemic partiality') writes, "[A]t the end of the day we are simply less likely to conclude that our friend acted disreputably, or that he is a bad person, than we would in the case of a nonfriend."[7] Contrary to the Redundancy Argument, then, in such cases loyalty frequently

---

[7] Stroud 2006, 506.

influences how an agent treats, and thinks and feels about, an accused friend or relative, in ways that will strike many as comprehensible and even admirable.

Now let us push further, by asking just what does it mean to be "less likely to conclude that our friend acted disreputably, or that he is a bad person"? For this is not, in fact, as simple a matter as it may at first appear; and seeing that this is so will open up still more space in which loyalty may play a substantial role in the deliberations and action of the virtuous agent. Suppose that a friend of mine, Peter, has been accused of performing a disreputable action. What does loyalty require, in terms of the kind of epistemic partiality we have been discussing? As always, it is important to say that it does *not* require that we continue to defend Peter *no matter what*. Where the action is extremely bad, and there is no doubt that he did it, loyalty, whatever it might require, must at least allow that we recognize Peter's guilt and respond accordingly.

Let us suppose that we have not (yet) reached *that* point. What kind of defense of Peter, then, might loyalty require? The most straightforward would concern factual matters: a loyal friend would find it difficult to believe that Peter actually performed the action in question, would carefully scrutinize the evidence that he had, would search for other possible explanations, and the like. This is one thing, and the most obvious thing, that might be meant by Stroud's assertion that "we are simply less likely to conclude that our friend acted disreputably." But there is another thing we might mean.[8] For we might, after all, admit that Peter performed the action in question, and even admit that it is the sort of action which is *generally* disreputable, but nonetheless claim that *in this particular set of circumstances* Peter had good reason to act as he did. Morality is, after all, complex, and there are few moral prohibitions that admit of no exceptions. Sometimes lying is justified; sometimes promises must be broken; sometimes one must be cruel to be kind;

[8] Cf. Stroud 2006, 506–510.

and so on. So another thing loyalty can do is make us more likely to deny the wrongness of the action even while admitting the factual truth of the accusation.

Similarly, a loyal agent might admit the wrongness of their friend's action while downplaying its significance, asking himself, and prompting others to ask, questions like: What does her having performed this action say about her overall character? How significant is it? Does it change our general opinion of her as a moral agent, as a person? A person, we often think, ought not to be defined by any single act. This is not to deny that we are sometimes justified in punishing a person for a single act. But in doing so, it is important to remember that punishment is always, of necessity, a response to a discrete action or set of actions; it does not, and cannot, reflect or acknowledge every aspect of a person's character. One of the tasks of a loyal friend, at such moments, is to help us bear this in mind and act accordingly.

We should not think that tendencies to favor one's friends in such ways involve nothing more than some sort of regrettable knee-jerk preference for those we love. Rather, they are largely rooted in the various roles that trust plays in friendship. Friendship requires trust; friendship engenders trust; and we tend to become friends with people whom we feel we can trust. Thus, if a friend has judged that an action was the right thing to do given the circumstances, the very fact that she has made this judgment will incline you to take that possibility seriously, and perhaps more charitably than you otherwise would.[9] If you know what your friend's reasons were, your loyalty to her will make you more likely to regard those reasons as valid and persuasive. If you do not know what those reasons were, you will be more likely to assume that she likely had

---

[9] Kyla Ebels-Duggan 2008 (158–159) makes a related point regarding goals and ends: "I claim that we should regard our partners as having what I call *authority in judgment*. In granting another this kind of authority, you treat her choice of an end as if it were evidence that the end is worthwhile."

good reasons for her action, based, possibly, on aspects of the situation of which you—and others, including the accusers—are likely unaware.

Thus, loyalty may exert an influence during at least three stages of the friend's deliberation and action. First, it will make her more likely to arrive at the belief that her friend is innocent, or likely to be innocent; call this the *verdictive judgment*. Second, it will affect her understanding and interpretation of the verdictive judgment, and the significance it has for her. And third, it will influence her practical responses to that judgment and her understanding of it. Loyal friends will tend to be more inclined to interpret their friends in a positive light, whatever verdictive judgments they have arrived at; and they will be more inclined to protect their friends, whatever interpretation of their friends' actions they may have settled on.

Of course, all of these tendencies have their limits. What's more, their force will vary from case to case, and from friendship to friendship. It is possible to be someone's friend while regarding them as having quite poor judgment. More commonly, we are often aware that our friends have somewhat poor judgment in some particular areas. If David has committed a violent crime, and I know that David has anger issues and struggles with self-control when provoked, I will be less inclined than I would otherwise be to trust that David's aggression was backed by good reasons. Our knowledge of the particular qualities of our friends will influence our judgments about what they are likely to have done. Where the likelihood of their guilt is increased, the friend-protecting impact of loyalty might be diminished. In some cases it might be entirely undermined.

The overarching point, again, is to make clear, in response to the Redundancy Argument, that there are a variety of substantial roles loyalty might play in the deliberations of the virtuous agent. Perhaps in extreme cases like *My Lai*, where, given the very nature of the loyalty-based demand being placed on the agent, it might appear that the only way to adhere to moral standards would be to be disloyal, there is little room for loyalty to play a legitimate role. (Though in the next section I will suggest that we should be hesitant even in drawing that conclusion.) But this is an uncommon and extreme case. In many other cases, loyalty seems to provide legitimate, nonredundant reasons for thinking, feeling, and acting in certain ways. When one's relative or friend has been accused of a serious wrongdoing, it might matter a great deal what one does—these are not, that is to say, trivial cases of the sort we noted earlier; yet it can still be true, for all that, that the commitments of the loyal agent will give them substantial reasons to respond quite differently from how they would otherwise.

The guilty friend

> Oh, I know he deserves to hang, you proved your stuff.
> But . . . don't ask me to tie the rope.
> —Holly Martins, in *The Third Man*

What if it is clear that one's friend is guilty of a nontrivial crime, and deserving of the punishment they stand to receive under the law? In *this* case, we might be tempted to think, loyalty must give way: morality demands that justice be done, and to help a guilty friend evade the punishment they merit cannot possibly be virtuous. Here, then, proponents of the Redundancy Argument might seem to get things right: if loyalty provides any reasons in such situations, they will necessarily be reasons that a morally virtuous agent would not act on. Here at least, loyalty has no legitimate role to play.

Even if this were correct, it is not at all clear that it would be enough to vindicate the view the Redundancy Argument was meant to support: that loyalty is no virtue. For if the argument of the preceding section is correct, then there is a range of cases in which loyalty does generate legitimate and nonredundant reasons for action, and in which, therefore, our principle (VR) seems to hold true of loyalty: the fact that an action would express loyalty would give a virtuous agent a (potentially defeasible) reason to perform it. (Perhaps one thing the discussion has begun to suggest, and which will become still clearer as this section proceeds, is that we should not restrict ourselves to *actions*: there are also thoughts, feelings, motives, styles of expression, and so on that are subject to such evaluation.) The case of the friend who is known to be guilty, by contrast, might merely be acknowledged as a kind of remainder—the sort of case in which, like *My Lai*, perhaps, loyalty turns out to have no role to play.

But must we say this, even in cases in which we know that our friend is guilty? It seems to me that the view that loyalty must be irrelevant in such cases rests on various oversimplifications, of which I will mention three. First, it overlooks the fact that situations of this sort are highly complex, offering a range of potential responses and behaviors. Second, it overlooks the fact that different agents, in such situations, may have good reason to adopt different roles and hence to respond in different ways; we do not all have just the same reasons to do just the same things. And third, it overlooks the significance of certain temporal aspects of loyalty.

Begin with the first point. To say that a good person should be loyal to a guilty friend is not necessarily to say that she ought to help that friend evade justice. For the choice of whether to do so is not the only choice that must be made. Let us suppose that a friend of mine has committed a serious offense, that I acknowledge that she has and that it is indeed serious, and that I've decided that I in no way intend to stand in the way of her being punished. This represents, to be sure, an important decision. But it need not represent the end of my moral thinking and decision-making in this area.

Moral conflicts and dilemmas are often described starkly, using the briefest of descriptors to identify the alleged options. Do I turn in my accused friend or hide her from the cops? Do I betray my country or betray my friend? But many other decisions may follow in the wake of such large ones; and as virtue ethicists have often reminded us, responding virtuously is not just a matter of choosing which (minimally described) action to perform but also of *how* one performs the chosen action. One must, as Aristotle says, do the right thing in the right way and for the right reasons. So we must distinguish between the person who feels no qualm about turning a friend in and ensuring her punishment, and the one who does so reluctantly, regretfully, and with heaviness of heart. The former might be acting in a manner that would be appropriate if the offender were a stranger, but quite inappropriate where she is an intimate. To assess virtue, then, we must go beyond the bare, result-oriented descriptions of one's actions, and also be concerned with the agent's attitudes and feelings, and the way they are expressed in their performance of the action—not to mention in what they say, think, and feel afterward, the kinds of reflections they engage in and questions they ask themselves (*might things have gone differently if I had been paying more attention?*), and other such matters. Moreover, it is not just feelings, attitudes, and so on that will be in play here, but actions as well. The line between expressed feeling and action is quite fuzzy here anyway; one can, after all, say that doing something enthusiastically and doing it reluctantly are in a sense different actions, and there will be cases here where this is indeed precisely the right thing to say. But it is also true that while turning one's friend in, or allowing her to be turned in and receive her punishment—refusing to shelter her, refusing to provide a false alibi, and the like—will be important parts of the story, the full story will be larger and more complex. There will be further decisions to be made, further actions to be performed, and, likely, further things loyalty will call on us to do.

As Ewin writes, "The loyal person sticks in there in the bad times as well" as the good.[10] This idea is reflected in typical wedding vows, in which one promises to stand by one's spouse for better or worse, for richer or poorer, in sickness and in health, and

---

[10] Ewin 1992, 411.

so on. Part of the importance of such vows is that they recognize that we are not always at our best. When we *are* at our best, and when things are going well for us, we have less need of support from lovers, friends, and others; we can, at least largely, take care of ourselves. It is when things go badly that we need such people. If people had only self-interested motivations, this would be a serious problem: for purely self-interested people will likely flock to us when things are going well and turn away from us precisely when we need the help of others most. But loyalty counteracts this tendency, motivating the people who care for us to be there when it is hardest and when their support is essential. As Robert Nozick notes regarding romantic love, such love "places a floor under your well-being; it provides insurance in the face of fate's blows."[11] The same can be said—though with different contours and nuances—of friendship, parenthood, and other personal relationships involving loyalty.

Promising to stand by someone through wealth or poverty, health or sickness—even "for better or for worse"—does not commit us to accepting, or excusing, everything they might do. It might be easier to stand by one's partner when undeserved misfortune strikes them—and, at least in some cases, clearer that one should—than when one's partner is to some degree responsible for their sufferings. Even in most of those cases, though, such promises presumably temper the temptation to judge one's partner swiftly and harshly or to abandon them immediately and unreflectively. Such promises urge that we regard our companions' shortcomings and wrongdoings in an understanding and generous light, that we be tolerant and, within reasonable (but capacious) limits, forgiving, and that we not abandon them at the first sign of imperfection. Again, this applies not only to marriages or romantic relationships, but to some degree to friendships as well. The loyal friend might admit that her friend has done wrong. (Indeed, admitting that she

---

[11] Nozick 1989, 71.

has—and helping the wrongdoer face the facts, and acknowledge her wrongdoing openly and honestly—might be better for the friend, particularly in the long run, than helping her hide from it.) But she will be hesitant to abandon her friend, even when doing so would be easier or more convenient. Even if the rest of the world turns its back on the offender, viewing her as nothing more than a common criminal and shunning her, her friend will still see her as a human being, a person. She is, admittedly, a person who has done wrong, perhaps serious wrong. Still, this is only one part of her—a part that, as large as it might loom now, might come in the fullness of time to seem a fairly small part of her. Each of us is much more than any particular act we commit, and even serial offenders are more than *just* offenders. A loyal person will insist on putting a friend's crime in a larger perspective, the perspective of a whole life, and in particular of a potential future that contains opportunities for regret, improvement, and various forms of redemption. Every criminal is a person who might not have been a criminal, who has often been something else, and who, in all likelihood, still has the possibility of being something else. To insist on seeing one's friend, and their acts, in the light of these facts is part of what it is to *be* loyal to someone.

It is not hard to find examples of actions that display this kind of loyalty. A person might show their loyalty to an incarcerated spouse by visiting and otherwise maintaining contact with them, by furthering and maintaining their joint projects, by taking care of their children, by not seeking a divorce, by not shunning their company once they are released (and, prior to that, by making decisions and plans on the basis of the assumption that the relation-ship will continue after the prison sentence has been served, and communicating this), and in a large number of other ways. They may also honor their commitment in smaller yet highly significant ways, such as by regularly reminding friends and others about the offender's good qualities and features, helping them not to forget, as they have not forgotten, that there is more to them than their crime.

There may also be certain things a loyal spouse or friend will not be willing to do. To admit that one's friend deserves to be brought to justice and punished is one thing; to help administer the punishment, or otherwise be complicit in it, is something else. This is related to the second sort of oversimplification mentioned earlier: we forget, sometimes, that in such situations, different people have different roles. It is a significant oversimplification of our moral thinking to think that belief in moral objectivity or in the reality of moral requirements demands that for each situation, there is one and only one proper way for all moral agents to respond. It is up to the authorities, not to me, to ensure that the offender is punished. I might well agree that the punishment is appropriate and deserved and yet have no desire to participate in it myself, or view doing so as inappropriate. Indeed, it is perfectly consistent for me to view the punishment as justified while also seeing my own role as that of friend and comforter who attempts to render the punishment less harsh or painful than it otherwise might be. Not all of us have to shun the offender, even if it is appropriate that they be shunned by most of society.

The third sort of oversimplification has to do with time. Recall again Blamires's statement of the Redundancy Argument:

> Loyalty to a good man, a good government, a good cause, is of course a different matter. But in these cases, where one stands by a man, or a government, or a cause, because it is good, one is standing by the good. The basis of action in these cases is moral in that one is serving the good; and thus the concept of loyalty is redundant.

There is certainly something to this. Again, however, even the good are not *always* good. Human beings are imperfect, and experience not only moments of weakness but periods of imperfection; a formerly good, indeed thoroughly admirable person might lose their bearings for a time. If we judged that person solely by their conduct during that particular time period, we would hold them unworthy of any sort of loyalty. But loyalty is precisely that virtue which reminds us that people are not to be judged by their conduct and nature during a limited time period. A person might, for a time, act like someone who, if they were always like that, would not deserve loyalty. But the basis of one's commitment—the fact that they do nonetheless deserve loyalty all things considered—is the fact that they are *not* always, or perhaps even ordinarily, like that.

Blamires's statement is, then, too simple. In standing by a friend who has gone astray, I need not be "standing by the good" in so straightforward a sense. I might instead be standing by a person who has been good, and who I hope will be good again. Perhaps my standing by her will increase the chance that this will happen— which is not to say that the rightness of my doing so necessarily depends on this being the case.

To hold this is perfectly compatible with allowing that some actions are sufficiently morally reprehensible that they may negate any claim to loyalty at all, regardless of the agent's conduct before or after them. Just as there are limits to forgiveness, there are limits to loyalty. Extreme cases of that sort will not count against the Redundancy Argument: in them, the party demanding loyalty does not merit it, and the appeal to loyalty should be rejected. But if we keep more ordinary cases in mind, we can see that the Redundancy Argument is quite limited in scope. Again, the idea of "for better or for worse" seems relevant here: if one's spouse, or friend, has on the whole behaved well, honored their commitments, attempted to act rightly, and so on, one does not drop them the minute they experience a moral failure. A loyal friend need not always overlook your imperfections, but they will not seize immediately upon them as a reason for abandoning you and ending their relationship with you.

Abstract principles and political communities

It might seem that the kinds of considerations I have been presenting apply to loyalty commitments that are directed toward individual persons, but not to those directed toward other kinds of objects. This might suggest that the Redundancy Argument can be resisted in the case of personal loyalties, but not with respect to, say, loyalty to a principle or ideal, or loyalty to a country or other political community.

I suspect that the Redundancy Argument may well possess considerable force when deployed against loyalties that are directed toward such abstractions as principles and ideals. The understanding of loyalty that seems to emerge from our discussion views it as something like a disposition to stick with a person through periods of time during which that person's objective merit, if we take a narrow and present-oriented view of it, might not otherwise justify one's support. But such 'loyalty' can have no application to something as abstract and unchanging as a principle. Whereas a flawed person might eventually recover and improve, there is no sense in which a flawed principle or ideal can improve without becoming a different principle. As a result, the idea of standing by someone through thick and thin, which serves as a natural expression of such hopes and commitments in the case of persons, seems quite out of place with respect to principles and other abstractions. While some people speak as if one can be loyal to a principle, in much the way one can toward a friend, lover, or relative, it seems to me that this stretches the meaning of 'loyalty' a bit too far. One can, of course, be *dedicated* or *committed* to a principle. But not all commitments involve loyalty, and reflecting on the contrasts between this sort of case and cases of the sort I have focused on in this paper may help clarify why it seems counterintuitive to many (including myself) to see commitments and ideals as proper objects of loyalty.[12]

---

[12] An interesting intermediary case is that of documents expressing ideals or principles: for example, to take the case focused on by Sanford Levinson in Chapter 8: the US Constitution. At any given time, the US Constitution presumably expresses a certain set of political principles. As Levinson observes, however, the document is subject to change depending on the will of the voters, and such changes are at least in principle without

(On the other hand, the considerations of the second section might suggest a limited role for loyalty here. Perhaps my loyal commitment to a certain principle, for instance, would give me reason to defend it when it comes under criticism, to be somewhat resistant to rejecting it when counterarguments are presented, and so on.) What about countries and other communities? A fair number of thinkers have found it intuitively plausible to see personal loyalties as tolerable or even valuable while viewing political loyalties as by nature dangerous and destructive.[13] While I agree that there is some reason to be more careful and more skeptical with respect to political loyalties than to personal ones, I do not think we must conclude that the critique of the Redundancy Argument I have developed here has no application in the case of patriotism or other political loyalties.

Let us again consider *My Lai*, in which the action that is claimed to be required by loyalty—participating in the massacre—is clearly prohibited by morality. I take it that stringent moral requirements, such as the requirement not to kill innocent persons, should trump loyalty, and that it follows that if the agent has any loyalty-based reason to participate in the massacre, it is outweighed by the countervailing moral prohibition. (The *if* is genuine, since it might be that loyalty-based reasons to participate in the massacre are not simply outweighed, but entirely annulled.) Does it follow that loyalty, in such cases, generates no reasons for the agent at all?

One might well hold that loyalty, in such cases, reinforces an agent's reasons for *refusing* to take part in the massacre: since such an atrocity would be highly detrimental to the moral integrity of her country, and would surely constitute a serious blemish on its

---

limit. Individuals, of course, also change—a fact that has been treated as significant in this chapter; but because people change in different ways and for different reasons, I tend to share Levinson's skepticism about the idea that loyalty to the US Constitution (as opposed to, say, some particular version of that document, relativized to a given moment in time) can be justified.

[13] See, for instance, Keller 2007.

character, someone who is loyal to her country has strong reason to want it not to happen. Moreover, given that military orders always issue from and are communicated by particular individuals, there may be room for a person on the receiving end of clearly immoral orders to refuse to obey them in the name of loyalty, by arguing that the orders and those who issued them violate the core principles of the country whose military employs them, and hence are not morally legitimate representatives of that country. (Presumably, a country that lacks such core principles merits no loyalty to begin with.)

Of course, a loyalty-based reason to disobey immoral orders is presumably another redundant reason, since the soldier already has more than enough reason to refuse to participate, and indeed to stop the massacre from happening if somehow she can do so. At this point in our discussion, however, that need no longer strike us as deeply troubling. Our initial worry was that loyalty's reasons were *always* redundant; had that turned out to be the case, it would, I think, have been problematic for the claim that loyalty is a virtue. But the possibility that loyalty's reasons are *sometimes* redundant—that they sometimes provide additional moral reason for doing what we already have good reason to do—does not seem problematic in the same way.

It is worth remembering, too, that other citizens of the country in question, while not as directly involved as the soldiers being given orders to commit evil acts, are nevertheless indirectly involved, and that loyalty might provide them with reasons as well. Not being on the battlefield, members of the general public back home do not face the choice of whether to participate in commanded massacres. But they may have some degree of political influence over whether such massacres happen, and over how the country responds after they happen. And again, while impartial justice already gives them sufficient reason to try to ensure that no such massacres are committed anywhere, by anyone, their special concern for their own political community will give them additional reason to ensure that *their* country avoids such evil acts. It was something like this that moved Thoreau to refuse to pay taxes that would have gone to supporting hunting down fugitive slaves and making war on Mexico; and it was for this sort of reason that Americans who opposed torture on grounds of universal principle had particular reason to object to the torture of prisoners at Abu Ghraib in the early 2000s—torture that was being carried out on their behalf, by their representatives, and in their name.

As with friends, we must also recognize that countries change over time. A country might begin with morally excellent core principles and then drift away from them, or it might begin with flawed principles and then struggle toward better ones. If it is currently engaged in immoral practices, the choice to refuse to engage in them, or to actively oppose them, might be an expression of patriotism in much the way that refusing to assist a friend's immoral projects can be an expression of friendship. Just as an individual can lose their moral compass for a while, so can a country; and in each case we might find ourselves with similar roles to play, in terms of trying to help them recover and return to their ideals. One's conception of what it is to be loyal to one's country must be formed both in the light of facts about what it has been and done in the past, and facts about what it might potentially do and become in the future.

During an 1871 US Senate debate concerning sales of surplus weapons to France for use in the Franco-Prussian War, Senator Matthew Carpenter accused his fellow Wisconsin Senator Carl Schurz of covert loyalty to Prussia and, hence, of a lack of patriotic commitment to the United States. His attack included a phrase that was already a well-known expression of patriotic sentiment: "My country, right or wrong." Schurz's reply included the following statement:

> The Senator from Wisconsin cannot frighten me by exclaiming, "My country, right or wrong." In one sense I say so too. My country; and my country is the great American Republic. My country, right or wrong; if right, to be kept right; and if wrong, to be set right.

This understanding of patriotism seems very much in the spirit of the interpretation of loyalty I have been working toward in this chapter.[14] Schurz clearly makes room for the requirements of morality and for the impersonal and objective assessment of actions that might be committed in the name of loyalty. Yet his commitment to his country is real, and is by no means redundant or eliminable, providing him with reasons to act on its behalf and, in particular, to take steps to set it right if it has gone wrong. Understood in this way, loyalty resists two objections that would challenge its status as a genuine virtue. On the one hand, it avoids the excesses of blind devotion or unconditional subservience. Yet at the same time it turns out to be the kind of character trait that is not simply reducible to something else—a set of impartial moral principles, for instance— but is rather capable of playing a real and substantial role in the thought and action of the virtuous agent.

Bibliography

Agassi, Joseph. "The Last Refuge of the Scoundrel." *Philosophia* 4:2–3 (1974): 315–317.

Blamires, Harry. *The Christian Mind*. London: S.P.K., 1963.

Ebels-Duggan, Kyla. "Against Beneficence: A Normative Account of Love." *Ethics* 119 (2008): 142–170.

Ewin, R. E. "Loyalty and the Virtues." *The Philosophical Quarterly* 42:169 (1992): 403–419.

Keller, Simon. *The Limits of Loyalty*. New York: Cambridge University Press, 2007.

Kleinig, John. *Loyalty and Loyalties*. New York: Oxford University Press, 2014.

Nozick, Robert. *The Examined Life*. New York: Simon and Shuster, 1989.

Rorty, Richard. "Justice as a Larger Loyalty." *Ethical Perspectives* 4:3 (1997): 139–151.

Stroud, Sarah. "Epistemic Partiality in Friendship." *Ethics* 116:3 (2006): 498–524.

---

[14] Compare Simon Keller's discussion of the slogan (Keller 2007: 69–70).

6

Loyalty and the Reception of Buddhism in China

Leah Kalmanson

Loyalty, as an explicitly theorized moral value or virtue, is not prominent in early South Asian Buddhist texts. The central moral value is that of compassion, and the central moral imperative is the alleviation of suffering through correct understanding of the *dharma* or "teachings." In general, Buddhism's emphasis on radical compassion, which extends impartially to *all* sentient beings, was at odds with indigenous moral sensibilities in Chinese traditions that prioritized context-specific personal and political obligations. In particular, the Buddhist institution of monasticism was seen as encouraging the abnegation of family and social responsibilities, the Buddhist pursuit of a seemingly otherworldly liberation was seen as threatening people's allegiance to the emperor, and the entire system of Buddhist rebirth was thought to disrupt the natural lines of loyalty extending back to the ancestors venerated at ancestral shrines. Nonetheless, Buddhism did indeed become well-established throughout East Asia, in large part through the work of adherents who foregrounded its relevance to both family and state concerns. Hence, although there are tensions between Buddhism's universalizing ethics of compassion and indigenous Chinese moral sensibilities regarding special and specific loyalties, these two positions were brought into productive dialogue in the course of a comparative philosophical exchange that played out over several centuries, two major language families (Indo-European and

Leah Kalmanson, *Loyalty and the Reception of Buddhism in China* In: *The Virtue of Loyalty.*
Edited by: Troy Jollimore, Oxford University Press. © Oxford University Press 2024.
DOI: 10.1093/oso/9780197612644.003.0007

Sino-Tibetan), and numerous cultural differences. In this chapter I trace some of the major aspects of that dialogue.

Loyalty in Chinese moral, social, and political thought

In the Chinese context, loyalty generally refers to socially situated moral commitments, such as familial, professional, and governmental responsibilities, framed within a hierarchical societal order in which age, rank, and gender often define the scope and strength of an individual's various obligations. Traditionally, young people would be expected to be deferential to older people, women would be deferential to men, and lower-ranking political officials would defer to higher-ranking ones. A cluster of terms all relate to this basic moral framework, including *zhong* (忠), often translated as "loyalty" or as "doing one's utmost"; but also *shu* (恕), which indicates a sense of reciprocity or empathy, often described as the ability to imagine oneself in another's place; *xiao* (孝), which refers specifically to family commitments or "family reverence"; *jing* (敬), which has connotations of reverence, deference, or respect; and *guanxi* (關係), which refers to social norms surrounding networks of mutual aid and obligation.

These values are most closely associated with the tradition that the West has come to call "Confucianism," a somewhat misleading term that portrays the historical figure of "Confucius" (Kongzi 孔子, 551–479 BCE) as the founder of a religious or philosophical movement. In fact, the tradition known in Chinese as *rujia* (儒家) well predates the life of Kongzi, and Kongzi himself denies being an innovator.[1] Rather, he was a member of the "lineage" or "family" (*jia* 家) of the *ru* (儒), a term better translated as "scholar"

---

[1] See *Lunyu* 論語, 3.14, where Kongzi declares himself a follower of the ways of the Zhou dynasty.

or "literati." The *ru* were members of China's educated elite: they were most often employed as educators or government officials, they were versed in the classic philosophical and literary texts of Chinese culture, and they were qualified to preside over various state rites and civic ceremonies as well as the rituals performed at ancestral shrines. Throughout this chapter, I use the alternative English terms "Ruism" and "Ruists" to refer to the tradition and its members. In what follows, I walk through a few representative examples of the cluster of terms related to loyalty in Ruism, drawn from both the classical literature as well as contemporary studies.[2]

The classic statement on the twin values of *zhong* and *shu* occurs in passage 4.15 of the *Lunyu* (論語) or *Analects* of Kongzi, where Kongzi declares that the unifying thread running through his entire philosophy consists in doing one's utmost (*zhong*) and putting oneself in another's place (*shu*). Although *zhong* is the term most commonly translated into English directly as "loyalty," Paul Goldin warns that it has a range of meanings, including being honest and being fair. He proposes to translate *zhong* in passage 4.15 as "being honest with oneself in dealing with others."[3] The sense, then, is that a person must be "vigilantly self-aware," as Goldin says, to realize the integrity demanded by *shu*.[4] This seems to suggest that getting one's own ego out of the way is necessary to commit to following another's perspective, which does gesture toward a mode of loyalty. But, as this brief discussion indicates, both *zhong* and *shu* either together or separately possess a range of meanings more complex than "loyalty" usually conveys alone.

Another important sense of loyalty in the Ruist context is captured by the term *xiao* or "family reverence." One of the most famous statements on *xiao* comes in *Analects* passage 13.18, where the governor of a local province explains: "In our village we have an

---

[2] For another good overview of these terms and concepts, see Higgins 2013.
[3] Goldin 2008, 169–170.
[4] Goldin 2008, 170.

upstanding person. When his father stole a sheep, he reported him to the authorities."[5] Kongzi replied: "Those who are true in my village conduct themselves differently: A father covers for his son, and a son covers for his father. And being upstanding lies in this."[6] This passage expresses one key Ruist moral value—namely, that family is paramount. Although we should not understand this simplistically as mindless obedience to one's parents, the passage is clear that the son's loyalty is to his father.

The passage also expresses a typically Ruist suspicion regarding the efficacy of penal law. In other words, the Ruist tradition will value a society that fosters the development of the moral character of its citizens over a society that keeps the peace by strictly enforcing punitive policies. So, in the earlier passage, the important message is not that the son should casually break the law to cover for his father. Rather, the focus of the passage is on whether a son should resort to the legal authorities without first attempting to address his father's moral failings in some other way.[7]

The complicated task of admonishing one's own parents is the topic of another famous *Analects* passage, 4:18, where we read, "In serving your father and mother, remonstrate with them gently. On seeing that they do not heed your suggestions, remain respectful and do not act contrary. Although concerned, voice no resentment."[8] This passage illustrates the sorts of moral dilemmas that arise from the emphasis laid on family loyalty. The dilemma, in this case, is that parents may indeed violate various moral norms, as in the case of the sheep-stealing father. In such cases, children must find ways to remain true to overarching ethical principles, without

[5] *Lunyu*, 13.18: 我家鄉有正直的人，父親偷羊，兒子告發了他。For my translations of all *Lunyu* passages, I consulted Ames and Rosemont, trans., *The Analects of Confucius*.

[6] *Lunyu*, 13.18: 我家鄉正直的人不同：父為子隱瞞，子為父隱瞞，正直就在其中了。

[7] There is certainly no single accepted interpretation of this much-discussed passage. For more on the tensions between family loyalties and an impartial sense of "justice as fairness," see Lambert 2021.

[8] *Lunyu*, 4.18: 父母有錯，要好言相勸，聽不進時，要尊重他們，要任勞任怨。

damaging the parent–child bond, and without failing to be a loyal
son or daughter.

We see a similar moral dilemma play out at the level of a minister
and a ruler. In the *Xiaojing* (孝經) or *Classic of Family Reverence*,
one disciple asks Kongzi "whether children can be deemed filial
simply by obeying every command of their father."[9] In the answer
Kongzi offers, quoted at length here, we see a much stronger statement on the importance of remonstrating with superiors to hold
them to a moral standard. The passage also provides a good sense of
the complicated bureaucratic hierarchies that those in Ruist social
contexts were negotiating. Kongzi responds with dismay:

> What on earth are you saying? What on earth are you saying? Of
> old, an Emperor had seven ministers who would remonstrate with
> him, so even if he had no vision of the proper way, he still did not
> lose his empire. The high nobles had five ministers who would re-
> monstrate with them, so even if they had no vision of the proper
> way, they still did not lose their states. The high officials had three
> ministers who would remonstrate with them, so even if they had
> no vision of the proper way, they still did not lose their clans. If the
> lower officials had just one friend who would remonstrate with
> them, they were still able to preserve their good names. If a fa-
> ther has a son who will remonstrate with him, he will not behave
> reprehensibly. Thus, if confronted by reprehensible behavior on
> his father's part, a son has no choice but to remonstrate with his fa-
> ther, and if confronted by reprehensible behavior on his ruler's part,
> a minister has no choice but to remonstrate with his ruler. Hence,
> remonstrance is the only response to immorality. How could
> simply obeying the commands of one's father be deemed filial?[10]

---

[9] *Xiaojing* 孝經, "Jianzheng" 諫諍: 敢問子從父之令，可謂孝乎？My translation
follows Ames and Rosemont, trans., 114.
[10] *Xiaojing*:   是何言與，是何言與！昔者天子有爭臣七人，雖無道，不失其天
下；諸侯有爭臣五人，雖無道，不失其國；大夫有爭臣三人，雖無道，不失
其家；士有爭友，則身不離於令名；父有爭子，則身不陷於不義。故當不義，

This passage provides a nuanced and complicated account of the significance of loyalty. True and robust loyalty means neither complacency nor uncritical obedience to those in power. Rather, being a good son means that you will be a moral compass for your father, and being a good minister means that you will be a sharp critic, when needed. In short, due to the complex, interlocking, overlapping social hierarchies of Ruist culture, the demands of loyalty require constant negotiation. This is likely why loyalty is one of the most highly theorized concepts, both within the tradition and in literature about Chinese social practices. We wrap up this discussion of terms related to loyalty with a few concrete examples drawn from both dynastic and contemporary contexts.

The Northern Song dynasty (960–1127) was a time of social and political upheaval, marking a transition from a military government to a civil one. With this transition came a rise in the power of civil bureaucrats and a renewed emphasis on the role of such officials as highly educated political advisors—that is, precisely the sorts of ministers who would remonstrate with their leaders. As the historian Tze-Ki Hon says: "While during the early Northern Song, members of the educated elite were still fighting against the old habit of mind that required civil officials to be subservient to the rulers, during the mid-Northern Song they were confident that they were the 'co-rulers' of the empire. As the co-rulers, they believed that they were ruling the country with the emperor rather than for him."[11] In response to this changing political climate, various philosophers and historians at the time offer very different opinions on the behaviors of scholar-officials caught in the midst of governmental intrigue. In particular, a major debate concerned whether a person's loyalties lay with the office and the institution, or

---

則子不可以不爭於父，臣不可以不爭於君；故當不義，則爭之。從父之令，又焉得為孝乎！The translation follows, with slight modification, Ames and Rosemont, trans., 114.

[11] Hon 2005, 22.

instead with the holder of the office. A thoughtful Ruist could offer a defense of either position.

The case in question here concerns Feng Dao (882–954), who served under four out of the five dynasties in what is known as the Five Dynasties Period, when (as the name suggests) political leadership changed rapidly. Again, in the words of Hon:

> He [Feng dao] was particularly good at remonstrating with the military leaders in humble and yet clear language mixed with military metaphors. As the subservient civil official par excellence, Feng Dao saw himself as a follower of Confucian teachings. In the preface to his "A Self-Portrait of the Ever-Happy Old Man" (*Changlulao zixu*), he presented himself as a contented old gentleman who was proud of watching his family flourish under him. He claimed that in public he might have shifted his loyalty from one imperial court to another, but in private he had done his utmost to perpetuate his family interests.[12]

Feng's own opinion of himself is echoed in the *Old History of the Five Dynasties*, published in 974, twenty years after Feng's death.[13] In that text, Feng is praised as a paradigmatic scholar-official, who was loyal to his office and carried out his duties regardless of who was in charge. Moreover, given the dangers of such a politically unstable time, Feng was praised for surviving to be an old man with a large family. In other words, as the *Old History* affirms, when the political situation is dangerous, it is praiseworthy to act in a way that preserves the happiness and health of your family in the long term.

Nonetheless, later opinions are divided. Less than one hundred years later, in 1053, the *New History of the Five Dynasties* expresses marked disapproval:

[12] Hon 2005, 23.
[13] Hon 2005, 23.

Having read Feng Dao's self-glorifying account in his "Self-Portrait of the Ever-Happy Old Man," I find him shameless. One can tell how shameless the society was at that time. In the Period of the Five Dynasties, I can only find three persons with full integrity, and fifteen civil officials died for their government. But there were many strange people wearing Confucian gowns and claiming to learn from the past. They received high salary and served in the government, but they never made sacrifice for the sake of righteousness and loyalty. . . . It seems that there was no true Confucian scholar [in the Period of the Five Dynasties].[14]

The *New History* advocates standing up for what is right, regardless of the consequences. The idea is not that Feng should have blindly died for his government, but rather, following Hon's analysis, the later appraisal of Feng Dao reflects a move toward the renewed power of ministers and scholar-officials. In other words, the criticism of the *New History* expresses the idea that Feng should have done more to direct the course of government—he should have been more involved, rather than simply keeping his head down while the higher-ups battled for power. True loyalty, says the *New History*, is not to the office, but to the moral center that the office represents, and the truly loyal minister will do his utmost to make sure that a morally exemplary person occupies the office.

Finally, the phenomenon of *guanxi* in contemporary China has received ample attention, both in philosophical work as well as in anthropological and sociological studies. This interpersonal network of mutual aid and obligation is sometimes discussed as the benign exchange of social capital but sometimes derided as an inescapable system of cronyism. However, as Andrew Lambert discusses, "*guanxi* relations are more particularistic and emotionally involved than mere lists of social contacts, favor exchange, or

---

[14] Quoted in Hon 2005, 24.

fee-for-service bribery."[15] Rather, the loyalties and bonds of *guanxi* reflect the deeply partial and context-based approaches of Ruist moral reasoning. As such, they open a route to mitigate and at times resist laws and governmental policies in contemporary China that, while "striving for impartiality, can nevertheless be insufficiently sensitive to local conditions and the needs of local populations."[16]

All in all, from the moral positions in classic texts such as the *Lunyu* and the *Xiaojing*, to the debates over loyalty following the Northern Song, to contemporary practices related to *guanxi*, we gain a sense of the prominent place of loyalty, as a complex and multivalent moral value, within Ruist ethical and political thought. In addition, we are able to see Ruist moral reasoning in operation, with its constant negotiations over how best to satisfy ever-shifting and context-specific obligations. Into this discussion, we now invite the Buddhist tradition. Beginning next with a short introductory story of the life of the Buddha, we can readily see that his biography alone would be liable to raise suspicion among Ruist scholars.

The life of the Buddha

The Buddha's birth is conventionally dated to 563 BCE, although other estimates vary. He was born to the king of a sizable territory encompassing parts of today's northern India and Nepal. Upon his birth, his father received a prophecy: his son would either grow up to be a great spiritual leader, saving countless people from suffering, or he would be a great military leader, uniting the entire subcontinent under his rule. Wanting his son to continue the family's reign, the king did what he could to make sure that the young Prince Siddhartha had political aspirations. As the story goes, the king shielded his son from knowledge of death, illness, suffering,

[15] Lambert 2021, 279.
[16] Lambert 2021, 280.

and anything else that might prompt the prince to take a spiritual path. Growing up surrounded by wealth and luxury, the prince at age sixteen married a beautiful princess, they had a son, and they were very happy for a number of years. From the Ruist perspective, all is in order: the family is prospering, and the son is fulfilling his duties.

But the story then takes a turn: at age twenty-nine, Siddhartha becomes disillusioned with his wealth and luxury, and he sneaks out of the palace unsupervised to explore the surrounding villages. He sees what is famously known in Buddhism as "The Four Passing Sights": an old man, a sick man, a corpse, and a wandering ascetic. Through these encounters he learns, suddenly, that every single human being will eventually grow old and die. Even his little boy, so young and happy, will eventually succumb to aging and suffering. He realizes that we cannot find true peace among others who, like us, are susceptible to illness, death, and suffering.

In records of his early teachings, the Buddha defines seeking peace in this misguided way as the "ignoble quest":

> What is the ignoble quest? In this regard, someone who is himself liable to ... old age, seeks after what is also liable to old age; being himself liable to sickness, seeks after what is also liable to sickness; being himself liable to death, seeks after what is also liable to death; being himself liable sorrow, seeks after what is also liable to sorrow.... What would you say is liable to old age? Sons and wife are liable to old age.... What would you say is liable to sickness? Sons and wife are liable to sickness.... What would you say is liable to death? Sons and wife are liable to death.... What would you say is liable to sorrow? Sons and wife are liable to sorrow.[17]

In the course of a normal human life, friends and family provide only temporary relief from the illness, death, and suffering that one

---

[17] Holder 2006, 4.

day overtakes us all. In response to this existential situation, the Buddha recommends the "noble quest":

> And what is the noble quest? In that case, someone who is himself liable to . . . old age, having seen the danger in what is liable to old age, he seeks the unaging, the unsurpassed escape from bondage that is *nibbāna*. Being himself liable to sickness, having seen the danger in what is liable to sickness, he seeks the unailing, the unsurpassed escape from bondage that is *nibbāna*. Being himself liable to death, having seen the danger in what is liable to death, he seeks the deathless, the unsurpassed escape from bondage that is *nibbāna*. Being himself liable to sorrow, having seen the danger in what is liable to sorrow, he seeks the sorrowless, the unsurpassed escape from bondage that is *nibbāna*.[18]

Nibbāna (Pāli) or *nirvāṇa* (Sanskrit) refers to complete liberation from the karmic cycles of birth, death, and rebirth that keep us tied to conditions of suffering. The nature of *nirvāṇa* is considered indescribable, though it is strongly implied to be a type of nonexistence beyond even the duality of being and non-being.[19] The path to *nirvāṇa* begins with the "right knowledge" of what Buddhism calls the Four Noble Truths, discussed later, which together express the basic insight that all of existence is marked by suffering and that suffering can be overcome through non-attachment.

Already, this unspecified and seemingly world-denying "liberation" was suspicious to Ruist sensibilities. But, as if to drive the point home for early Ruist readers, the Buddha describes in excruciating emotional detail his abandonment of his family for the ascetic life: "Then, after a time, when I was a young man, my hair shiny black, endowed with radiant youth, in the prime of life—my unwilling parents wailing tearfully—I shaved off my hair and

---

[18] Holder 2006, 4–5.
[19] See, for example, "Discourse to Vacchagotta on Fire," in Holder 2006, 117–122.

donned yellow robes, I went forth from home to homelessness."[20] Here, in the prime of life, an heir to a throne abandons his duty to continue his family's prosperity, a father turns his back on his wife and son, and a capable member of society walks out the door of his home and into the life of an itinerant begging ascetic.

Certainly, from the Ruist perspective, the story has gone off the rails. Not only was it appalling that the main character would so definitively reject his duties to his parents, his wife and child, and his kingdom; but the path of asceticism was also seen as dangerous, in that Buddhism appeared to divide people's loyalties by suggesting that spiritual enlightenment might legitimately express a higher calling. As such, for the Ruist audience, it threatened to undermine people's natural and special loyalties to their families and governmental leaders.

Buddhist morality: non-attachment and the question of loyalty

Although it may be true that loyalty is not a particularly important value in the Buddhist tradition, Buddhism is not lacking in its own moral philosophy. The core teachings, mentioned earlier, are known as the Four Noble Truths, which express the insight into nature and cause of suffering that the Buddha obtained upon his eventual enlightenment. They tell us that all life is marked by dissatisfaction or suffering (Sk. *duḥkha*); the cause of suffering is desire, or craving (*taṇhā*); to overcome suffering, one must overcome desire; and the way to overcome desire is to follow the Eightfold Path. This is a path of moderation, avoiding the extremes of self-indulgence and self-denial, and placing heavy emphasis on avoiding doing harm to others, through our words, our deeds, our livelihoods, and so forth. Philosophically, suffering is also included,

[20] Holder 2006, 6.

along with impermanence (*anitya*) and "no-self" (*anātman*), as one of the "Three Marks" or three features that characterize all of existence. The Three Marks express the basic claim that all existing forms are temporary, including the mortal and composite entity that we routinely refer to as our "self."

Due to the temporary and ultimately non-substantial nature of all that exists, Buddhism advises non-attachment (*alobha*). Indeed, as the Buddha famously teaches in the "parable of the raft," students should practice non-attachment even with regard to the teachings (*dharma*) of the Buddha himself. In the parable, the Buddha compares the *dharma* to a raft that a person constructs to cross a river. Finding the near shore of the river to be "dangerous and frightening"[21] (i.e., the karmic cycles of death and rebirth), the person will build a raft to reach the further shore (i.e., attaining liberation or *nirvāṇa*). The Buddha poses the question to his students: suppose that this person, after having crossed the river, continues to carry the raft around? The students all agree that this would not be the appropriate use of the raft; rather, they say, the raft should be left behind, either floating in the water or hauled to dry ground. The Buddha concludes his parable: "Just as, in the parable of the raft, the *dhamma* [Sk. *dharma*] taught by me is for crossing over, not for retaining. *Bhikkhus* [students], by understanding the parable of the raft, you should abandon the *dhamma*, all the more what is not the *dhamma*."[22]

In other words, the *dharma* is useful for attaining liberation, but one should not allow one's allegiance to the *dharma* to become a source of renewed attachment. Here, "loyalty" seems to be a problematic value, since attachments are seen as giving rise to the kind of desire or craving that contributes to further suffering. Later Mahāyāna writings such as the *Diamond Sutra* push this point about abandoning the *dharma* even further, declaring

---

[21] Holder 2006, 107.
[22] Holder 2006, 108.

that indeed there is no *dharma*, and that anyone who says otherwise slanders the Buddha.[23] The logic of the *Diamond Sutra* holds
that, since there is no "self" in the first place, then there is no "self"
to overcome and no liberation to attain. This leads to well-known
Mahāyāna pronouncements on the non-duality of delusion and
enlightenment and the non-difference between buddhas and ordinary beings. In general, Buddhism has a habit (at least rhetorically)
of undercutting its own authority. As such, it is not a tradition that
demands "loyalty" from adherents.

Rather, what Buddhism demands is radical compassion for the
suffering of others. The scope of such compassion reaches out impartially to include *all* others, often pushing individual humans to
extremes in the attempt to uphold such a value. In the Theravāda
tradition most prominent today in South and Southeast Asia, we
find Buddhist folktales about total self-sacrifice, such as Prince
Mahasattva, who sacrificed his own body to feed a starving ti-
gress and her cubs.[24] In the Mahāyāna tradition, which is the form
of Buddhism that entered East Asia, we find the moral exemplar
known as a "bodhisattva," who takes a vow to postpone his or her
own *nirvāṇa* until all other sentient beings are saved from suffering. Of course, we might talk about loyalty as a kind of commitment to this high ideal, but this seems to be stretching the term. In
the end, the explicitly theorized values in Buddhism are compassion (*karuṇā*) and the principle of non-harm (*ahiṃsā*), not loyalty.
The paradigmatic image might be that of the thousand-eyed and
thousand-armed bodhisattva Avalokiteśvara (Ch. Guanyin 觀音),
who can see and respond to the suffering of all beings.

This mismatch between Ruist and Buddhist moral commitments
accounts for the various objections to Buddhism raised by the
Chinese educated elite. In addition to the tension between Ruist
context-based moral reasoning and Buddhist rhetoric surrounding

---

[23] *The Diamond Sutra*, see especially chapters 13 and 18.
[24] For context, see Ohnuma 2006.

the impartial scope of radical compassion, Chinese scholar-officials also contended with institutional structures and ritual practices that initially seemed foreign. First, a formal institution of monasticism was, more or less, absent in China before Buddhism. There were instances of Daoist hermits, and hermit communities, but there was no institutionalized path by which the Chinese could socially sanction the purposeful renunciation of family roles and responsibilities.[25] Second, beliefs about reincarnation were not popular in China prior to Buddhism. Chinese views on death tended to emphasize the importance of returning the body back to the ancestors, whole and intact. This expresses a moral charge to be a good steward of your body and mind, because some aspect of your spiritual life force will become part of your family's ancestral shrine after you die. Rites performed at these shrines express the spirit's continued relationship with the family, even following death. In contrast, Buddhist burial practices were aimed at helping a person leave this world behind entirely.[26] All in all, Buddhism was seen as disrupting natural bonds of loyalty at a multitude of levels: familial, social, political, and spiritual.

Han Yu remonstrates with his emperor

We see all of these lines of critique come together in an 819 letter to the emperor by the scholar-official Han Yu. The letter serves as an example of a minister remonstrating with his leader and as a cautionary tale of the consequences—Han Yu was sent into exile after saying his piece.

During the Tang dynasty (618–907) in which the letter was composed, imperial attitudes toward Buddhism varied, with some

[25] Later Daoist monasticism developed as such through contact with Buddhism. For more, see Bokenkamp 2011.
[26] For context, see Hershock on "the disparate meanings of being dead in India and China" (2005, 35–38).

emperors seeking to stem the rising tide of this foreign import, and others trying to harness its growing popularity for their own political ends. On that point, we should note here that Buddhism might have been criticized among the educated elite, but its message about salvation from suffering was attractive in other strata of society. Buddhism attracted women, for example, for exactly the same reasons that monasticism was viewed with suspicion by the Ruist patriarchy—women found in Buddhist institutions a socially sanctioned alternative to the lives they would otherwise be expected to lead as daughters, wives, and mothers. Women in nunneries were educated, and they pursued their own intellectual and spiritual agendas, marking a degree of agency not available to them in the traditional Chinese framework.[27]

We should also note that much of the Buddhism in China at this time was associated with "pure land" (*jingtu* 淨土) practices derived from a cluster of Mahāyāna texts devoted to a figure known as Amitābha Buddha (Ch. Amituofo 阿彌陀佛).[28] (The word "buddha" simply means an "awakened" being, and so the Buddhist tradition recognizes other buddhas besides the prince Siddhartha whose life story was summarized earlier.) Upon their awakening, buddhas are thought to acquire supernormal powers, including the ability to manifest concretely the realm of their influence. Such realms come to be called "pure lands" in Chinese discourse.[29] One such buddha, known as Amitābha, has taken a vow that any person who calls on his name will be reborn in his pure land, even if they suffer from the weight of accumulated karmic baggage. Once in

[27] However, see Idema and Grant 2004 for a comparative discussion of the literary output of elite women in the Ruist context of the imperial palace versus the output of practitioners in Buddhist nunneries (5).

[28] These include the *Longer Sukhāvatīvyūha Sūtra*, the *Shorter Sukhāvatīvyūha Sūtra*, and the *Amitāyurdhyāna Sūtra*. The original Sanskrit texts were translated into Chinese multiple times and contributed significantly to the development of Buddhism in East Asia. Generally, I refer to the text's central buddha by his Sanskrit name (Amitābha) when referring to the early sources but by the Chinese translation of his name (Amituofo) when referring to the East Asian context.

[29] For context, see Rowell 1934.

Amitābha's realm, such reborn practitioners will be able to obtain spiritual liberation quickly under his direct tutelage, after which they will fulfill the bodhisattva vow by reincarnating to this world to help others. Hence, calling on Amitābha Buddha by various means (recitation of his name, visualizing his presence) became widely popular. Such teachings, commonly referred to together in English-language literature as Pure Land Buddhism, promised a blissful afterlife accessible without strenuous Buddhist practices such as meditation. The Pure Land approach was especially attractive to a wide swath of workers, farmers, and merchants who could not commit to a lifetime of monasticism. As this indicates, the philosophical and political objections of the Ruist elite did not mark the last word on Buddhism, and the spread of Pure Land and other popular movements outpaced the ability of scholar-officials to control.

This is the situation in which we encounter Han Yu, whose emperor was preparing to venerate the finger bone of the Buddha in an official court ceremony. This was and still is a common practice—after death, a monk will be cremated, and in the case of particularly important monks, their bones and other remains will be kept as relics, housed in special containers, and revered. To keep and venerate a relic was thought to bestow a large amount of karmic merit. In Han Yu's letter, we easily see his deep suspicion toward such practices and beliefs.

He opens his letter as follows: "Your servant begs leave to say that Buddhism is no more than a cult of the barbarian peoples, which spread to China in time of the Latter Han."[30] He continues: "Buddha was a man of the barbarians. . . . He understood neither the duties that bind sovereign and subject nor the affections of father and son."[31] With this statement, Han Yu reflects the standard Ruist

---

[30] Yu 1999, 583.
[31] Yu 1999, 584.

concern that Buddhism divides loyalties, disrupts families, and undermines state commitments.

Han goes on to say (rhetorically, we surmise) that surely the emperor's change in attitude toward Buddhism must be politically motivated. His argument is worth quoting at length:

> Now Your Majesty, wise in the arts of peace and war, unparalleled in divine glory from countless ages past, upon your accession prohibited men and women from taking Buddhist orders and forbade the erection of temples and monasteries. . . . Even if the suppression of Buddhism should be as yet impossible, your servant hardly thought that Your Majesty would encourage it and, on the contrary, cause it to spread. Yet now your servant hears that Your Majesty has ordered the community of monks to go to Fengxiang to greet the bone of the Buddha, that Your Majesty will ascend a tower to watch as it is brought into the palace, and that the various temples have been commanded to welcome and worship it in turn. Though your servant is abundantly ignorant, he understands that Your Majesty is not so misled by Buddhism as to honor it thus in hopes of receiving some blessing or reward, but only that, the year being one of plenty and the people joyful, Your Majesty would accord with the hearts of the multitude in setting forth for the officials and citizens of the capital some curious show and toy for their amusement. . . . But the common people are ignorant and dull, easily misled and hard to enlighten, and should they see their emperor do these things they might say that Your Majesty was serving Buddhism with a true heart. . . . Then will our old ways be corrupted, our customs violated, and the tale will spread to make us the mockery of the world. This is no trifling matter![32]

---

[32] Yu 1999, 583–584.

Many things are at stake for Han Yu: the welfare of the people, who are easily corrupted when bad examples are set for them; the preservation of indigenous tradition, which is threatened by a foreign cultural force; and the authority of the emperor, who must serve as the moral anchor of the office he occupies.

Han concludes his letter by voicing his disgust at the relic itself, and reminding the emperor that spiritual forces, when unmoored from the ancestral shrine system, are dangerous:

> How then, when he has long been dead, could his rotten bones, the foul and unlucky remains of his body, be rightly admitted to the palace? Confucius said, "Respect spiritual beings, while keeping at a distance from them." So when the princes of ancient times went to pay their condolences at a funeral within the state, they sent exorcists in advance with peach wands to drive out evil, and only then would they advance. Now without reason Your Majesty has caused this loathsome thing to be brought in and would personally go to view it. No exorcists have been sent ahead, no peach wands employed. The host of officials have not spoken out against this wrong, and the censors have failed to note its impropriety. Your servant is deeply shamed and begs that this bone be given to the proper authorities to be cast into fire and water, that this evil may be rooted out, the world freed from its error, and later generations spared this delusion.[33]

In this final passage, we see that Han Yu is not only concerned with moral and political affairs, but he is worried about insidious spiritual forces as well. The spiritual remnants of people are properly cared for via the Ruist ancestral shrines and the rites that take place at them. When not cared for in the prescribed ways, such forces easily become harmful, unpredictable, and uncontrollable.

[33] Yu 1999, 584.

Overall, Han Yu's letter is a good case study demonstrating both the resistance to Buddhism on the part of the Ruists, revolving around issues of divided loyalties, as well as the status of Buddhism "on the ground," as it were, in China at this time, where the populace at large was attracted to Buddhism's promise of salvation in the afterworld alongside the this-worldly benefits of accumulating karmic merit. And, in fact, Buddhism reconciles with Ruism over time, eventually becoming deeply and fully embedded with Chinese thought and culture. We turn next to question of how some of these specific accommodations were made.

Wang Rixiu on bodhisattvas in government

Over time, the Buddhist system of karmic merit becomes important in reconciling the detached ethical view of Buddhism, and its emphasis on compassion for all beings, with the Ruist view that placed such importance on partial commitments and specific obligations. For example, in reconciling monasticism with family responsibilities, a son or daughter who joins a monastery could be seen not only as practicing for the benefit of *all* sentient beings but also as serving family interests in a variety of ways. As for a daughter, she ceases to be the financial responsibility of her parents, since her basic living expenses are taken care of through the monastic institution. Also, both monks and nuns had the ability to move up in rank, from novices to institutional heads, and so the system brought with it some measure of prestige.[34] And, as Albert Welter details in a recent book on Buddhism and the Chinese state, many Buddhist monks served as political advisors and so were accorded a more Ruist sense of social prestige, as well.[35] Finally, entirely apart from

---

[34] Keep in mind, however, that even the highest-ranking nun is outranked by even an initiate monk.

[35] Welter 2018.

Ruist standards, the practices of a son or daughter at a monastery were believed to generate karmic merit that benefitted the family's health, wealth, and well-being, and which boded well for their eventual rebirth in a pure realm such as Amituofo's (Amitābha).

Speaking of Pure Land practices, in particular, a popular and influential text by the lay Buddhist Wang Rixiu (d. 1173) is notable for its merger of Ruist morality with Pure Land soteriology. Contemporary scholar Daniel Getz argues against a simplistic dualism between the otherworldly orientation of Pure Land practices and the this-worldly focus of Ruist family and political commitments. As he says, Wang's text is evidence of the extent to which Ruist social values shaped Buddhism in China. In the text, Wang criticizes those who think the Pure Land concerns the afterlife alone: "The ignorant simply regard this teaching merely as an affair of the afterlife. They are entirely unaware that Pure Land teaching is of great benefit in the present life. How is this the case? It is because the Buddha's purpose in teaching people was nothing other than the promotion of goodness. How then is this different from the goal of Confucianism in teaching people? It differs only in name."[36]

In the rest of the text, Wang enumerates a long list of the ways in which Ruist moral values align with Buddhist values, and then provides an even longer list of reasons why every type of citizen in the empire should adopt Pure Land practice, that is, reciting the Buddha's name. The two items in Wang's lists that concern us most here have to do with family and political loyalties. Regarding the first, Wang addresses himself to "filial sons," and he goes so far as to assert that commitment to one's parents' well-being in the afterlife is a higher type of filial piety than commitment to their worldly well-being, though he certainly never says that the latter is not necessary: "Thus the filial piety of this world is for one lifetime and is yet a lesser type of filial piety. The filial piety of the other world is

[36] Getz 2019, 609.

never exhausted. Helping your parents be born in the Pure Land where happiness and longevity are without limit, lasting for *kalpas* [eons] as many as the sands of the Ganges, is the greatest type of filial piety."[37]

Regarding political loyalties, Wang addresses himself to Ruist scholar-officials, noting that their esteemed place in society certainly reflects karmic rewards from their past lives. Yet, he asks rhetorically, would they not be even better governmental servants were they to obtain enlightenment in the Pure Land and return to serve the people as bodhisattvas? He poses the question: "If officials care deeply for the people and cannot bear to abandon them, what would prohibit them, after first being born in Pure Land and transcending the cycle of *saṃsāra* [transmigration], from returning to this world and appearing in the form of a minister of state in order to accomplish a great benefit?"[38] Overall, Wang's approach is generally characteristic of how Ruism and Buddhism come to accommodate each other over time: Being a good Ruist, in the sense of being a loyal son, or a loyal civil servant, is believed also to be karmically meritorious, in a Buddhist sense; and, accordingly, Buddhist practices aimed at spiritual liberation are seen as fulfilling Ruist loyalties one way or another, either here and now or in the world to come. In this way, the universalizing scope of Buddhist compassion and liberation is made relevant to everyday personal and family affairs.

Conclusion

As we have seen, loyalty does not receive much philosophical attention in early Buddhist literature. However, over the course of its acculturation in China, Buddhism becomes embedded within a network of family and state allegiances and responsibilities. On

[37] Getz 2019, 620.
[38] Getz 2019, 615.

the one hand, much of its success in East Asia can be attributed to the spread of Pure Land conceptions of the afterlife. The conventional picture of Buddhist reincarnation and eventual liberation from the cycles of rebirth clashed with traditional Chinese ancestor worship, which sought to maintain family ties with the spiritual energies of the deceased via the rites at ancestral shrines. By contrast, the Pure Land depiction of Amituofo's realm offered a compromise—technically speaking, a rebirth in the Pure Land is only a temporary stopover in the cycles of reincarnation; but practically speaking, families could still think of the ancestors as living on in a paradisaical afterworld for the imaginable future. As such, rebirth with Amituofo did not conflict directly with shrine activities. In this way, the Pure Land allowed the bonds of family and community loyalties to remain alive.

On the other hand, the system of karmic merit was also instrumental in Buddhism's transition to China, as it provided a nonmaterial but nonetheless potent means by which practitioners could contribute to their family's prosperity. The benefits of fulfilling Ruist social obligations were effectively doubled, when they came to be seen as karmically meritorious, and the benefits of earning positive karma were deepened when they came to be seen as contributing to a family's long-term spiritual welfare. Perhaps no one takes better advantage of these various Buddhist–Ruist compromises than does the aforementioned Wang Rixiu, with his claim that the most devoted government officials should consider attaining liberation in the Pure Land as a precondition for effective governance.

All in all, family and state loyalties largely determine the framework that Buddhism had to navigate and accommodate upon its arrival in China, a fact which speaks both to the enduring values of Ruist morality and the nondogmatic flexibility of Buddhist thought and practice. Tensions between context-based and universalistic approaches to moral reasoning remain relevant in philosophy today (as in debates over care-based versus rule-based ethical theories).

In the Chinese context at least, these tensions were brought into fruitful dialogue. For today's world, with its ever-increasing political and religious tension, the history of Buddhist–Ruist relations provides multiple examples of productive and transformative cross-cultural exchange.

Bibliography

Ames, Roger T., and Henry Rosemont, Jr., trans. *The Analects of Confucius: A Philosophical Translation*. New York: Random House, 1998.

Ames, Roger T., and Henry Rosemont, Jr., trans. *The Chinese Classic of Family Reverence: A Philosophical Translation*. Honolulu: University of Hawai'i Press, 2008.

Bokenkamp, Stephen R. "The Early Lingbao Scriptures and the Origins of Daoist Monasticism." *Cahiers d'Extrême-Asie* 20 (2011): 95–124.

The Diamond Sutra. In *The Diamond Sutra and the Sutra of Hui-neng*, edited and translated by A. F. Price and Wong Mou-lam, 17–53. Boulder, CO: Shambhala, 2005.

Getz, Daniel, trans. "A Confucian Pure Land? 'Longshu's Treatise on Pure Land' by Wang Rixiu." In *Pure Lands in Asian Texts and Contexts: An Anthology*, edited by Georgios T. Halkias and Richard K. Payne, 602–630. Honolulu: University of Hawai'i Press, 2019.

Goldin, Paul R. "When *Zhong* 忠 Does Not Mean 'Loyalty.'" *Dao* 7 (2008): 165–174.

Han Yu. "Memorial on the Bone of the Buddha." Translated by Burton Watson. In *Sources of Chinese Tradition: From Earliest Times to 1600*, edited by Wm. Theodore de Bary and Irene Bloom, 583–585. New York: Columbia, 1999.

Hershock, Peter D. *Chan Buddhism*. Honolulu: University of Hawai'i Press, 2005.

Higgins, Kathleen. "Loyalty from a Confucian Perspective." *Nomos* 54 (2013): 22–38.

Holder, John J., ed. and trans. *Early Buddhist Discourses*. Indianapolis: Hackett, 2006.

Hon, Tze-Ki. *The Yijing and Chinese Politics: Classical Commentary and Literati Activism in the Northern Song Period, 960–1127*. Albany: State University of New York Press, 2005.

Idema, Wilt, and Beata Grant. *The Red Brush: Writing Women of Imperial China*. Cambridge, MA: Harvard University Press, 2004.

Lambert, Andrew. "Love's Extension: Confucian Familial Love and the Challenge of Impartiality." In *Love, Justice, and Autonomy: Philosophical*

Perspectives, edited by Rachel Fedock, Michael Kühler, and Raja Rosenhagen, 259–288. New York: Routledge, 2021.

Lunyu 論語. In *Chinese Text Project*, edited by Donald Sturgeon. 2011. http://ctext.org/analects/zh.

Ohnuma, Reiko. *Head, Eyes, Flesh, Blood: Giving Away the Body in Indian Buddhist Literature*. New York: Columbia, 2006.

Rowell, Teresina. "The Background and Early Use of the Buddha-Kṣetra Concept. Introduction and Chapter One." *The Eastern Buddhist* 6:3 (1934): 199–246.

Welter, Albert. *The Administration of Buddhism in China: A Study and Translation of Zanning and the Topical Compendium of the Buddhist Clergy*. Amherst, NY: Cambria Press, 2018.

Xiaojing 孝經. In *Chinese Text Project*, edited by Donald Sturgeon. 2011. http://ctext.org/xiao-jing/zh.

Yu, Han. "Memorial on the Bone of the Buddha." Translated by Burton Watson. In *Sources of Chinese Tradition: From Earliest Times to 1600*, edited by Wm. Theodore de Bary and Irene Bloom, 583–585. New York: Columbia University Press, 1999.

7

Exemplars of Loyalty

Mathew A. Foust

Introduction

In *The Philosophy of Loyalty*, Josiah Royce writes, "Everybody has heard of loyalty; most prize it; but few perceive it to be what, in its inmost spirit, it really is,—the heart of all the virtues, the central duty amongst all duties."[1] On Royce's theory, which places loyalty at the center of morality, loyalty is a value to be promoted, a virtue to be cultivated, and a duty to be followed. Moreover, Royce's approach to examining the nature and value of loyalty makes heavy use of virtuous exemplars—persons who instantiate this virtue to a high degree. Royce's use of exemplars is interesting in its own right, and it is also useful in thinking more generally about the kinds of role exemplars may play in accounts of morality that emphasize the virtues.

The idea of making exemplars central to moral theory has gained traction recently due largely to the work of Linda Zagzebski (2017). In *Exemplarist Moral Theory*, Zagzebski aims "to show how to use exemplars to construct a comprehensive ethical theory," a theory that "serves the same purposes as deontological, consequentialist, and virtue theories."[2] While, as this remark suggests, she takes her theory to constitute a rival to virtue ethics, there is clearly some significant common ground—more common ground, perhaps, than

[1] Royce 1995, xxiv.
[2] Zagzebski 2017, 3.

Mathew A. Foust, *Exemplars of Loyalty* In: *The Virtue of Loyalty*. Edited by: Troy Jollimore,
Oxford University Press. © Oxford University Press 2024. DOI: 10.1093/oso/9780197612644.003.0008

exists between her moral exemplarism and either consequentialist or deontological views. This suggests both that there is indeed some distinction between her view and virtue ethical views, but also that the distance between the two should not be exaggerated. Whereas virtue ethics guides the individual primarily through description of character traits to be realized toward ideal personhood, Zagzebski seeks to create "a type of moral theory that arises out of direct reference to particular persons—not their traits of character, but the persons themselves."[3] Both approaches focus on virtuous *persons* rather than rules, principles, or consequences; and it is quite common for virtue ethicists to include in their writings examinations and discussions of particular virtuous individuals— something we also find Royce doing, as we will see.

For his part, Royce announces as his aim in *The Philosophy of Loyalty* "to indicate some ways whereby we may clarify and simplify our moral situation,"[4] and attempts such clarification and simplification via his philosophy of loyalty, an ethical theory that shares features of deontological, consequentialist, and virtue theories.[5] Although Royce does not explicitly draw attention to his use of exemplars, he deploys them as illustrations of his philosophy of loyalty with such frequency that it raises the question of how closely Royce and Zagzebski are aligned on the role of exemplars.

I will begin with a brief overview of Zagzebski's exemplarist moral theory in which I canvass Zagzebski's treatments of three moral exemplars, each of whom she takes to represent a type—the hero, the saint, and the sage. Moving on to Royce, I will consider *his* treatment of three moral exemplars—the Japanese samurai, William

---

[3] Zagzebski 2017, xi. Indeed, some would argue that a person just *is* their traits of character. But I take it that Zagzebski means that she wants to start with morally excellent persons and build from there, rather than starting more abstractly with certain values or virtues.

[4] Royce 1995, 6.

[5] These terms, "deontological," "consequentialist," and even "virtue ethics" predate Royce.

Lenthall, and Antigone.[6] Examining the theories of Zagzebski and Royce in tandem will shed some light on issues connected with the relation between loyalty and exemplarity, on one hand, and the relation between loyalty and the other virtues, on the other. In doing so, I expand on my previous discussions[7] of Royce's philosophy of loyalty, bringing into clearer relief resonances of Royce in contemporary moral discourse, and attempting to inject some of Royce's important insights into that discourse.

Zagzebski, exemplars, and loyalty

Linda Zagzebski's *Exemplarist Moral Theory* originated over two decades ago when Zagzebski had the idea of creating a type of moral theory "that arises out of direct reference to particular persons—not their traits of character, but the persons themselves."[8] She first developed a distinctively Christian form of the idea in *Divine Motivational Theory*, published in 2004, arguing that all value flows from God, the supreme exemplar.[9] Since then, various occasions allowed opportunities for further development of the theory. Notably, a year prior to the publication of *Exemplarist Moral Theory*, Zagzebski delivered the 2015 Gifford Lectures on moral exemplarism.

One might ask: "Why exemplarism?" According to Zagzebski, exemplars are "supremely admirable persons who show us the

---

[6] Royce highlights several other figures in the course of his discussions of loyalty. I have chosen the examples of the Japanese samurai, William Lenthall, and Antigone, as they serve well my purposes in this essay. A more fraught example is that of Robert E. Lee, as Fischer 2012 has observed (130). Royce's discussions of Lee vis-à-vis his philosophy of loyalty are complex and merit a more extensive treatment than can be provided here.

[7] The most extensive of these discussions is Foust 2012. Much of the content in the sections, "Royce's Definition of Loyalty" and "Royce's Principle of Loyalty to Loyalty" is found in that work, as are more detailed discussions of these facets of Royce's philosophy of loyalty and critiques of Royce's philosophy of loyalty.

[8] Zagzebski 2017, xi.

[9] Zagzebski 2004.

upper reaches of human capability, and in doing so, inspire us to expect more from ourselves."[10] There are various types of exemplars, not all of whom are morally salient (e.g., geniuses and the athletically or artistically gifted), but moral exemplars are touchstones for moral decision-making. They are supremely excellent and supremely admirable. Moral exemplars are persons we emulate; we see the good in their actions and in their lives, and we strive to be like them, linking their kind of goodness with the flourishing that we desire. In short, exemplarism "gives us directions on what to do and how to live, and it can be used to make us want to do so."[11] Moral exemplars perform a more fundamental function, as identifying moral exemplars establishes a reference for the term "good person." Just as picking out exemplars of gold or water allows us to say that gold is stuff *like that* or water is stuff *like that*, "basic moral terms are anchored in exemplars of moral goodness . . . Good persons are persons *like that*."[12] With the identification of moral exemplars as a starting point, "we know what to investigate to find out what virtue, right action, and a good life are."[13] Zagzebski's particular version of exemplarism focuses on three types of moral exemplar: the hero, the saint, and the sage.

A hero is "a person who takes great risks to achieve a moral end, often the end of helping others in distress" and whose moral character is "dominated by . . . courage."[14] Zagzebski describes Leopold Socha, a Polish sewer inspector and former thief, as a hero.[15] Socha risked his life to hide a group of Jews with their families in the sewers beneath the Polish city of Lvov, helping them to avoid attack by the Germans and Ukrainian militia. In addition to protecting the Jews

[10] Zagzebski 2017, 1.

[11] Zagzebski 2017, 3.

[12] Zagzebski 2017, 15 (emphasis in original). Zagzebski uses the Putnam-Kripke theory of the semantics of natural kind terms in the construction of a moral theory. For this theory, see Putnam (1975).

[13] Zagzebski 2017, 22.

[14] Zagzebski 2017, 1, 96.

[15] Zagzebski 2017, 70–72.

from the Nazis, Socha took great risks to care for them. Expressing remorse for his past life as a thief, he described his actions as his mission, a form of atonement for past misdeeds. Socha later died in an unrelated act of rescue while riding bicycles with his twelve-year-old daughter, Stefcia. While Stefcia rode ahead, a Soviet army truck careened down a narrow street toward her. Socha pedaled forward and knocked her safely out of the way, but he was crushed to death.

Socha's selfless actions—placing himself at great risk to defend those Jewish families whose safety he had pledged to protect, and sacrificing his life to save his daughter—are undoubtedly examples of admirable courage. But inasmuch as they display and are motivated by commitments to the well-being of particular individuals, they also serve well as exemplifications of different species of loyalty: loyalty toward a vulnerable community, on the one hand, and toward a family member, on the other. Elsewhere in her book Zagzebski discusses the case of Thomas More, as depicted in Robert Bolt's play *A Man for All Seasons*. Noting that Bolt intended More to be seen as a kind of hero, she remarks:

> Most of us design our lives in a way that eliminates the possibility of having to make a tragic choice. The failure to be committed to anything (or anyone) far enough to possibly cause us misery is one way to do that. As Bolt sees it, such a person lacks a self.[16]

Here, too, then, the value of loyalty in conjunction with courage is recognized in relation to the nature of heroism: to avoid being committed in the suggested manner is, after all, precisely to avoid being loyal to anything or anyone.

A saint, Zagzebski writes, is "someone who is both spiritually and morally exemplary" and whose moral character is "dominated by

---

[16] Zagzebski 2017, 164.

charity."[17] Zagzebski describes Jean Vanier, a philosophy professor and former naval officer, as a saint.[18] Vanier and several volunteers aimed to create a family life for the mentally infirm. Toward this aim, they established L'Arche, a community named after Noah's Ark. Starting with a small house in Trosly-Breuil, a village north of Paris, the communities multiplied and now can be found across the globe. These communities have been life-changing not only for their residents but also for their caregivers. Vanier's accounts of the L'Arche communities relate "the transformative power of those who can see the humanity in persons whom no one believed in and letting it blossom."[19] For Zagzebski, "Vanier's moral genius was in being able to create a revolutionary kind of human community, one that had never before been thought possible."[20] As with Socha, it takes little effort in the case of Vanier to find loyalty residing alongside and indeed wrapped up tightly with the virtue, charity, that Zagzebski takes to be characteristic of the saint; the fact that his efforts were consistently and over a long period of time dedicated to the well-being of a particular community of people indicates as much. As she writes, Vanier's life was shaped by "an irrevocable decision to live with two disabled men, Raphael and Philippe, for the rest of their lives or his."[21]

A sage, or wise person, is someone "whose admirable features include both moral and intellectual excellences, and sometimes spiritual excellences," and whose character exemplifies wisdom.[22] Zagzebski describes Confucius, the ancient Chinese philosopher, as a sage.[23] While heroes and saints are typically identified primarily by admirable overt acts, sages are typically identified primarily by "words of wisdom" or "wise decisions." They may also convey

[17] Zagzebski 2017, 1, 96.
[18] Zagzebski 2017, 80–82.
[19] Zagzebski 2017, 82.
[20] Zagzebski 2017, 82.
[21] Zagzebski 2017, 81.
[22] Zagzebski 2017, 1, 96.
[23] Zagzebski 2017, 84–87.

a sense of serenity and emotional tranquility. The primary source consulted by scholars of Confucius's life and thought is the *Analects*. Zagzebski explains that the *Analects* reveal Confucius's moral character in more than acts but also in physical bearing, movement, and manner of speaking, as well as the "graceful and devoted way"[24] in which Confucius performs *li*, or rituals. Identifying *ren*—variously translated as "benevolence," "goodness," "authoritative conduct," "human excellence," or "virtue"—as the "fundamental Confucian virtue,"[25] Zagzebski notes that the authors of the *Analects* "do not attempt to present an abstract conception of *ren* but offer Confucius as a primary exemplar of *ren*."[26]

For Zagzebski, the hero, the saint, and the sage are distinct classes of exemplars, with each exemplar type dominated by a particular virtue. The hero is dominated by courage, the saint by charity, and the sage by wisdom. Exemplars exhibit other virtues as well, but "the other virtues are accompaniments to the dominant virtue, perhaps necessary accompaniments."[27] These models serve both practical and theoretical aims. Practically, "we want to have an idea of the kind of life to which we can aspire, and the kinds of lives worthy of being the goal of people to whom we are connected . . . or whose lives are affected by our financial choices and our choice of political leaders."[28] Theoretically, mapping "the connection between a good life in the sense of an *admirable* life or a life of virtue, and a good life in the sense of a *desirable* life, or a life of happiness and flourishing"[29] requires accounts of what a good life is in both senses, and these accounts can be derived from moral exemplars.

On a more general level, Zagzebski suggests that the very terms *virtue* and *virtuous act* can be defined in terms of moral exemplars.

---

[24] Zagzebski 2017, 86.
[25] Zagzebski 2017, 86.
[26] Zagzebski 2017, 87.
[27] Zagzebski 2017, 96.
[28] Zagzebski 2017, 156.
[29] Zagzebski 2017, 156–157 (emphasis in original).

A virtue, she suggests, is "a trait that makes an exemplar admirable in a certain respect." Virtues, then, are what make admirable persons admirable in particular ways; they are "disposition[s] out of which admirable acts arise."[30] This, she says, tells us what the word *virtue* means. As for what a virtue *is*, she proposes the following account: "A *virtue* is a deep and enduring acquired trait that we admire upon reflection, consisting of a disposition to have a certain emotion that initiates and directs action towards an end, and reliable success in reaching that end."[31] As for *virtuous acts*, they are simply, as she writes, "the acts that express virtues."[32]

Interestingly, Zagzebski does not identify a class of exemplar whose dominant virtue is loyalty. One wonders whether Zagzebski believes that there is any such an exemplar, or whether loyalty is always relegated to being an accompanying, and essentially secondary, virtue.[33] If this is what she thinks, it would present a clear disagreement with Royce, who would reject any notion of loyalty being auxiliary to other virtues, such as the courage of the hero, the charity of the saint, or the wisdom of the sage. That said, an accompanying virtue can still play a significant role, and the examples she provides of heroism and sainthood—Socha, More, and Vanier—quite clearly manifest various forms of loyalty as well as the particular virtues she associates with those categories. One might also observe that her chosen example of a saint, Confucius, explicitly placed great significance on loyalty in his ethical thinking. What is more, a discussion included in the chapter titled "A Good Life" finds Zagzebski reflecting critically on the cosmopolitan ideal

---

[30] Zagzebski 2017, 114.

[31] Zagzebski 2017, 113.

[32] Zagzebski 2017, 114.

[33] There are, too, occasional explicit mentions of loyalty in Zagzebski's text. She describes Chief Plenty Coups (1842–1932), the last hereditary chief of the Crow Nation, as a "modern sage who combined visionary wisdom with practical skills" in order to "invent forms of courage, honor, loyalty, and justice" (Zagzebski 2017, 89–90). And in response to Jonathan Haidt's thesis that there are distinct modes of value that affect moral and political positions (Haidt 2012), she describes Confucius as "sensitive to dimensions of loyalty/betrayal" among other morally salient dichotomies (181).

and suggesting that a desirable human life will likely be one built around stable attachments to particular communities:

> Staying in one place enhances human relationships. Always eating food in the same cuisine fosters culture in a sense that most educated persons have given up. Education opens the mind, but it weakens attachment to one's origins. St. Benedict made stability one of the three central vows of his monastic communities. As an anonymous hermit in Egypt said long before Benedict, "A tree cannot bear fruit if it is often transplanted" (Ward 2003, 72). Stability is necessary for spiritual growth. A life of movement is more adventuresome, but someone who travels out of restlessness lacks inner peace. There is more than one way to flourish. The Buddha probably led a more flourishing life because of his travels, but St. Benedict flourished because he stayed put. We sometimes romanticize the wanderer who has the kind of freedom that comes from lack of attachment, but unless the wandering ends, the story does not usually end well.[34]

Royce, for his part, explicitly identifies loyalty not only as *a* virtue, but as *the* central virtue, writing that "*all the commonplace virtues, in so far as they are indeed defensible and effective, are special forms of loyalty to loyalty*."[35] One thing he means by this is that proper practice of these virtues results in the increase and strengthening of loyal bonds. To better understand this claim, it will be instructive to consider overviews of Royce's definition of loyalty and his principle of loyalty to loyalty.

[34] Zagzebski 2017, 171.
[35] Royce 1995, 61 (emphasis in original). Royce describes the virtues of honesty (66), justice (68), and benevolence (69) as all forms of loyalty to loyalty.

Royce's definition of loyalty

The Philosophy of Loyalty is a collection of eight lectures delivered in November and December of 1907 before the Lowell Institute in Boston and published in March of 1908. In the opening lecture, "The Nature and the Need of Loyalty," Royce defines loyalty as "*The willing and practical and thoroughgoing devotion of a person to a cause.*"[36] Before going further, it will be helpful to consider this definition closely.

First, loyalty is the devotion of a person to a cause. One might argue that this part of the definition is too narrow, for loyalty may be directed at a person, an institution, an ideal, or any number of other things. But by "cause" Royce does not have in mind—at least not exclusively—social movements, such as the cause of promoting social justice or the cause of ending world hunger. Rather, Royce's notion of a cause encapsulates all possible objects of loyal devotion. For Royce, a cause is simply the tie uniting individuals in loyal service. Royce first cites "the devotion of a patriot to his country" and "the devotion of a ship's captain to the requirements of his office"[37] as examples, but soon adds the loyalty of lovers to his list, noting that they "are loyal not merely to one another as separate individuals, but to their love, to their union, which is something more than either of them, or even than both of them viewed as distinct individuals."[38] We may love persons, institutions, ideals, or any number of other things, but love is an emotion. The faithfulness and commitment we demonstrate toward the tie that binds us to the object of our love is loyalty. Thus, to act disloyally is to act in a way that weakens the tie or bond.[39]

[36] Royce 1995, 9 (emphasis in original). Royce indicates that this definition is preliminary and tentative, and though he does add to it later in the book, it is the operative definition for the majority of the text as well as in subsequent texts.

[37] Royce 1995, 9–10.

[38] Royce 1995, 11.

[39] Troy Jollimore (correspondence, July 19, 2021) raises as a possible counterexample the case of a person who deems it in the best interest of their spouse to end their marriage. Attempting to follow Royce's philosophy of loyalty, the person judges that loyalty

Second, loyalty is willed. One cannot be loyal if one does not choose to be. "The loyal man's cause," Royce asserts, "is his cause by virtue of the assent of his own will."[40] To build on Royce's example of the patriot's loyalty, the notion of an involuntary patriot would strike one as peculiar. One cannot authentically be a patriot if one is not willingly devoted to one's country. The need for loyalty to be voluntary is brought into sharper relief by the supposition that loyalty requires devotion that is both practical and thoroughgoing.

By practical, Royce means that loyalty requires the loyal agent to act. Loyalty is not merely a feeling or emotion. "Adoration and affection may go with loyalty," Royce explains, "but can never alone constitute loyalty, . . . The loyal man serves."[41] Thus, the loyalty of the patriot to his country is not simply his feeling of pride to be a citizen of his country; loyalty requires action expressive of that feeling. He might, for instance, fly the flag of his country outside his home. He might vote in a national election. He might enlist in the military. Whatever he chooses, he engages in pursuits aimed at furthering the cause of promoting the flourishing of his country. Similarly, the loyalty of the ship captain to the requirements of his office requires him to fulfill those requirements; he cannot merely feel that it is his duty to do so.

In claiming that the willing and practical devotion of a person to a cause must be thoroughgoing, Royce means that the devotion must be sustained. A fickle or weak loyalty is, for Royce, a contradiction in terms. If one is loyal to a cause, one does not waver in one's devotion to it. Furthermore, while the cause of one's loyalty is "viewed by [one] as something outside of [one]," with respect to some causes, the loyal is also "ready to live or die as the cause

to the spouse would require ending the marriage (since it is best for the spouse), but notes that it seems that one cannot be loyal to the marriage if one destroys that very marriage. Royce's allowing for revision of one's loyalties—to be discussed shortly—aids in addressing this type of scenario.

[40] Royce 1995, 10.
[41] Royce 1995, 10.

directs."[42] The patriot, then, recognizes that his country, while it includes himself, is much larger than his private self. It has its own value, which it would maintain even if his private interest were not considered. It is this value, prized as it is by the patriot, that may make him ready to live or die for his cause of promoting the flourishing of his country.

Royce adds another feature to his sketch of loyalty, namely, that loyalty is social. "If one is a loyal servant of a cause," Royce states, "one has at least possible fellow-servants."[43] For Royce, the cause to which a loyal person is devoted always concerns other persons. The patriot has his compatriots; the lover has his beloved. The ship captain's loyalty to his ship clearly concerns other persons, among whom are his crew and any other passengers on his ship, as well, perhaps, as those anticipating the ship's arrival on successful completion of its voyage. The captain's crew might counsel him as to how best to loyally serve the cause, or they may act as fellow servants by showing confidence in decisions that he has made in this regard. The fact that loyal service to a cause bears consequences for more than the individual serving the cause necessitates that loyalty to a cause is, as Royce suggests, always at least potentially a social affair.

One might notice that Royce confines loyalty to the domain of human persons and objects that nonhuman animals are capable of loyalty (e.g., dogs are "man's best friend"). Royce explicitly denies the capacity of dogs to be loyal, holding that "the fidelity of a dog to his master is only a pathetic hint of loyalty, or a fragment of the disposition that, in human beings, expresses itself in the full reasonableness of loyal life."[44] Because loyalty to a cause entails the *duty* of willing, practical, and thoroughgoing devotion to a cause, dogs and other nonhuman animals are, for Royce, precluded from being loyal in any meaningful sense. The level of awareness and reflection

---

[42] Royce 1995, 10.
[43] Royce 1995, 11.
[44] Royce 1995, 118.

required to recognize and honor the duty of loyalty, Royce would contend, is beyond what dogs and other nonhuman animals typically display.[45]

Royce's principle of loyalty to loyalty

We have seen that for Royce, loyalty is always directed at a cause, but we have yet to say what constitutes a worthy cause. We are also unclear as to how to adjudicate between or among what appear to be conflicting worthy causes. Royce's responses to these questions come in the form of his notion of loyalty to loyalty:

> A cause is good, not only for me, but for mankind, in so far as it is essentially a *loyalty to loyalty*, that is, is an aid and a furtherance of loyalty in my fellows. It is an evil cause in so far as, despite the loyalty that it arouses in me, it is destructive of loyalty in the world of my fellows. My cause is, indeed, always such as to involve some loyalty to loyalty, because, if I am loyal to any cause at all, I have fellow-servants whose loyalty mine supports. But in so far as my cause is a predatory cause, which lives by overthrowing the loyalties of others, it is an evil cause, because it involves disloyalty to the very cause of loyalty itself.[46]

In short, a cause is worthy of loyalty to the extent that it promotes loyalty and is unworthy to the extent that it impedes loyalty.

What if one is torn between loyalties that that do not admit of a course of action that is clearly more loyal to loyalty? "[I]f,"

---

[45] Fletcher (1993, 10–11) takes the same position (and groups human babies with nonhuman animals): "We need not isolate a single distinguishable characteristic to realize that animals and babies could not bear duties of loyalty. As a matter of social practice, we attribute obligations only to those beings that can understand that they are under an obligation."

[46] Royce 1995, 56 (emphasis in original).

states Royce, "at the critical moment, I cannot predict which of two modes of serving the cause of loyalty to loyalty will lead to the more complete success in such service, the general principle certainly cannot tell me which of these two modes of service to choose."[47] Nonetheless, loyalty to loyalty is a guide in the face of such ignorance, for "it now becomes the principle, *Have a cause; choose your cause; be decisive.*"[48] In other words, "*Decide, knowingly if you can, ignorantly if you must, but in any case decide, and have no fear.*"[49] How is it that loyalty to loyalty *becomes* the new principle? Acknowledging influence from Harvard colleague William James's "The Will to Believe" essay, Royce instructs, "*As soon as further indecision would itself practically amount to a decision to do nothing,*—and so would mean a failure to be loyal to loyalty,—*then at once decide. This is the only right act.*"[50] Because the failure or refusal to choose any cause would fail to promote loyalty, when the question becomes "Choose a cause or do not," loyalty to loyalty always instructs, "Choose." "Henceforth," Royce states, "with all your mind and soul and strength belong, fearlessly and faithfully, to the chosen personal cause until the issue is decided, or until you positively know that this cause can no longer be served without disloyalty. So act and you are morally right."[51]

It is noteworthy that Royce allows for revision of loyalties. On the face of it, it would seem that thoroughgoing devotion of a person to a cause would be mutually exclusive with opting out. Being loyal to loyalty, however, demands conscientious self-reflection. Royce explains, "My causes must form a system. They must constitute in their entirety a single cause, my life of loyalty. When apparent

---

[47] Royce 1995, 88.
[48] Royce 1995, 88 (emphasis in original).
[49] Royce 1995, 89 (emphasis in original).
[50] Royce 1995, 89 (emphasis in original). James's 1896 essay "The Will to Believe" pertains to the rationality of adoption of religious belief in the face of a lack of coercive evidence for or against the existence of God. James believes that all persons must believe in God or not, conceiving of agnosticism as amounting to deciding to not believe.
[51] Royce 1995, 90.

conflicts arise amongst the causes in which I am interested, I shall deliberately undertake . . . to reduce the conflict to the greatest possible harmony."[52] Thus, "my loyalty will aim to be, even within the limits of my own personal life, an united, harmonious devotion, not to various conflicting causes, but to one system of causes, and so to one cause."[53] Accordingly, one ought to discontinue loyal behavior upon recognizing it as disloyal to loyalty. If loyalty to a particular cause was formerly judged to be loyal to loyalty, but mounting evidence suggests that this judgment was in error (or, perhaps, events have arisen that transform loyalty to a particular cause from having been loyal to loyalty to presently being disloyal to loyalty), the cause should be suspended or abandoned.[54]

One detects strands of several different moral theories in Royce's principle of loyalty to loyalty. The principle of loyalty to loyalty is a unique loyalty-centered form of consequentialism. Royce seems to implicitly distinguish his variety of consequentialism from utilitarianism when holding that his philosophy of loyalty "aim[s] at something much larger and richer than the mere sum of human happiness in individual men."[55] Rather, Royce instructs that one "so choose and so serve [one's] individual cause as to secure thereby the greatest possible increase of loyalty amongst men."[56]

The principle of loyalty to loyalty may also be viewed as a form of deontological theory. Royce's student, Annie Lyman Sears,

---

[52] Royce 1995, 62.

[53] Royce 1995, 63.

[54] To return to the counterexample raised by Jollimore (note 39), while the devil is in the details, it is certainly possible for the dissolution of a marriage to be compatible with Royce's philosophy of loyalty, assuming the continued devotion to this cause engenders disloyalty to loyalty. For example, remaining in a marriage in which one is controlled by one's spouse, whose domineering behavior has proven intractable in the face of attempted intervention, can lead to a diminished sense of self, a negation of autonomy, and estrangement from others, among other effects. Continued loyalty in the context of this marriage may *already* no longer be continued loyalty in Royce's sense, if it is not, in fact, a "willing" devotion. Choosing dissolution of the marriage, and thus promoting one's own potentiality as a willing, practical, and thoroughgoing devotee to some other cause(s) would thus be more loyal to loyalty than continued devotion to the marriage.

[55] Royce 1995, 177.

[56] Royce 1995, 90.

summarizes the affinity of Royce's principle of loyalty to loyalty with Kant's categorical imperative:

> We want to find some universal principle which shall not only unify "the many" of fleeting individual experience, but one which shall harmonize the conflicting variety of ideals of the world of many individuals. . . . I know of no better expression of such an ethical principle than that of Kant's categorical imperative. This universal law is a command to every one to so act that the principle of his action might become a law for all intelligent beings. Or, otherwise expressed, Will always the good-will. This universal statement of the ought is, of course, highly abstract, and to religious experience it seems cold. Professor Royce has given more concreteness and warmth to the principle in his statement of it. "Be loyal to the spirit of loyalty, everywhere."[57]

Whereas Kant insists that we imagine that we act, through our maxims, as a lawmaking member of the Kingdom of Ends, Royce has us imagine that our prospective actions are those of a vital constituent of humanity at large. The contrast is between a view of morality that views human agents as generalized abstractions and one that sees them as concrete particulars with specific individual cares, concerns, and motivations. From here it is a natural step to a view that knowledge of particular moral requirements is closely associated with, and is most visible in the context of, the actions and character traits of those particular individuals who are most successful in incorporating morality into their lives and actions—that is, the exemplars.

Finally, consider the compatibility of Royce's principle of loyalty to loyalty with virtue ethics. The extent of such compatibility is

---

[57] Sears 1915, 388. It is worth noting that Royce authored a ten-page introduction to Sears's book. It is improbable that Royce would write such a note without having read the entirety of Sears's text, and improbable that he would allow Sears's description of loyalty to loyalty stand if he thought it inaccurate.

perhaps limited by the primacy given in virtue ethics to the agent's cultivation of virtues. While Royce certainly wants people to become loyal, the principle of loyalty to loyalty surpasses the individual agent in scope, implicating humanity at large. Perhaps in this respect loyalty to loyalty resembles the virtue ethics of Confucius, sometimes referred to as a role ethic, with virtue being explicitly tied to interpersonal relations rather than to individual traits of character.[58] Royce would find compelling the Confucian notion of moral development as beginning in the context of family and proceeding, as if outwardly in a series of concentric circles, into one's roles in community, country, and the cosmos.

At any rate, there are considerable affinities between Royce's theory and virtue ethics. For Royce, loyalty establishes selfhood and strikes a harmony between self-will and self-sacrifice. Employing loyalty to loyalty as a regulative ideal guides one's ensuring that one's loyal action is good, rather than bad, or better rather than worse. *Aretē* ("excellence" or "virtue" in fulfillment of a particular function) with respect to being loyal to loyalty is necessary for a Roycean notion of *eudaimonia* (well-being or happiness, the flourishing that results from *aretē*), with the development of a kind of *phronesis* (practical wisdom) required for its achievement. Although Royce does not fully detail this "art of loyalty," he suggests that "[m]uch of the art of loyalty depends [. . .] upon training yourself to observe the loyal who are all about you, however remote their cause is from yours, however humble their lives."[59]

Royce, exemplars, and loyalty

It could be said that Royce's philosophy of loyalty is prompted in large part by the desire to revise a popular notion of moral

---

[58] For a key scholarly resource on Confucian role ethics, see Ames 2010.
[59] Royce, 1995, 134.

exemplarity. Among Royce's stated motivations in *The Philosophy of Loyalty* is to "break up" the "disastrous association" that has long endured between war and loyalty.[60] Royce casts the title of his own work as something of a response to Rudolf Steinmetz's then recently published *The Philosophy of War*, which perpetuated that association.[61] Although Royce wishes to distance 'loyalty' from its popular association with war, he frequently cites examples of loyalty connected with battle, such as the loyalty embodied by the Swiss patriot Arnold von Winkelried, who purportedly rushed on the Austrian spears at the Battle of Sempach, dying for the cause of liberty.[62] Royce recognizes this tension and claims that he cites such examples solely on account of their familiarity.[63] Even if Royce does not align himself with the chosen causes of the individuals in question, he finds exemplary certain aspects of their loyalty to their chosen causes.

Consider the Japanese samurai. Royce alludes to the Japanese samurai in several works, but he first does so explicitly in the second lecture of *The Philosophy of Loyalty*, "Individualism." In this lecture, Royce argues against the notion that loyalty amounts to slavishness and thus fundamentally undermines the individual. On the contrary, Royce holds that the individual expresses himself in his fullest when embodying thoroughgoing loyalty to a chosen cause. Relying on the testimony of Inazo Nitobe in *Bushidō: The Soul of Japan*,[64] Royce writes, "The loyal Japanese Samurai, as he is described to us by those who know, never lacked his own sort of self-assertion."[65] Indeed, according to Nitobe, the moral code of "Bushido did not require us to make our conscience the slave of any lord or king."[66]

---

[60] Royce 1995, 7.
[61] Steinmetz 1907.
[62] Royce 1995, 153.
[63] Royce 1995, 48.
[64] Some scholars have criticized Nitobe for giving an inaccurate portrait of the Japanese samurai. See, for instance, Hurst, III 1990.
[65] Royce 1995, 35.
[66] Nitobe 1969, 80.

While Nitobe does not exactly articulate a principle analogous to loyalty to loyalty, he does make it clear that the samurai can and should "use every available means"[67] to persuade his master if he sees things differently than he does; this is "the loyal path for him to pursue."[68] Royce closes the lecture on "Individualism" by holding, "There is only one way to be an ethical individual. That is to choose your cause, and then to serve it, as the Samurai his feudal chief ... in the spirit of all the loyal."[69] Thus, the samurai exemplifies loyalty in service of his master, including when remonstrating with his master about the proper path of action. Royce's reference to the samurai's serving one's cause "in the spirit of all the loyal" foreshadows his introduction of the concept of loyalty to loyalty in the next and third lecture, "Loyalty to Loyalty."[70] Perhaps indeed Royce would add that the samurai should remonstrate with his master precisely when the master fails to be loyal to loyalty.

As a "representative instance"[71] of loyalty, introduced in the "Loyalty to Loyalty" lecture, Royce offers the following example centered on William Lenthall,[72] the Speaker of the House of Commons during the reign of Charles I:

> In January, 1642, just before the outbreak of hostilities between King Charles I and the Commons, the King resolved to arrest certain leaders of the opposition party in Parliament. He accordingly sent his herald to the House to demand the surrender of these members into his custody. The Speaker of the House in reply solemnly appealed to the ancient privileges of the House, which gave to that body jurisdiction over its own members, and which forbade its arrest without its consent. The conflict between the

---

[67] Nitobe 1969, 80.
[68] Nitobe 1969, 80.
[69] Nitobe 1969, 47.
[70] For further discussion of the connection of Royce and Nitobe, see Foust 2015.
[71] Royce 1995, 48.
[72] Although he never refers to him by name, it is evident that William Lenthall is the Speaker of the House to whom Royce refers.

privileges of the House and the royal prerogative was herewith
definitely initiated. The King resolved by a show of force to assert
at once his authority; and, on the day following that upon which
the demand sent through his herald had been refused, he went
in person, accompanied by soldiers, to the House. Then, having
placed his guards at the doors, he entered, went up to the Speaker,
and, naming the members whom he desired to arrest, demanded,
"Mr. Speaker, do you espy these persons in the House?"[73]

In response, Royce continues, the Speaker "at once fell to on his
knee before the King and said: 'Your Majesty, I am the Speaker of
this House, and, being such, I have neither eyes to see nor tongue
to speak save as this House shall command; and I humbly beg
your Majesty's pardon if this is the only answer I can give to your
Majesty.'"[74] For Royce, when one is loyal, one "can say with the
Speaker: 'I am the servant of this cause, its reasonable, its willing, its
devoted instrument, and being such, I have neither eyes to see nor
tongue to speak save as this cause shall command.'"[75]

That the loyal should be described as an "instrument" with "neither eyes to see nor tongue to speak" except as the cause commands
may lead one to think that loyalty prohibits critical reflection.[76] But
as Royce points out, the moment at which the Speaker responded
to the King "was an unique one in English history. Custom, precedent, convention, obviously were inadequate to define the Speaker's
duty in this most critical instance."[77] Rather, while the words of the
Speaker were consistent with custom, they also created a new precedent. The Speaker "had to be inventive to utter them."[78] Although
the King might take offense at the Speaker's refusal to consent to

---

[73] Royce 1995, 49.
[74] Royce 1995, 49.
[75] Royce 1995, 50.
[76] For precisely this criticism, see Baron 1984, 8–9. For further discussion of Baron
and Royce, see Foust 2012, 35–40.
[77] Royce 1995, 49.
[78] Royce 1995, 50.

the arrest of the members of the House, the King "could not fail to note that, for the moment, he had met with a personal dignity greater than kingship,—the dignity that any loyal man, great or humble, possesses whenever he speaks and acts in the service of his cause."[79] The dignity of the Speaker is manifested not just in his loyal service of his cause, but in his honorable way of being loyal. He does not dishonestly deny that the members of the House who the King seeks to arrest are in the House. As in the case of the loyal Japanese samurai, the Speaker maintains his self-assertion, literally not allowing his conscience to be the slave of a king.

Among those types of loyal figures who Royce views as exemplary are those who are so thoroughgoing in their devotion to their cause as to persist in loyalty should it become "lost in the visible world."[80] Any number of causes may be rendered "lost" on the occasion of a death. Although the death of one to whom we are loyally bound removes the object of our loyalty from our earthly vision, loyalty to lost causes is, according to Royce, "attended by two comrades, grief and imagination,"[81] each of which sustains the loyal in continued devotion to the cause. The strain and sacrifice endured in the suffering of another's death may be the precursor to new forms of loyal expression.

Royce often cites one figure in particular whose loyalty in the midst of such suffering he admires—Antigone, the eponymous protagonist of Sophocles's drama (c. 441 BCE). Early in *The Philosophy of Loyalty*, Royce states, "moral standards, as Antigone said, are not of today or yesterday."[82] In other words, genuine moral standards bind eternally. It may be said that Royce's academic career is bookended by this line from Antigone. As an undergraduate Classics major at the University of California, Berkeley, he delivered a commencement address, "On a Passage in Sophocles"—*this*

[79] Royce 1995, 50.
[80] Royce 1995, 131.
[81] Royce 1995, 132.
[82] Royce 1995, 7.

passage in Sophocles—in 1875. In notes for his 1915–1916[83] extension course on ethics, he describes the tragedy of Antigone as "founded upon a sister's consciousness of Loyalty toward the obligations which require her, despite the command of the king, to celebrate the rites of her slain brother" and holds that the "majesty of the fraternal tie is nowhere more deeply felt and expressed than in Antigone's famous words with regard to what the gods of the underworld have required of her as an expression, both of her duty and of her love, towards her brother. She goes willingly to death, because these commands of the gods of the underworld, as she says: 'Are not an affair of today or of yesterday, and no man knows whence they came.'"[84] Royce's sustained attention to Antigone suggests the possibility that her exemplarity inspired the shaping of his moral theory.[85] This sequence would be consistent with the model of exemplarist moral theory, described as beginning with people and ending with theory.[86]

With the Japanese samurai, William Lenthall, and Antigone, I have considered figures who took significant risks in loyal service of their chosen cause. Arguably, Zagzebski would classify them as heroes. But Royce seeks to avoid suggesting that fatalistic heroism is the watchword of loyalty. Rather, steadfast commitment is the essential quality.[87] Service to one's cause, whatever the cause is, provides an answer to what Royce dubs "the hardest of human practical problems, the problem: 'For what do I live? Why am I here? For what am I good? Why am I needed?'"[88] As Royce puts it:

[83] Royce dies in 1916.

[84] Royce, "1915–1916 Extension Course on Ethics: Principles of the Art of Loyalty," in Oppenheim 2001, 154.

[85] For further discussion of the connection between Royce and Antigone, see Shew and Foust 2010, 355–356.

[86] Zagzebski 2017 cites Amy Olberding's description of the Confucian *Analects* as following this model (86). See Olberding 2012.

[87] Of course, if one is "too strongly" loyal to a cause (i.e., remaining committed to a cause when that commitment engenders disloyal to loyalty), then one must revise one's loyalties.

[88] Royce 1995, 28.

the mightiest and the humblest members of any social order can be morally equal in the exemplification of loyalty. Whenever I myself begin to look about my own community to single out those people whom I know to be, in the sense of our definition, especially loyal to their various causes, I always find, amongst the most exemplary cases of loyalty, a few indeed of the most prominent members of our community, whom your minds and mine must at once single out because their public services and their willing sacrifices have made their loyalty to their chosen causes a matter of common report and of easy observation. But my own mind also chooses some of the plainest and obscurest of the people whom I chance to know . . . whose loyalty is even all the more sure to me because I can certainly affirm that they, at least, cannot be making any mere display of loyalty.[89]

For her own part, Zagzebski perceives an incongruity between renowned historical exemplars and our ordinary lives, remarking, "Most of us do not know someone whose life is saintly enough or sagely enough to make a good narrative for large numbers of other people, but we may know someone whose admirability is an inspiration in our own lives."[90] On this point there appears to be some tension between Royce and Zagzebski. For Royce, the "plain" and "obscure" people whom he "chances to know" fit the relevant descriptor of moral excellence. Rather than being saintly or sagely enough, they are *loyal* enough to make a good narrative for large numbers of other people; it just so happens that few people know of them. For Zagzebski, the ability to observe moral exemplars via personal experience "is very limited in scope. Few people have had personal interactions with a Mother Teresa or a Pope Francis, much less with someone on the caliber of Confucius or Jesus."[91] Although

---

[89] Royce 1995, 53.
[90] Zagzebski 2017, 128.
[91] Zagzebski 2017, 68.

she includes unrenowned persons in a list of those she considers admirable "in very different ways" (e.g., "A woman I know who is impeccably groomed and keeps her house always ready for company, while caring for her husband with Alzheimer's" and "Any man who can sing the last verse of "Walk the Line"),[92] the admirable qualities of these persons align more with temperament and natural talent, not the acquired traits—the moral virtues—on which her theory is focused. Because moral learning involves emulation of exemplars, and emulation is the product of admiration and imitation, it would seem that a theory allowing for exemplars to be nearer at hand would be more conducive to moral growth.[93] Royce's philosophy of loyalty has this advantage over Zagzebski's exemplarist moral theory.

Conclusion

In this essay, I have discussed some elements of Royce's philosophy of loyalty, focusing especially on his use of moral exemplars in developing and expounding that philosophy. To do so, I have drawn on Zagzebski's recent work on exemplarist moral theory. Although it would be facile to view Royce's philosophy of loyalty as an early form of exemplarist moral theory, there is ample evidence that Royce recognized the power of admiration and imitation of exemplars in helping one to live a moral life. While Royce may not

---

[92] Zagzebski 2017, 36.

[93] Although she stops short of stating that one's (unrenowned) grandmother could be classified as a moral exemplar, in a critique of a Gallup poll about admiration, Zagzebski acknowledges that one could admire one's grandmother more than an admirable person of renown. Respondents were asked to identify what man and what woman "that you have heard or read about, living today in any part of the world, do you admire most?" Zagzebski comments that the poll "can easily be interpreted as asking for the name of a well-known person. Nobody is going to name his grandmother in an answer on a Gallup Poll . . . the poll does not necessarily show that people are more likely to admire persons of high status than persons of low status, but that they interpret the poll to be asking which among the persons of high status they admire the most" (2017, 49).

build exemplars directly into the content of his moral theory as Zagzebski does, he clearly recognizes that they play a useful and likely non-eliminable role in thinking, talking, and teaching about morality and virtue. As for the virtue of loyalty, Royce explicitly places it front and center in his discussions of exemplars, while Zagzebski focuses on other virtues. But the importance of loyalty is, I would venture, implicit in Zagzebski's discussions of exemplars. Surely loyalty to their respective causes animated Socha, Vanier, and Confucius. Indeed, the accounts we have of the heroism of Socha, the saintliness of Vanier, and the wisdom of Confucius would not be intelligible if not for the willing, practical, and thoroughgoing devotion of each of these men to their chosen causes.

Considering Royce and Zagzebski in tandem, then, underscores the vitality of loyalty to the moral life. One may object that because there are bad loyalties, championed by what could be called anti-exemplars, loyalty is not a quality befitting of an exemplar.[94] In my view, Royce's principle of loyalty to loyalty addresses—if not obviates—this objection. It is one thing to be loyal; it is another to be loyal to loyalty. Those who are exemplary in their loyalty, and who thus manifest a genuinely virtuous loyalty, will be loyal to loyalty.

Bibliography

Ames, R. T. *Confucian Role Ethics: A Vocabulary*. Albany: SUNY Press, 2010.

Baron, M. *The Moral Status of Loyalty*. Dubuque, IA: Kendall/Hunt, 1984.

Birondo, N. "Review of Linda Trinkaus Zagzebski, *Moral Exemplarist Theory*." *Notre Dame Philosophical Reviews* 10 (2017). https://ndpr.nd.edu/reviews/exemplarist-moral-theory/

---

[94] For the suggestion that Zagzebski's moral theory is incomplete without discussion of anti-exemplars, see Birondo 2017. Although Zagzebski confesses that she is "not comfortable naming names of contemptible persons," she admits that "it is always a safe bet to mention Hitler." Adolf Hitler is exactly the sort of example I have in mind; he was certainly loyal to his chosen cause, but his loyalty to this cause was disloyal to loyalty.

Bovermann, T. "Findings of L'Arche International's Inquiry into Jean Vanier," 2000. https://www.larcheusa.org/news_article/findings-of-larche-interna tionals-inquiry-into-jean-vanier/

Damon, W., and A. Colby. *The Power of Ideals: The Real Story of Moral Choice.* Oxford: Oxford University Press, 2015.

Fischer, M. "Locating Royce's Reasoning on Race." *The Pluralist* 7:1 (2012): 104–132.

Fletcher, G. P. *Loyalty: An Essay on the Morality of Relationships.* New York: Oxford University Press, 1993.

Foust, M. A. *Loyalty to Loyalty: Josiah Royce and the Genuine Moral Life.* New York: Fordham University Press, 2012.

Foust, M. A. "Nitobe and Royce: Bushidō and the Philosophy of Loyalty." *Philosophy East and West* 65:4 (2015): 1174–1193.

Haidt, J. *The Righteous Mind: Why Good People are Divided by Politics and Religion.* New York: Vintage Books, 2012.

Hurst, III, C. "Death, Honor, and Loyality [*sic*]: The Bushidō Ideal." *Philosophy East and West* 40:4 (1990): 511–527.

James, W. "The Will to Believe." *The New World* 5 (1896): 327–347.

Nitobe, I. *Bushido: The Soul of Japan.* Vol. 1 of *The Works of Inazo Nitobe.* Tokyo: University of Tokyo Press, 1969.

Olberding, A. *Moral Exemplars in the* Analects: *The Good Person Is That.* New York: Routledge, 2012.

Oppenheim, F. M., ed. *Josiah Royce's Late Writings: A Collection of Unpublished and Scattered Works.* Vol. 2. Bristol, England: Thoemmes Press, 2001.

Putnam, H. "The Meaning of 'Meaning.'" *Minnesota Studies in the Philosophy of Science* 7 (1975): 131–193.

Royce, J. *The Philosophy of Loyalty.* Nashville, TN: Vanderbilt University Press, 1995.

Royce, J. *The Sources of Religious Insight.* Washington, DC: Catholic University of America Press, 2001.

Sears, A. L. *The Drama of the Spiritual Life: A Study of Religious Experience and Ideals.* New York: Macmillan, 1915.

Shew, M., and M. A. Foust. "Loyalty and the Art of Wise Living: The Influence of Plato on the Moral Philosophy of Josiah Royce." *The Southern Journal of Philosophy* 48:4 (2010): 353–370.

Steinmetz, S. R. *Die Philosophie des Krieges.* Leipzig, Germany: J.A. Barth, 1907.

Ward, Benedicta. *The Desert Fathers: Sayings of the Early Christian Monks.* New York: Penguin Books, 2003.

Zagzebski, L. T. *Divine Motivation Theory.* Cambridge: Cambridge University Press, 2004.

Zagzebski, L. T. *Exemplarist Moral Theory.* New York: Oxford University Press, 2017.

8

Loyalty to the Constitution

Sanford Levinson

The pervasiveness of loyalty oaths (and, therefore, of conflicts of loyalty)

Our lives are enmeshed in oaths, many of them involving professions of loyalty and the concomitant promise of giving priority to the person or institution to whom loyalty is professed. Paradoxically or not, perhaps the most telling examples of oaths set out in the Bible are not only those taken by human beings acknowledging Divine rule, but, rather, those given by God to the People of Israel. As stated in Hebrews 6:16, "So when God desired to show more convincingly to the heirs of the promise the unchangeable character of his purpose, he guaranteed it with an oath," as if the unadorned promise were not enough. However, as indicated in Isaiah 45:23, reciprocity was expected: "To me every knee shall bow, every tongue shall swear allegiance," and a common trope among the Prophets in explaining the ills besetting the people of Israel was the failure to be faithful to oaths taken of obedience to the sovereign God, who would in turn punish the people for their failures to comply. But, of course, it is not only a possibly "jealous God" who demands oaths of loyalty.

Oaths are, in fact, all around us, and it is the rare individual who has not taken multiple such oaths. Probably the most common oath in modern times is that given during formal marriage ceremonies. Oaths, even if written by the participants instead of taken from given liturgies, are the centerpiece of the ceremonies. And promises

Sanford Levinson, *Loyalty to the Constitution* In: *The Virtue of Loyalty*. Edited by: Troy Jollimore, Oxford University Press. © Oxford University Press 2024. DOI: 10.1093/oso/9780197612644.003.0009

of lifetime commitment are given even as participants are presumably well aware of the availability of easy divorce (and the fact that many marriages will, in fact, dissolve). Perhaps in the modern world promises of sexual fidelity are treated with more latitude; one wonders, especially during a pandemic, if this is also the case with promises to provide succor "in sickness and in health."

But the list is surely not exhausted by wedding vows, however important they may be to the participants. Governments are often quite zealous—and, perhaps, jealous—in demanding that citizens and, even more so, employees, swear fidelity to the state in whose name they rule. As the list of oath demanders increases, the opportunity for conflicts of loyalty does as well. Does the promise to take care of an ill spouse take priority over the demands of one's job and any affirmations of loyalty to *it* that might have been demanded along the way? And so on. It will not be difficult for most readers to realize that loyalty, however much it may be a virtue in the abstract, can become extremely complicated when conflicts of loyalty present themselves. These conflicts may involve multiple institutions and their competing demands or, instead, they may be presented when there are good-faith differences of opinion on what counts as living up to the loyalty that one has pledged. No doubt many marital arguments are sparked by differences about the meaning of the very abstract promises made. Does one have a duty to provide endless care for what might be termed self-induced sickness, that is, the patent failure of a partner to "take care of himself"? And who gets to determine whether pledges to God of "righteous behavior" are in fact being carried out?

My own primary interest, both personally and professionally, lies in claims to loyalty demanded by governmental institutions. The most dramatic, of course, involves our president, who, as the late Ross Perot insisted, should be envisioned as an "employee" of the public with attendant duties to his or her employer. The Constitution specifies in Article II the oath required of presidents upon taking office, in which they "solemnly" promise "to the best of my Ability, [to] preserve, protect and defend the Constitution of the United States." Almost all presidents (and others) add at the conclusion "So help me God," as a further signification of the solemnity of the occasion. A minor slip-up in Chief Justice John Roberts's presentation of the oath to Barack Obama upon his inauguration in 2009 led to a repeat performance the next day lest anyone believe that Obama had not "really" complied with the Constitution's command. Even if as cynical sophisticates we are tempted to view oaths as the homage that hypocrisy pays to virtue, almost all of us would undoubtedly be shocked if an American president emulated the late Venezuelan President Hugo Chavez. Not only did he add the word "moribund" to his 1999 oath to uphold the Venezuelan Constitution, but he also went on to proclaim to the assembled audience that "[t]he Constitution, and with it the ill-fated political system to which it gave birth 40 years ago, has to die. It is going to die, Sirs! Accept it!"[1]

Article VI commands that all members of Congress, as well as "the Members of the several State Legislatures, and *all* executive and judicial Officers, both of the United States and of the several States, shall be bound by Oath or Affirmation, to support this Constitution" (emphasis added). There was nothing "innocent" about this requirement; a major challenge facing partisans of the new system created in Philadelphia and then ratified thereafter was to create a national consciousness that would ultimately triumph over existing primary identifications with the constituent states of the United States. From then until now it has been a continuing issue whether one gives priority to the adjective or the noun. After all, 750,000 persons died between 1861 and 1865 over the answer to this question, and among those repudiating their oaths to the generalized *United* States in favor of their home *states* were a former Senator and Secretary of War, Jefferson Davis; the leading general

---

[1] Available at https://www.nytimes.com/1999/02/04/world/new-president-in-venezuela-proposes-to-rewrite-the-constitution.html

in the United States Army, Robert E. Lee; a prominent senator, Judah P. Benjamin, of Louisiana; and a member of the U.S. Supreme Court, John Campbell, who also went home to Louisiana and the Confederacy.

It is, of course, altogether possible that these particular persons, as well as many others, had taken multiple oaths of political loyalty, to their states as well as to the United States, perhaps not realizing at the time that they might in fact end up in conflict instead of being truly complementary. Oaths are of special interest in pluralistic societies. Not only may they operate as efforts to transform the identity of individuals—the most obvious example is immigrants—by creating a new sense of what constitutes the self as, say, a loyal American instead of whatever had been the case before. They may also signify the competition, so to speak, among the many groups and institutions that daily compete for the loyalty of individuals who may well feel themselves torn by conflicting demands. Lewis Coser years ago coined the term "greedy institutions" to capture the sociological (and phenomenological) reality that any given institution will try to inculcate a sense of priority in the consciousness of those who belong to it, with concomitant consequences for the other groups seeking the inevitably scarce time, energy, and psychic commitments of the beleaguered individual. Most institutions do not require formal expressions of loyalty; economic incentives may be sufficient. But some institutions *do* demand formal oaths, and then one must ask both why they do so and what are the actual implications for persons taking such oaths.

With or without formal oaths, one can certainly not be confident that the conflicts of political loyalty manifested in the American carnage of the 1860s have been resolved, just as we know that wedding oaths have not in fact brought an end to having affairs or seeking formal divorce. After all, with whatever degree of seriousness, over 100,000 Texans signed a petition following the 2012 presidential election on behalf of Texas being allowed to withdraw from the Union, and a majority of youngsters gathered at the American

Legion's "Boy's State" in Texas in 2017 voted to secede. A 2014 poll taken by Reuters showed that approximately a quarter of American respondents supported secession by their state,[2] and it would be surprising if the presumed alienation from the Union and its government had not grown (or at least remained stable) since what may strike some of us as the halcyon days of the Obama administration.

As I write my final revisions to this essay in November 2023, Great Britain has in fact seceded from the European Union; it remains an open question whether the hopefully titled United Kingdom will in fact survive long into the future should Scotland, led by members of the Scottish National Party, follow through on their threat to hold another secession referendum. Approximately 45 percent of Scots voted in 2014 to secede from the United Kingdom, and it is widely believed that a majority could well be found for secession, given some of the realized costs attached to Brexit. After all, what we call the American Revolution is itself most accurately described as a secession from the British Empire. Both potential and actual conflicts of political loyalty abound in today's world.

At a more mundane level, recent figures indicate that approximately 21.734 million persons—approximately 12 percent of the total American workforce—work for one or another level of government and are thus subject to the requirement of Article VI.[3] Although one might question whether professors at public universities are "officers" of a state, many states do in fact require their faculty to take an oath of loyalty to the United States Constitution and, quite often, the state constitution as well. Attorneys, as "officers of the court," are also required to take suitable oaths, sometimes, as in Texas, even in order to sit for the bar exam prior to formal admission to the bar. If one adds to formal loyalty oaths the "pledge of allegiance" to "the flag of the United States and to the republic for which it stands," which begins for most Americans very early in their lives as they enter public schools, then it is undoubtedly the case that the overwhelming majority of Americans have been and remain exposed to the phenomenon of being expected to express loyalty to the state and to its political arrangements.

In my own case, I have certainly taken not only marriage vows but also vows of loyalty to both the United States and various state constitutions when I interned at NASA in 1962; worked for a U.S. Senate subcommittee in 1963; became a member of the California Bar; began employment as a clerk to a federal district judge in North Carolina; and when I joined the faculty of the University of Texas Law School in 1980. I certainly wouldn't be surprised if there were other occasions as well that I have forgotten. As someone who avoided the draft in the 1960s by taking advantage of student deferments, I did not join the armed forces, which most certainly requires a loyalty oath, even (or perhaps especially?) from those noncitizens who in fact enlist, perhaps as a path to quicker citizenship.

Nor should anyone believe that such oaths are signs of American exceptionalism. Thomas More lost his life in part because he refused to acknowledge the legitimacy of the new Church of England with Henry VIII as its head. And some historians view as a pivotal moment in the French Revolution the passage of the Civil Constitution of the Clergy in 1790, which required that (Catholic) bishops, prior to their consecration, "take a solemn oath, in the presence of the municipal officers, of the people, and of the clergy, to guard with care the faithful of his diocese who are confided to him, *to be loyal to the nation, the law, and the king, and to support with his power the constitution decreed by the National Assembly and accepted by the king*."[4] This is, of course, an effort to limit the sovereignty of the Roman Catholic Church as constituted institutionally by the

---

[4] https://history.hanover.edu/texts/civilcon.html (emphasis added).

Vatican and, ultimately, the Papacy. Here, too, there was nothing innocent about these requirements.

Returning to the United States, it is not hard to see similar impulses behind the imposition of oaths, including one adopted by Congress in exercising its constitutionally assigned exclusive power over naturalization of immigrants from other countries and thus making them full citizens within the American political community. Prior to their being juridically (and psychologically) reborn as naturalized citizens of the United States, they had to pledge, "I hereby declare, on oath, that I absolutely and entirely renounce and abjure all allegiance and fidelity to any foreign prince, potentate, state, or sovereignty of whom or which I have heretofore been a subject or citizen; that I will support and defend the Constitution and laws of the United States of America." Loyalty to prior sovereigns was now erased, to be replaced by a distinctly new self-understanding as a citizen of the United States. "[S]overeignty could reside only in the nation and principally among the people"[5] who were, as proclaimed at the beginning of the Constitution's Preamble, the "ordainers" of the polity. The good news is that immigrants could in fact become part of the "American people," unlike societies that adhered rigidly to a set of ascriptive characteristics and excluded all others from membership. But, perhaps, the bad news is that one was in fact called upon to acknowledge the death in some important sense of prior loyalties and identities based on them—such as being "a subject of his Majesty the King."

Not at all coincidentally, the earlier Declaration of Independence also was founded on the ability of "one people" to be able to "alter or abolish" any constitutional order that no longer met the attribute of government by "consent of the governed." One might well now believe that the notion that "the voice of the people is the voice of God," a term originally used derisively in the ninth century, had now become decisively transvalued. And, of course, an atheist

[5] Miller 1990, 481, 493.

could simply proclaim that "the voice of the people" has the same authority once ascribed to the ostensible voice of God. It might be worth noting, incidentally, that the original oath was quite sensibly interpreted to make dual citizenship—that is, the retention by a new citizen of his or her prior status as a citizen of another country (or subject of a monarch)—juridically impossible. Thus the necessity for "renunciation and abjuration." However, for whatever reason, this clause is apparently no longer taken to have that most obvious meaning, at least since a 1967 law authorizing dual citizenship. Thus two participants at the conference at which these papers were initially discussed explained that they had not in fact given up their original political loyalty. Perhaps they should be classified as "political bigamists."

Not all countries are so generous. China and India, for example, automatically rescind the citizenship of their nationals upon naturalization in another country, and Spain allows dual nationality only with regard to certain Latin American countries that were part of the Spanish Empire. (This obviously excludes the nationals of South America's largest country, Brazil.) At the very least, one might wonder whether the tolerance of dual citizenship is at least as much a product of the declining seriousness with which we are prone to treat the idea of overarching political identity as it is an admirable willingness to be more tolerant of divided loyalties. Is it relevant, for example, that there is not a significant movement to be more tolerant of plural marriage?[6] Or is it that we believe that marriage is more "serious" than is the profession of political loyalty?

One might, of course, take the foregoing as simply a set of factoids of interest to political theorists or, on occasion, to lawyers

---

[6] Though perhaps it is worth noting that Chief Justice Roberts, in his angry dissent in the Supreme Court's *Obergefell* decision that recognized a constitutional right to same-sex marriage, suggested that the majority's basically libertarian logic would inexorably lead to the constitutionalization of polygamy. As a predictive matter, one can be confident that no such constitutionalization is likely to take place in the foreseeable future, but this empirical observation is completely orthogonal to the argument about the strict logic of *Obergefell*. See also Levinson 2005.

with given clients, but not as something truly pressing. Ironically, such a response almost certainly requires that one treat such oaths as "mere" formalities or what the Supreme Court of the United States once described as "no more than an amenity."[7] Or perhaps, as with even the oath of succor "in sickness and in health," until "death do we part," they are taken as aspirations that are nonetheless defeasible under a variety of circumstances, ultimately to be determined by the promise-giver and accepted thereafter as legitimate by what has become a more libertarian state and culture. No one need fear any longer that the state will view those particular oaths as binding, whatever might be the view, say, of the Catholic Church on such matters. Still, one wonders if the state itself is necessarily so blasé about those professions of loyalty it itself elicits from those who serve it or even wish to become citizens.

A turn toward the personal and beyond

I first wrote of loyalty oaths in 1986 and 1987.[8] Both of those essays were revised and became part of my first book, *Constitutional Faith*, originally published in 1988. That book concluded with a highly personal narrative about my response to an exhibit in Philadelphia, on the occasion of the Constitution's bicentennial in 1987. The exhibit concluded by giving each participants an opportunity to join the Founders, as it were, by signing a long scroll accepting the Constitution. I wrote of my doubts, primarily because of the rank injustices of the original Constitution vis-à-vis accommodations with slavery; I ultimately decided, however, to add my signature on the grounds that if Frederick Douglass, even before the Civil War and the addition of the so-called Reconstruction Amendments, could affirm the Constitution, then so could I. (Though Douglass

---

[7] 397 U.S. at 240, quoted in Cole v. Richardson, 405 U.S. 676, 685 (1972).
[8] Levinson 1986, Levinson 1987.

had earlier, in 1849, written of his inability to "swear to support" the Constitution, even if he changed his position a decade later.[9]) Though not a formal loyalty oath, it certainly constituted a close analogue, an affirmation of the "constitutional faith" that was the topic of the overall book.

I also addressed similar questions in a 1990 essay that specifically examined the interrogations of Catholic nominees to the Supreme Court with regard to their giving priority to the commands of the Church over those of the Constitution itself.[10] I prefaced that essay with a statement of Columbia historian Istvan Deak that described the Roman Catholic Church as "beautiful anachronism in our age of crazed nationalism; virtually every devout Catholic preserves in his heart some remnants of his denomination's transnational loyalty and the duty of Catholics to defy immoral laws."[11] That is, the "transnational loyalty," in this case to the demands incumbent on being a Roman Catholic, take precedence over merely national loyalties should they command that one engage in "immoral" actions. But nationalism, "crazed" or not, is the central motif of politics since the development of the so-called Westphalian system,[12] organized around the "sovereignty" of separate states. This generates the associated duty to obey duly enacted laws independent of one's own private views about their "immorality."

---

[9] Quoted in Re (2016): 307.

[10] Levinson 2003: 192.

[11] Levinson 2003: 192.

[12] The Treaty of Westphalia brought the Thirty Years War of 1618–1648 to a formal end in effect by recognizing the existence of geographically bounded states that would be treated as "sovereign," that is, all-powerful, within their particular domains. This gave, among other things, the rulers of a given state the authority to determine that the state would be Catholic or Protestant, with suitably "established churches" to which one was expected to affirm loyalty and help finance through taxes, coupled, in some countries with active persecution and perhaps exile of those unwilling to affirm the state-required identities. It was, of course, especially important that rulers themselves be of the "proper" religion and theological commitments. Thus King James II was basically run out of Great Britain because of his Catholic sympathies, to be replaced by the Protestants William and Mary. And thus the importance of the ban in Article VI of "test oaths" for American political officials. But such oaths were religious; ironically, the same Clause prohibiting *religious* "test oats" required oaths to become public officials.

Most of my own essays now go back more than a quarter of a century, written in what increasingly feels like another time. What this means, as a practical matter, is that in a second edition of *Constitutional Faith*, published in 2011, I explained in an extensive afterword why in 2003, at the opening of the National Constitution Center in Philadelphia, for which I had served as one of many expert advisors, I refused to endorse the Constitution. The Center concludes its generally impressive exhibit on the history of American constitutional development with an opportunity to visit Signers' Hall, which features impressive life-size statues of all of the delegates to the Philadelphia Convention. The visitors, as was the case in 1987, were invited to emulate the signers by adding their own names to the document and thus reaffirming their own constitutional faith. This time around, however, I chose to stand, as it were, with George Mason, Elbridge Gerry, and Edmund Randolph, the three nonsignatories of the Constitution who occupy their own place at one side of the Hall (perhaps suggesting the corner in a classroom to which disruptive children are sent). The reason for my change of mind (and heart), as I explained, is that my own central interest with regard to the Constitution has dramatically shifted from one that emphasizes the presence (or absence) of certain protections of individual rights to one that instead focuses on the *structures*, remarkably unchanged since 1787, that provide the framework for actual government of the United States.

As I have elaborated in two further books written since then, I now believe that the Constitution is indefensibly undemocratic.[13] The chief exhibits offered as proof are the electoral college, which twice in the five most recent election cycles has given the Oval Office to the loser of the popular vote; and the U.S. Senate, in which, at present, the half of the American population that lives in nine states has a total of eighteen senators, while the less-than-half that lives in the remaining forty-one states receives eighty-two votes.

[13] See Levinson 2006.

The small states that benefit from this patent denial of our ostensible commitment to one-person/one-vote are, by and large, ever more unrepresentative of the United States as a whole. They tend, among other things, to have populations that are older, whiter, more religious, and less urban. And then there is Article V, which deals with the process of constitutional amendment. Over our 235-year history, the exclusive actual method of amendment has required attaining the support of two-thirds of the membership of each of the House and Senate and then ratification by a full three-quarters of the states. This means, as a practical matter, that thirteen states with less than 10 percent of the total population can veto what the majority believes to be vitally needed changes. Article V itself helps to contribute to a sense of hopelessness about the very possibility of constitutional reform. These criticisms might be dismissed were people generally happy with the actual output of the national government, but that is certainly not the case. Public opinion polling reveals near contempt for Congress and only uncertain support for whoever is president and even the Supreme Court. Most Americans believe the country is headed in the wrong direction. My own view is that our travails are the result of more than the deficiencies of particular political leaders; instead, they are attributable to the pathologies produced by the unamended Constitution itself. I believe that the Constitution, as a practical matter, now comes close to constituting a clear and present danger with regard to the ability of the national government effectively to meet the challenges facing the United States in the twenty-first century.

I think it is safe to say, for better or worse, that I am probably the most vociferous critic of the U.S. Constitution in the American legal academy. I have come to believe that one of the true pathologies of American political consciousness is the literally mindless "veneration" directed at it. It has become sacralized and, as a sacred document, thought to be above criticism. In fact, I admire its Framers because of their ruthless willingness to criticize the existing system of government established by the Articles of Confederation. Alexander Hamilton in *Federalist* 15 referred to the "imbecilic" nature of the existing framework as part of the argument why it needed to be replaced. In *Federalist* 1, Hamilton had praised the American people for its ability to engage in "reflection and choice" as to how they were to be governed. "Reflection" does not coexist very well with "veneration," a word used in *Federalist* 49, written by James Madison to explain his appalled opposition to Thomas Jefferson's suggestion that there should be frequent future conventions to correct defects in the Constitution. Madison comes close to suggesting that "reflection and choice" are a one-time achievement, never to be repeated at a later date. This, I think, is ultimately a dangerous view inasmuch as it almost forecloses the possibility of a truly national conversation about the adequacy of the Constitution to our present needs. I am no longer willing to profess any "faith" at all in the Constitution. My own present attitude is probably close in some ways to that earlier expressed by Hugo Chavez with regard to the Venezuelan constitution.

Two other chapters in *Constitutional Faith* are relevant to the central topic of this paper—and this book. One concerns what kinds of "loyalty" should be expected from those who teach within the American legal academy—and not, for example, in a department of political science.[14] In fact, I have a joint appointment in both the University of Texas Law School and the University of Texas at Austin Department of Government (perhaps because I have both a PhD and JD). Are the demands of teaching interestingly different depending on the specific venue? Chapter Five discussed at some length an attack by Duke University Professor Paul Carrington on adherents of what was called Critical Legal Studies (CLS; of which I was at least a fellow traveler). CLS offered fundamental critiques, often influenced by Marxism, of the ideological pretenses of the legal system. The "rule of law," for example, is most often a device by which the ruling class is enabled to establish its hegemony rather

---

[14] See Levinson 1988, Chapter 5.

than a genuine path toward liberation of the oppressed. Carrington suggested, in no uncertain terms, that they/we did not have the requisite faith in the law to teach fledgling lawyers. "One cannot believe in the worth of one's professional skill and judgment," wrote Carrington, "unless one also has some minimal belief in the idea of law and the institutions that enforce it."

We can obviously quibble about the meaning of "minimal belief," I suppose. Ethical codes governing lawyers, for example, do seem to impose a "solemn duty . . . to encourage respect for the law and for the judges and institutions thereof."[15] What if one finds one or both of these demands to be problematic? It is, after all, one thing to tell a client that "the law," understood, for example, as a prediction of the actual use of public force, "requires" certain actions unless one is willing to take the risk of punishment for noncompliance. But such prudential advice has little or nothing to do with encouraging "respect for the law" and those who enforce it. One could, after all, offer the identical prudential advice to someone about to visit China or North Korea or, for that matter, Germany during the 1930s.

Political scientists (or political theorists) are presumably under no such obligations derived from their particular roles or identities. Those who teach courses on the presidency are not expected to be cheerleaders for those who have held that office or even to prefer its maintenance (as distinguished, say, from switching to a parliamentary form of government). Why are law professors any different? In my response to Carrington, I offer an analogy (and distinction) between religious seminaries and secular "departments of religion." The former can expect its faculty to be faithful adherents of the religious precepts being taught and can even presumably sanction any faculty who attack fundamental norms, including structures of authority, of the religion in question. There is no reason to believe that

---

[15] American Bar Association, Code of Professional Responsibility, quoted in Levinson 1988: 158.

a "Jew for Jesus" should or would be welcomed to teach within the Jewish Theological Seminary any more than a Jew who denies that Jesus was the Messiah should expect to be hired as a member of the Baylor or Wheaton theology departments.

But no one should reasonably expect anyone in an ordinary department of religion within a secular university to "believe in" the religious precepts that he or she teaches. Similarly, a political scientist can presumably be as detached from (and potentially critical of) the American constitutional system as she might well be, say, with regard to that of Iran or Saudi Arabia. Why not, unless, of course, the fact that the political scientist (at a public university) has been forced to pledge fealty to the Constitution places significant limits on what otherwise might be her academic freedom to speak without fear about all aspects of her subject?

Finally, another chapter of that book was devoted to one of the most truly fascinating cases in our entire history, which involved the attempt of the United States to denaturalize William Schneiderman, an avowed communist who had become an American citizen in 1925.[16] Lawyers representing the United States argued that as a committed Marxist-Leninist, Schneiderman could not have offered his vow of loyalty to the U.S. Constitution in good faith. The argument (and the ensuing opinions) represents the most completely "meta-moment" in the United States Reports, inasmuch as the central issue is what exactly constitutes "the Constitution" to which one bears loyalty. Represented by defeated 1940 Republican presidential candidate Wendell Willkie, Schneiderman argued that so long as he didn't directly advocate the *violent* transformation of the United States to a proletarian dictatorship, then he was within the four corners of the Constitution. After all, Article V contemplates the possibility of constitutional change through amendment, and there are almost no limits placed on transformations. (The exceptions involve the maintenance of the international slave trade

---

[16] See Levinson 1988, Chapter 4. The case is Schneiderman v. U.S., 320 U.S. 118 (1943).

until 1808 and a guarantee that any change to the allocation of equal voting power in the Senate in effect receive the unanimous assent of all states in the Union, and not merely the three-quarters necessary for "ordinary amendment.") So, Willkie argued, *all* parts of the Communist Program could be made part of an amended U.S. Constitution. He quoted Thomas Jefferson and others as to the non-sacredness of private property, as well as other worthies who criticized other aspects of the constitutional status quo.

So from this perspective the essence of the Constitution is simply that any proffered change must surmount the hurdles of Article V, but, otherwise, there are no substantive limits on what can be imagined. One might contrast this, incidentally, with the modern German Constitution, which is notable for treating its commitment to "dignity," as well as to German federalism, as eternal, incapable of being amended away, even if one can, of course, imagine a violent revolution that simply sweeps the constitution aside. But the central point is that *only* a revolution could displace the "dignity clause," whereas it appears true, as a matter of pure constitutional theory, that the United States could become a Christian country or could reinstate slavery through the procedures of Article V.

The Court, in a sharply divided 6–3 decision, voted in favor of Schneiderman. Justice Murphy, writing for the majority, specifically declined to accept the full reach of Willkie's argument. He instead held that the Government had not demonstrated Schneiderman's disloyalty even under its own preferred test. It may not be irrelevant, of course, that we were at the time allied with the Stalinist Soviet Union against Germany and that it might have been awkward to argue that Schneiderman's loyalties as a communist to the U.S.S.R. automatically made him disloyal to the United States. Still, one wonders where the actual limit would be reached.

The alliance with the Soviet Union, of course, collapsed after the end of World War II, and anti-communism itself became a defining feature of American politics. One form this took was the imposition of loyalty oaths, especially on those teaching the young, in which one was asked to swear both affirmative loyalty to the U.S. Constitution and opposition to the doctrines of communism. The Supreme Court systematically invalidated the latter, finding them too vague to survive the demands of the First Amendment and its protection of freedom of thought. The last such case was *Cole v. Richardson*, decided in 1972.[17] A research sociologist at the Massachusetts State Hospital was fired for her refusal to "solemnly swear (or affirm) that I will uphold and defend the Constitution of the United States of America and the Constitution of the Commonwealth of Massachusetts and that I will oppose the overthrow of the government of the United States of America or of this Commonwealth by force, violence or by any illegal or unconstitutional method." The Supreme Court, through Chief Justice Burger, upheld the oaths against the challenge that they were "so vague that 'men of common intelligence must necessarily guess at its meaning and differ as to its application.'"[18] Such vagueness generates an "uncertainty as to an oath's meaning [that] may deter individuals from engaging in constitutionally protected activity conceivably within the scope of the oath" (405 US 681). According to Burger (and the majority), pledging to "uphold" the Constitution translated only into a "'recognition that ours is a government of laws and not of men,'" implying the illegitimacy of "the use of force to overthrow the government."[19] Concomitantly, the last part of the oath was simply "a commitment not to use illegal and constitutionally unprotected force to change the constitutional system" (405 US 684).

Interestingly enough, the Court offered no citation to or discussion of In re *Anastaplo*,[20] in which a bitterly divided 5–4 Supreme Court upheld the refusal of the Illinois Bar to admit George Anastaplo to membership because he refused to renounce Thomas Jefferson's support in the Declaration of Independence for the

---

[17] Cole v. Richardson, 405 U.S. 676 (1972).
[18] Cole v. Richardson, 405 U.S. 682.
[19] Cole v. Richardson, 405 U.S. 683.
[20] 366 U.S. 82 (1961).

forcible overthrow of an ostensibly tyrannical government. One might, of course, argue that the Constitution makes impossible the rise of a tyrannical government, though this is contradicted by the very fact that the 1787 Constitution included important concessions to the maintenance of chattel slavery, which is surely for most of us a paradigmatic example of tyranny. Nor, if one accepts the logic of *Schneiderman*, can one say that there is any *necessary* relationship between what is constitutional and what is moral or immoral, just or unjust. It's all a matter of what can get the assent of the those whose approval is necessary for proposal and ratification of amendments under Article V.

But Article V presents more than a logical difficulty. As already noted, it also establishes what as a practical matter are close to insurmountable hurdles to the achievement of needed constitutional reform. In a seminal essay, Donald Lutz measured the "degree of difficulty" of constitutional amendment in all American constitutions, both state and national, and some thirty other national constitutions.[21] At the time Lutz was writing, only the now-defunct Yugoslav constitution surpassed the U.S. Constitution in terms of the difficulty of amending it. American state constitutions are, by and large, far more easily amendable.

So what does, or should, the loyalty oath mean to a sophisticated academic, who professes to take ideas, and oaths, seriously, in the twenty-first century? The most recent contemplation of this problem is that of University of Virginia Professor Richard Re.[22] He notes assertions by the Supreme Court that run contrary to the earlier suggestion that loyalty oaths in the modern age have become merely an "amenity." Thus a 1987 opinion states that "we are given no basis for believing that legislators are inclined to subvert their oaths."[23] In her dissenting opinion on the substance of

[21] See Lutz 1995.
[22] Re 2016.
[23] Illinois v. Krull, 480 U.S. 340, 352 n. 8 (1987).

the case, Justice O'Connor, the last member of the Court actually to serve as a legislator, stated that "I heartily agree with the Court that legislators ordinarily do take seriously their oaths to uphold the Constitution."[24] Yet Re acknowledges that "the oath's legal and practical import remains uncertain," given that it "has been invoked as support for almost every imaginable proposition, as well as its opposite."[25] Nor do the Supreme court cases themselves provide much in the way of genuine clarity. But, he says, "[t]he oath deserves to be taken more seriously," and he attempts to provide a scaffolding that allows us to do that, rooted in the notion of *promising*. But, of course, that requires us to answer the question of what exactly is being promised.

"An official who has assumed the oath," Re writes, "has done so in order to undertake a position of trust and so, on balance, has a greater moral duty to the Constitution than the average citizen."[26] Ordinary citizens may well have never taken a formal oath (though, as noted earlier, it is highly likely that she will have pledged explicit "allegiance . . . to the republic" that the American flag symbolizes). So thus we (or I) can ask if I personally, as a professor of law who has taken the oath, have a special "moral duty to the Constitution" and what that might consist of, given my own increasingly vehement opposition to many of its arguably most important structural features.

To be sure, as a mere academic, I am rarely given the opportunity to violate (or, for that matter, support) the Constitution in my quotidian actions. Or, to be more accurate, perhaps the principal opportunities to violate the Constitution would be associated with being unfair to students in violating their rights to freedom of expression or to be treated fairly, and I would like to think that I live up to those responsibilities. Still, I increasingly take every opportunity

---

[24] Illinois v. Krull, 480 U.S. 340, 302 n. 3, citing Illinois v. Krull, 480 U.S. 340 (1987).
[25] Illinois v. Krull, 480 U.S. 340, 302.
[26] Illinois v. Krull, 480 U.S. 340, 312.

to indicate to students that I believe the Constitution is significantly defective and, as suggested earlier, perhaps even a danger with regard to our future. I avidly support a new constitutional convention that could presumably put *all* features of the Constitution up for discussion. On prudential grounds, I certainly believe that one generally ought to adhere to the rules as enunciated by ostensibly "authoritative" institutions, but that is entirely contingent on the proposition that the demands made of us do not in fact violate fundamental precepts of morality or justice. Indeed, I regard as one of the strengths of the legal positivism associated with someone like H. L. A. Hart that it so explicitly separates "law" from "morals" and enjoins us, perhaps as suggested by the earlier quotation from Deak, never to confuse the two.

From my particular perspective, as a critic of the Constitution, the most interesting section of Re's essays comes at the very end, where he considers the implications of the oath for those advocating "revision," or even "revolution," concerning the Constitution. "Can someone who has taken an oath to the Constitution ethically work to change it," he asks, "such as by supporting a constitutional amendment?"[27] The answer to this question *must* be yes, if for no other reason than that the text of the Constitution itself, in Article V, authorizes its own amendment. This logically requires, as a condition precedent, that respected leaders, including members of Congress and state legislatures, believe that such change is desirable. Re basically agrees. The obvious problem is going beyond Article V.

Although the most obvious problem is raised by out-an-out attempts to overthrow the constitutional order, Re discusses the endlessly fascinating problems presented by the addition of the so-called Reconstruction Amendments to the Constitution between 1865 and 1870.[28] After all, the Congress that proposed the

[27] Illinois v. Krull, 480 U.S. 340, 351.

[28] What follows concerns entirely the process by which the Amendments, particularly the Fourteenth Amendment, were adopted. As I complete these revisions, in November

amendments was what Yale Professor of Law Bruce Ackerman has described as a "rump Congress." In December 1865, the Republican majorities in the House and Senate formally refused to seat representatives and senators who had been elected by state governments recognized as legitimate by President Andrew Johnson. The two-thirds support necessary to propose amendments simply never could have been attained had the Democrats sent to Washington by the "unreconstructed" former Confederate states been recognized as legitimate. Moreover, given the necessity for ratification by three-quarters of the states (with the defeated Southern states being recognized as part of the denominator), military Reconstruction was imposed by Congress precisely to assure that reformed state governments would in fact ratify the amendments. Indeed, renewed membership in Congress was made contingent on their ratifying the Fourteenth Amendment. It is, therefore, exceedingly difficult, perhaps impossible, to describe them unproblematically as "Article V" amendments, given these procedural irregularities. The defeated white southerners expected full re-entry into the Union simply by acknowledging the illegitimacy of secession and the demise of slavery signified by the Emancipation Proclamation and then the Thirteenth Amendment. Andrew Johnson, after all, warmly supported the Thirteenth Amendment and made its ratification a condition of the return to the Union of the defeated would-be Confederate States.[29]

The Fourteenth Amendment, which radically transformed American federalism, was another matter, and Johnson fought it

---

2023, however, one often-ignored section of that Amendment has become a source of intense debate. Section Three seemingly bars those who engage in "insurrection" against the United States, which among other things could easily be viewed as a violation of one's loyalty oath(s), from holding any future political office. Literally hundreds of Americans have been charged with insurrection following the January 6, 2021, attack on the Capitol in Washington, DC. Most of the contemporary discussion, though, focuses on one particular alleged "insurrectionist," Donald J. Trump, and whether he should be barred from taking any future office. Trump, of course, twice was impeached by the House and twice was acquitted by the Senate.

[29] See, e.g., Downs 2015.

with all of his might. As noted earlier, ratification was procured only by Congress's willingness to adopt Military Reconstruction devoted to what we might today refer to as full-scale "regime change." Ackerman is arguing not against the irregularities of the Reconstruction Amendments but, instead, against our obtuse unwillingness to recognize the extent to which American constitutional development cannot be explained by reference to our civic-book understanding of Article V as the sole procedure by which the Constitution has been (or could in the future legitimately be) amended.

So it appears that there are two analytically distinguishable problems: There may be "amendments" to the Constitution that do not conform adequately with the procedures set down in Article V. But precisely because the amendments in question, including the Reconstruction Amendments, are viewed as distinctly justifiable moral improvements to what had in fact been a morally defective Constitution, there is no serious contemporary dispute about their legitimacy. Indeed, the central temple of our American civil religion is the Lincoln Memorial, regardless of Lincoln's questionable fidelity to narrowly legalistic views of his own presidential oath.

But the second problem is presented by the possibility of an impeccably legally "correct" Article V amendment that is nonetheless abhorrent. Consider an amendment overriding *Brown v. Board of Education* and legitimizing the reinstatement of Jim Crow segregation or even reinstating slavery. Would a judge be obliged to enforce such an amendment and law professors required to acknowledge its legitimacy as a part of the Constitution to which one ought to be faithful (at least until repealed by a future Article V amendment)? The theoretical question for Re becomes what it means to pledge fealty to "this Constitution," as required by Article VI, in light of the fact that one might well argue that its current meaning, whether because of declarations by the Court and other seemingly authoritative officials or ostensible Article V amendment, departs significantly from what one might have thought constituted the Constitution at the time one gave the oath itself. Does "this Constitution" necessarily include, say, future decisions of the Court that one might view as indefensible departures from legitimate constitutional meaning? Does it require that one give priority to the procedural aspects of Article V and disregard any arguable substantive limits?

This is at the heart of a famous anecdote about Kurt Gödel, the world-famous mathematician who demonstrated the limits of mathematical logic. A refugee from Austria, Godel was naturalized as an American citizen in Trenton, New Jersey. The judge assured Gödel that what had happened in Austria (and Germany) could not possibly happen here, within the American constitutional order. Gödel intervened and said that he had discovered a problem with the U.S. Constitution that negated the judge's reassuring proposition.[30] The colleagues who had accompanied Gödel, who, it is said, included Albert Einstein, encouraged him to remain silent, and the naturalization ceremony proceeded apace. Though there is no hard-and-fast evidence, it has often been assumed that Godel had realized the problems presented by Article V and its apparent lack of substantive limits (save for the assignment of two senators to each state).

Re, presumably like Gödel, is ultimately unwilling to adopt pure proceduralism. Certain changes might "leave 'this Constitution' unrecognizable." It would not simply be "worse" than the Constitution to which one had pledged loyalty but also would no longer be "*this* Constitution."[31] Its "identity" would have fundamentally changed.[32] Indeed, Re ends up defending Jefferson and other American revolutionaries. After all, "[t]he American colonists had sworn allegiance to a Crown that tolerated significant home rule" and then in effect changed the unwritten conventions.[33]

[30] See, e.g., Guerra-Pujol 2013.
[31] Guerra-Pujol 2013, 353.
[32] The notion of "constitutional identity" is crucial in Jacobsohn and Raznai 2019.
[33] Jacobsohn and Raznai 2019, 354.

"[N]o colonist had promised timidity in the face of royal oppression." This, of course, is the basis of Anastaplo's support of Jefferson that led the Illinois Bar to reject his admission as unworthy. Re notes the "Continental Congress imposed an oath of allegiance to the United States that, in the same breath, required federal officers to 'renounce, refuse, and abjure any allegiance or obedience' to King George."[34] As Re writes, the renunciation of earlier solemn oaths did not lead to the moral that such oaths were generally a bad idea; instead, they were replaced with oaths to a presumably more worthy government. It should go without saying, incidentally, that the Crown scarcely shared these legal conclusions, as was true, incidentally, of most judges in the colonies, who had been appointed by the Crown, and who became Loyalists, as did many other lawyers.

Conclusion

The most obvious ways that states (or, for that matter, all other organizations or, indeed, individuals and spouses) can elicit loyalty involve behavior generating the affection that must underlie the notion of a genuinely internalized consciousness of loyalty (as distinguished from prudential behavior based on fear). But behavior is not thought to be enough. Instead, oaths continue to be an almost omnipresent part of our culture, presumably with the expectation, as enunciated by Justice O'Connor, that enough people will take them truly seriously to make a change in their own behavior when faced with conflicts between their raw desires and the demands ostensibly attached to their oaths.

Having begun by referring to religious oaths, let me conclude by mentioning a riveting discussion of oaths by Moses Mendelssohn in his great book *Jerusalem: On Religious Power and Judaism*. He was specifically discussing demands placed on Jews in Germany

---

[34] Jacobsohn and Raznai 2019, 234.

and other Christian countries to convert and to affirm loyalty to Christian precepts. He went, on, however, to offer a quite devastating critique of almost all oaths in general inasmuch as they referred to professions of state of mind—such a "loyalty" or "belief." He contrasted such oaths with oaths to tell the truth about matters about which one has direct sense impressions, so that one can say "'I saw, I heard, received, gave, did not see,' and so on."[35] For Mendelssohn, "Oaths beget no new duties."[36] They may, perhaps, serve as a goad to "reawaken[ing] conscience" by reminding one of preexisting duties, such as to tell the truth to a court about what one saw. (I put to one side potentially endless discussions of the source of *those* duties.) But, with regard to basically metaphysical beliefs, he emphasized that the frequency of changes of mind: "Many positions for which I would suffer martyrdom to day, will perhaps appear very problematical to me to-morrow." And, given the inevitable vagueness of much language, where one is asked to swear to "words and symbols," [i]t is impossible that I and my neighbor can unite the selfsame inward sensations to the selfsame words." We are being asked to affirm not concrete things for which we have true sensory impressions, but, rather, "metaphors." So, he asks, "How will not the ideas vary, which different men, in different times and ages, link to the selfsame symbols and words?"

For some readers, an even better source of such skepticism about generalized oaths is probably James Madison, who in *Federalist* 37 presents a similarly radically skeptical view of the limits of language. "The faculties of the mind itself," Madison reminds us, have never yet been distinguished and defined, with satisfactory precision, by all the efforts of the most acute and metaphysical philosophers." Language itself is "so copious as to supply words and phrases for

[35] Mendelsohn, Jerusalem, Section 13, "Church government. Oaths," at pp. 19 and 22, available at https://www.earlymoderntexts.com/assets/pdfs/mendelssohn1782.pdf. All quotations from Mendelsohn come from this section.

[36] Mendelsohn, Jerusalem, Section 13, at 20, available at https://www.earlymodernte xts.com/assets/pdfs/mendelssohn1782.pdf

every complex idea, or so correct as not to include many equivo-
cally denoting different ideas." He is writing of the "unavoidable in-
accuracy" that "must be greater or less, according to the complexity
and novelty of the objects defined." Then comes the most stunning
passage in the entire essay, and perhaps for some readers in the entire *Federalist* itself: "When the Almighty himself condescends to
address mankind in their own language, his meaning, luminous as
it must be, is rendered dim and doubtful by the cloudy medium
through which it is communicated."[37] So who indeed could believe
that oaths taken to affirm necessarily vague theological (or political) concepts could possibly have any kind of universal meaning?
The reason, after all, that one can make a career of teaching "constitutional law" is precisely that most of the Constitution contributes
to what I have called "The Constitution of Conversation," the source
of endless, often acrimonious, arguments about indeterminate language in the constitutional text. This differs from what I call "The
Constitution of Settlement," based on certain passages of text that
can be debated for their wisdom—each state's being assigned two
senators, for example—but not their "meaning," at least in any ordinary, pragmatic, sense. "What part of two do you not understand"
is a perfectly good riposte to anyone who objects, on legal grounds,
to Wyoming and California each having two senators. One might
well ask why anyone would pledge loyalty to such a Constitution,
but at least we have a clear idea of what the Constitution means
(or commands) in this particular instance. But it is hopeless to believe that we have more than the slightest idea, if that, of the force
of an oath to devote oneself to "equal protection of the laws" or to
maintaining the "Republican Form of Government" guaranteed to
each state in Article IV of the Constitution.

So loyalty oaths present an interesting problem for "modern"
intellectuals. They often rest on premises in which we have little
or no remaining faith. But, at the same time, as I have discovered

---

[37] Available at https://avalon.law.yale.edu/18th_century/fed37.asp

particularly when asking students whether they would even modify, let alone eliminate, the loyalty oaths required by the Constitution, we seem unable to free ourselves from their grip. We might well wonder why. Is it just too frightening to imagine a political world in which we must rely exclusively on the judgment and good faith of political leaders (or spouses) independently of the making of specific promises that we deem to be solemn oaths?[38]

Bibliography

Gregory Downs, Gregory. *After Appomattox: Military Occupation and the Ends of War*. Cambridge, MA: Harvard University Press, 2015.

Guerra-Pujol, F. E. "Gödel's Loophole." *Capital University Law Review* 41 (2013): 637–673.

Jacobsohn, Gary Jeffrey, and Yaniv Raznai. *Constitutional Revolution*. New Haven, CT: Yale University Press, 2019.

Levinson, Sanford. "The Confrontation of Religious Faith and Civil Religion: Catholics Becoming Justices." 39 *Depaul Law Review* 1047 (1990). Reprinted in Levinson, Sanford, *Wrestling with Diversity*, Duke University Press, 2003: 192–232.

Levinson, Sanford. "Constituting Communities Through Words That Bind: Reflections on Loyalty Oaths." 84 *Michigan Law Review* (1986): 1440–1470.

Levinson, Sanford. *Constitutional Faith*. Princeton, NJ: Princeton University Press, 1988.

Levinson, Sanford. *Our Undemocratic Constitution: Where the Constitution Goes Wrong (And What We the People Can Do About It)*. New York: Oxford University Press, 2006.

Levinson, Sanford. "Ratifying the Civil Religion (Or, Would You Sign the Constitution?)" 29 *William and Mary Law Review* (1987): 113–144.

Levinson, Sanford. "Thinking About Polgyamy." 42 *San Diego Law Review* 1049 (2005). Available at https://digital.sandiego.edu/sdlr/vol42/iss3/18

Lutz, Donald. "Toward a Theory of Constitutional Amendment." In *Responding to Imperfection: The Theory and Practice of Constitutional Amendment*,

---

[38] This chapter was originally prepared for presentation at a conference on "Loyalty" at the University of Oklahoma, June 14–15, 2019. I am grateful for comments received from other conference participants at the time, as well as further specific comments offered by Vito Breda.

edited by Sanford Levinson, 237–274. Princeton, NJ: Princeton University Press, 1995.

Mendelsohn, Moses. *Jerusalem: Religious Power and Judaism.* Available at https://www.earlymoderntexts.com/assets/pdfs/mendelssohn1782.pdf

Miller, David C. "A.-G. Camus and the Civil Constitution of the Clergy." *The Catholic Historical Review* 76 L 3 (1990): 481–505.

Re, Richard M. "Promising the Constitution." *110 Northwestern University Law Review* 299 (2016): 299–355.

9

Love and Loyalty

Sharon Krishek

Introduction

It is commonly accepted that when it comes to love, loyalty is a virtue. Love *demands* loyalty—without it, one's love is tainted or flawed. Although particularly evident in the case of romantic and marital love—the focus of the present paper—it also holds true with regard to any kind of love. This raises the question, however, of what exactly *is* the relation between loyalty and love? Is loyalty *essential* to love, so that a failure in loyalty attests to a lack of love, or is loyalty rather a necessary condition for the *endurance and flourishing* of love? In this chapter I argue that the latter is the case, and in doing so I aim to highlight the virtue of loyalty. My claim is that loyalty is not only an adherence to the commitments entailed in a love relationship but something more, a *wholehearted assent* to them. By examining the crucial role that loyalty (understood in this way) plays in ensuring that love can thrive, I explore the nature of loyalty as a "work" of love, and the importance of what such a work yields.

I begin by presenting a Kiergaardian view of love.[1] In this view, love is a specific kind of caring that is grounded in a particular type of correspondence between the lovers. I then demonstrate the nature of loyalty as a wholehearted assent to commitments

---

[1] This view is 'Kierkegaardian' and not 'Kierkegaard's' because, although relying on a number of the philosopher's ideas, it goes beyond his explicit position.

Sharon Krishek, *Love and Loyalty* In: *The Virtue of Loyalty*. Edited by: Troy Jollimore,
Oxford University Press. © Oxford University Press 2024. DOI: 10.1093/oso/9780197612644.003.0010

and delineate the central place of loyalty in the endurance of love, showing that it enables the kind of correspondence that serves as the grounds for love. In the last part of the chapter, using the conceptual framework demonstrated throughout, I look closely at a relevant literary work: *Black Dogs* by Ian McEwan, which vividly portrays the aftermath of a love defeated, so I claim, by a lack of loyalty. Reading this work in light of the philosophical analysis presented in this chapter therefore helps reveal the phenomenology of the close connection between love and loyalty. In doing so, I hope to clarify how loyalty is indispensable for the flourishing of love.

Love

The nature of love

When attempting to define love, it is important to distinguish between the question of what love *is* and that of how love *should* be. After all, the phenomenon of unhappy love is a familiar one: love can go wrong or be weakened, leaving the lovers unsatisfied or miserable. We should therefore be careful not to conflate the conditions for love and those for *happy* (i.e., successful) love. Regarding the former question ('what love is'), I follow Kierkegaard in understanding love to be a kind of selfless caring, that is, willing the good of the beloved for the beloved's sake (as opposed to being motivated by the will to promote one's own interests).[2] However, and here I depart from Kierkegaard, such a conception seems incomplete, because love is essentially experienced as emotional. And even if there is a case for arguing that selfless caring necessarily entails the feeling of compassion,[3] compassionate caring does not seem

[2] Cf. Frankfurt 2004.
[3] I discuss the relation between compassion and love in Krishek 2022, chapter 5. The argument, in short, is as follows: Compassion is provoked in response to the suffering of another. Every person, by virtue of her temporality and finitude, is lacking in *some* respect and susceptible to loss. As such, every person is in a state of (explicit or implicit,

enough to count as love, because loving a person is emotionally richer than that. My claim, then, is that for compassionate caring to be *love*, it should also include *joy*: an affirmative feeling of vitality that is provoked in the (real or imagined) presence of the beloved.[4]

Having defined what love is, another distinction to draw is that between the focus of love and the reasons for love[5]: *who* our love is directed at, and *why* our love is thus directed are two separate questions, and here I will be interested only in the latter.[6] However, as my thesis is that love is rooted in the correspondence between the selves of the lovers, we first need to clarify what it means to be a self.

The beloved's selfhood

By using the term 'self' I refer to a person in her distinctiveness. When we think of someone as a 'self' (in my use of the term), we think of her not just as 'a person' like everybody else—one among many—but as *that particular person*, a person with a name. In this sense, 'self' designates a person in her individuality; in her being, say, June. We can think about her individuality (as I construe it) as the qualitative 'makeup'—the qualitative composition or setup— that makes her the distinctive person that she is: June. When reading *Black Dogs*, for example, the reader forms a mental picture of June: a portrait of her comprised of her mental, temperamental, and physical traits. In talking about one's 'self', I refer to this kind of portrait.

---

astir or latent) suffering, and it only requires our attention to see this. Selflessness allows precisely for this kind of attention. Hence, caring selflessly for another necessarily entails compassion toward that other.

[4] For a detailed discussion of love as joyful compassionate caring, see Krishek 2022, Chapter 3.

[5] Cf. Kolodny 2003.

[6] For a discussion of the former question, see Krishek 2021.

Such a portrait, however, is not fixed and frozen. June's ensemble of qualities changes and develops. The young June with whom Bernard fell in love is different in important senses from the old June who died alone, far away from Bernard, whom she had left many years prior to her death. How to reconcile these two aspects of being 'June'—that is, of her being both 'the same' and different? To answer this, let me introduce my conception of selfhood as an *individual essence*. This conception relies on Kierkegaard's analysis of the self, which is rather intricate and beyond the scope of the present discussion. I therefore intend neither to present this analysis here nor to clarify how my conception of selfhood relates to that of Kierkegaard.[7] For the purpose of the present discussion it is enough to focus on Kierkegaard's claim that every human being is "intended to be a self, destined to become himself" and on his assertion that a human being is "a synthesis . . . of the temporal and the eternal."[8]

On my view, the way to make sense of the claim that Bernard (say) is 'destined to become himself' is to understand Bernard as created[9] not just as *a* person but as *Bernard*, a *particular* person. At the same time, the need to *become* himself (i.e., the Bernard that he is destined to be) attests to his possessing the quality of 'Bernardhood' (i.e., selfhood) in a *potential* state. In the same way that to become a writer, for example, requires an actualization of one's potential for writing, so the quality of selfhood requires an actualization: one has to *become* the self, the Bernard, that one is *in potential*. What kind of quality is selfhood? I find the answer to this question in Kierkegaard's characterization of the human being as both temporal and eternal.

---

[7] For this, see Krishek 2022, Chapter 6.

[8] Kierkegaard 1980, 33, 13.

[9] The terminology of being 'created' (by God) is in line with the theistic frame of thought of Kierkegaard's analysis of the self. However, although I do not demonstrate it here, there may well be a secular equivalent to this theory—for example, an Aristotelian one—at least at a few crucial points.

Human beings are finite creatures who experience constant change and loss throughout their lives and are doomed to eventually die. It therefore seems clear enough why Kierkegaard characterizes human beings as 'temporal'. But in what sense is a human being also 'eternal'? To be eternal, I suggest, designates the existing connection to God that, according to Kierkegaard, every human has, regardless of his or her beliefs; that is, it designates the ontological connection of being created *by* God and *in His image*.

Now, to be created in God's image means (arguably) to possess *essentially* the qualities that characterize (traditionally) God: reason, will, creativity, care. However, although humans are created in the image of God, they are also very different from God—hence their characterization as 'temporal'. Whereas God possesses ultimate reason/creativity/power/caring, a human being, as a finite being, is rational/creative/powerful/caring only in various limited and particular ways. For example, one person has an admirable understanding of social situations but is entirely incompetent when it comes to understanding music, while another person is a genius in music but fails to comprehend people, and so on. Further to Kierkegaard's characterization of the human being as both eternal and temporal, then, the first thing I want to say about selfhood—the quality that makes one a self—is that it is composed of a set of particular qualities that best manifest, relative to each person, the image of God. Hence, under the assumption that God creates each human with a singular selfhood unique to him or her,[10] this individuating quality can be understood as reflecting God's image *in a particular shape*.

---

[10] In this sense selfhood can be thought of as a *qualitative* haecceity (note that this is distinct from the way that haecceity is typically understood, namely, as a *non-complex* quality that is, accordingly, *not* composed of any other qualities). Here it should be clarified that although composed of many qualities, selfhood is *one unified* quality. The fitting analogy is to a mixture of colors. In the same way that when combining white and blue and red we experience this combination as 'lilac' (and not as white plus blue plus red), so is one's selfhood experienced as a unified 'persona' (and not as a list of individual qualities).

However, conceiving of selfhood as an accumulation of qualities, including *contingent* qualities (such as physical ones), may sound incompatible with the characterization of selfhood as one's individual *essence*. Hence, to reconcile the idea of 'essence' with that of contingency, there is a need to distinguish between two senses of 'essence' (both of which are accommodated in the theory). In its more rigorous usage, 'essence' is that which determines the identity of X, and as such it is constant and unchangeable. In its more casual or everyday usage, however, 'essence' simply stands for 'what (or who) one is'—without being committed to constancy and unchangeability (as in Sartre's 'existence precedes essence'). The conception of one's individual essence conflates these two senses by means of the distinction between the two states of selfhood: potentiality and actualization. What does this mean?

Here Kierkegaard's characterization of humans as both temporal and eternal is pertinent again, as it invites the distinction between potential and actualization. In its potential state, one's selfhood can be characterized as 'eternal' because it is invariant and independent of time and circumstances. Accordingly, in its potential state one's selfhood stands for essence in the first sense (constant and invariable). The actualization of the potential, however, is temporal. It takes place 'in the world' (by virtue of one's existence) and as such it is changing and dependent on time and circumstances. Hence, in its actualized state one's selfhood stands for essence in the second sense (changing and contingent).

Let us consider June. We can think of June's selfhood in its *potential state* as her 'kernel of individuality', which is realized in the context of her life circumstances. Accordingly, the actualization (June's 'temporal' essence) consists not only of the qualities that constitute the potential (June's 'eternal' essence) but also of contingent qualities that may be present in one version of June, but not in another. Thus, June at the age of sixty possesses qualities that she did not possess at the age of twenty, but these two versions are nevertheless 'June', in the sense of being two different (and contingent) actualizations of the same potential. Hence, one's selfhood—one's being June—is both invariant and changing, both 'the same' (in its potential state) and changing (in its actualized state).

To be a self, then, is to possess an individual essence in its two states—predetermined and invariable *potential* and a changing *actualization*—while the latter is as significant to 'being oneself' as the former. This, as we now turn to see, proves crucial when it comes to the *reasons* for love.

The correspondence between the selves of the lovers

Two common convictions (or intuitions) regarding love are, first, that love responds to the beloved's being who she is, namely, to the 'beloved herself' (as opposed to her beauty, wisdom, or endorsement of communism); and, second, that our relationships with our loved ones, be they parents, friends, children, spouses, and so on, play a prominent role in shaping the person, the *self*, that we are. In what way? I suggest that it is not only a matter of the education given to us by our parents, the values we share with our friends, the lessons we learn as parents, or the projects we develop with our spouses. The extent and nature of their impact go deeper than that. Our loved ones influence our selfhood by provoking emotions, desires, and aspirations in us; by the things they enable us to do, as well as the limits that they impose on us; by the way they challenge us and the way they strengthen us, and by both accepting us for who we are and encouraging us to improve and evolve. They cultivate our character traits, foster our capacities and talents, build up our beliefs and values, and accommodate our temperament. Thus, our interactions with those close to us constitute an incessant journey of self-discovery and self-shaping.

The experience of becoming ourselves by virtue of our relationships with those we love fits the conception of selfhood as a worldly (i.e., time and space dependent) actualization of a predetermined potential. As I posited earlier, to become the individuals that we are is to actualize our 'kernel of individuality' in the context of our worldly existence—including, thereby, human interactions. Further, in *Works of Love* Kierkegaard makes the stronger claim that "we can be like God only in loving [the neighbor]" (63). Arguably, 'being like God' indicates a successful actualization of one's potential. And if so, then Kierkegaard's claim is, in fact, equivalent to the claim that the best actualization of our potential is achieved only by loving. Accordingly, 'becoming ourselves' depends on loving relationships with others. Relying on both our experience and Kierkegaard's analysis, then, we can suggest that relationships of love are the 'venue' for actualizing our potential and becoming who we are.

It is against this background that I propose 'the correspondence thesis'. Assuming that becoming ourselves is *good* for us (even if we are not necessarily aware of that) and hence something that we *want* (even if in an unarticulated way),[11] then, if we become ourselves only by loving, we have reason (albeit unacknowledged) to love—and, in particular, to love those who help us become ourselves. Accordingly, we can say that the very actualization of lover L's potential by means of loving beloved B is the *reason* for L's love for B *in particular*.[12] Simply put, we are attracted to those who help us fulfil our essence, who help us enact our potential and become who we are intended (given this potential) to be. Where does the correspondence lie?

Returning to the conviction (again, based on our experience) that love responds to the beloved herself, to her being 'who she is', we can say (further to the conception of selfhood) that if Bernard loves June, he responds to June's being who she is—to her

---

[11] Indeed, in Kierkegaard's analysis a failure to become ourselves is a state of despair, that is, an undesirable state that is not good for us. For a discussion of the state of despair and its relation to one's selfhood, see Krishek 2022, Chapter 6.

[12] This is true with regard to *any* relationship of love, but here I will focus only on romantic love.

individual essence as June, to her selfhood. However, this response, we should now note, is crucially dictated also by the *lover* being who *he* is. After all, while it is true that when loving June, Bernard responds to the value of her selfhood, the latter does *not* provoke the same response in everybody else. In this sense, there is a *correspondence* between who *she* is and who *he* is. What is the nature of this correspondence?

Rather than a simple or straightforward similarity, or being akin to each other, for June to correspond to Bernard means that June has the capacity to help Bernard to become himself. Which means that June, due to the accumulation of her qualities—temperament, character traits, talents, preferences, looks—stimulates and positively affects *his* talents, character traits, and so on. She makes him feel at ease, liberated from pretense, and vital; 'comfortable in his own skin', as it were. She helps him deepen traits and talents that he values, she strengthens or challenges his preferences and intuitions, she helps him—simply by being who she is—understand what is right and good for him. *This* is the nature of the correspondence of June to Bernard, and this is the reason for his love for her.[13]

Loyalty

Loyalty as a wholehearted assent to commitments

Loyalty is often understood as a state of adhering to commitments and obligations that one has taken upon oneself. When it comes to loyalty to a *person*, then, the adherence is to the explicit and implicit

---

[13] It should be emphasized that Bernard does *not* love June *in order* to gain self-actualization. Even if it is true that he is motivated by the way she affects him, this is not 'for the sake' of anything other than loving *her*. Further, it is important to note that the correspondence in question is from the point of view of the lover: Bernard loves June because June corresponds to him (i.e., helps him to become himself). Therefore, for a *requited* love, there should be a *double* correspondence, so that not only June helps Bernard become who he is, but Bernard helps June become who *she* is.

committing of promises and expectations that the relationship with that person yields. But loyalty is stronger than that. It requires not only that one fulfil one's commitments but that one fully assent to them: one accepts them wholeheartedly, and fulfils them willingly, that is, with full agreement (as opposed to begrudgingly or with resentment).[14]

For example, in the Preface to *Black Dogs*, the narrator, Jeremy, tells, in a seemingly offhand manner, the episode of his betrayal of Sally, his beloved niece. Although a central and benefactory figure in her life (being the one to take care of her instead of her nonfunctioning mother), when the time came to begin his studies at Oxford, he left her behind to what he knew was going to be a grim fate. His feeling of being disloyal to her is rooted in his refusal to fulfil the implicit commitment to continue taking care of her. We could easily imagine a different scenario: Jeremy deciding to renounce his studies in order to continue being a substitute parent to Sally, but doing so unwillingly, with bitterness and antagonism. In such a case, we (and he himself) would still deem him to be failing in his loyalty to Sally, despite fulfilling his commitment to her. To be loyal, then, it is not enough to keep one's (explicit and implicit) commitments; one must unreservedly assent to them.

In the spirit of this example, I will now indeed use the context of *love* (this time romantic) to examine the nature of loyalty as assent to commitments. As was demonstrated earlier, for an attitude to be love, it must include (at least as a disposition) caring for the beloved, compassion for her, and joy in her presence. Further, when an attitude is *love*, it responds to the beloved's selfhood—that is, to the beloved's being who he or she is—and is rooted in a *correspondence* between the lovers' selfhoods: in the capacity of each to help the other become who he or she is. These are, then, the conditions for love to be provoked. However, the arousal of love is not sufficient for love to endure and thrive. Literature, and life, is packed with

---

[14] I'm grateful to Ariel Meirav for helping me to clarify this point.

stories of unhappy love: love that began well, but, while still being *love*, goes wrong, grows weak, or in some other way deteriorates. Once provoked, then, what is it that *secures* love?

To begin with, it should be clarified that, just as with one's self-hood, the correspondence between lovers is a function of both potential and actualization. 'Correspondence', recall, is the term I use to designate the special effect that the selfhood of the beloved, say June, has on the selfhood of lover, say Bernard, while the selfhoods of both June and Bernard are actualizations of respective predetermined potentials. Thus, the reason for Bernard's love for June is the correspondence between her selfhood and his; her ability (being who she is) to help him become who he is intended (by virtue of his potential) to be. And the same holds true from June's point of view: the reason for her love for Bernard is his correspondence to her; his ability to help her become who *she* is intended to be. Here, however, we should distinguish between 'metaphysical' (or potential) correspondence and 'in practice' (or actualized) correspondence.

On one level—that of the potential—the correspondence between Bernard and June is predetermined. It is independent of the lovers' will, decision, or action; it exists by virtue of *that* aspect—the potential—of their respective selfhoods. Let us call this 'metaphysical' correspondence: June has the potential (no matter what actualization it takes) to positively affect the actualization of Bernard's potential (i.e., help Bernard to become the self that Bernard can be). However, on another—and no less crucial—level, the correspondence between June and Bernard depends on the *actualization* of their respective potentials. It is the actualization of each's potential that determines whether the existing, predetermined correspondence (of their potentials) will be realized. Let us call this 'in practice' correspondence.

Further, when it comes to 'in practice' correspondence, we must make another distinction, this time between spontaneous correspondence and what we can call 'attentive correspondence'—a correspondence that is the result of deliberate effort. Suppose that June is metaphysically correspondent to Bernard, and vice versa. Given such correspondence, and assuming a not-too-distorted actualization of their respective potentials, it is likely that Bernard and June will be attracted to each other. In such a case, their love can be said to be the result of a spontaneous correspondence between their (actualized) selfhoods. However, June's selfhood, as well as Bernard's, is in a constant process of actualization, and is hence changing and developing. Accordingly, despite the spontaneous, initial, correspondence, June (or Bernard) may change in a way that *works against* the correspondence. In other words, the actualization of June's potential, for example, might result in a version of herself that blurs or hides her metaphysical correspondence to Bernard (a correspondence that, between lovers, is *always* present); that is, it makes her *ability* to help Bernard actualize his potential less evident.

It is here, then, that the attitude of the lover becomes crucial. What it takes to recognize (and deepen) the correspondence— namely, to recognize the ability of the beloved to affect the lover in the relevant way—is a clear appreciation, a *clear vision*, of the beloved.[15] Having such vision, the lover is able to recognize the potential through the actualization and hence, accordingly, perceives the ability of the beloved's selfhood to impact positively upon him. Such a clear-sighted perception is particularly needed if there is an unwelcome change in the beloved's selfhood, as occurred, from Bernard's point of view, with June. In such a case, the challenge is to be able to discern the underlying potential—the same potential that informed the version with which the initial, spontaneous, correspondence occurred. Thus, while metaphysical correspondence is beyond the lovers' control, *attentive correspondence* is entirely their responsibility. In other words, when metaphysical correspondence

---

[15] For a different substantiation of the crucial relation between vision and love, see Jollimore 2011.

does exist, the onus is on the lovers to recognize and deepen it. This, as I now turn to demonstrate, is precisely where loyalty becomes crucial.

The virtue of loyalty

For love to endure and flourish, the *reason* for love—that is, the correspondence between the selfhoods of the lovers—must be available to the lovers. Now, given the correspondence at the metaphysical level, in an important sense the reason for love is *always* available. However, being always available does not mean that it is always *discerned* by the lovers. The latter is achieved by virtue of attentive correspondence. The endurance and flourishing of love, then, depends on the lovers' being attentively correspondent to each other. That is to say, each needs to approach the 'correspondent' beloved in a way that allows a clear-sighted appreciation of the beloved. By *this*, it becomes possible for them to discern each other's 'kernel'—and the way it has informed their initial correspondence—even in cases when this kernel is less successfully actualized. Attentive correspondence, however, is not spontaneous but, rather, is attained through effort, through *work*.[16]

And the 'work' at issue, I suggest, is precisely loyalty. This is the attitude that enables the lovers to experience, through clear-sighted vision of the respective beloved, the metaphysical correspondence between them; particularly when they cease to experience it spontaneously. How does loyalty, then, allow a clear-sighted appreciation of the beloved (and hence attentive correspondence with her)? To answer this question, we need to understand better the nature of

---

[16] I am inspired here by Kierkegaard, who in his pivotal *Works of Love* speaks in terms of 'work' when he analyzes love in its ideal form. For Kierkegaard, however, such work consists only in self-denial while I suggest that it also includes self-affirmation (see Krishek 2022, Chapter 4). This double structure, as I now demonstrate, is found also in loyalty (thus making it a work of love).

loyalty: that is, we need to understand what it means for the lover (say, Bernard) to *wholeheartedly assent* to his (implicit or explicit) commitments to his beloved.

First and foremost, such an attitude involves *self-denial*. To borrow again from Kierkegaard, self-denial (in his use of the term) is the conscious effort of the lover to be wholly focused on the beloved. The denial in question, then, is of everything that might divert the lover's attention from the well-being of the beloved; everything that might 'stain' the lover's selfless interest in the beloved. In other words, the lover knowingly and deliberately resists and pushes aside anything that might hinder him from being interested in the beloved *for the beloved's sake*. Loyalty, as a wholehearted assent to one's *commitments*, evidently involves self-denial. A state of assent to commitments implies the possibility of conflicting interests and, in this sense, loyalty attests to a submission of the lover's interests to those of the beloved (say, further to the earlier example, renouncing one's desire to study away from home in order to support the well-being of a beloved child).

However, important as it is, self-denial does not exhaust the position of loyalty. As a wholehearted *assent*, loyalty further involves self-*affirmation*. What does self-affirmation (in this context) mean? Having denied oneself, self-affirmation is the position of affirming anew one's interests, inclinations, and desires. It is the challenging position of 'returning' to oneself, of assessing one's interests anew from this position of self-denial, and possessing them in a purified, unselfish, way. In other words, if the natural (and often selfish or egocentric) stance is that of focusing on *oneself*, and the stance of self-denial is that of focusing on the *other*, then the stance of self-affirmation, coupled as it is with self-denial, is that of a shared focus (as it were): one attends both to oneself and to the beloved in a harmonious (rather than conflicting) way.

This desirable stance, it should be emphasized, is necessarily twofold. That is to say, self-denial must exist alongside self-affirmation and be integral to the relevant work of love. This is so because self-denial secures the kind of purified attitude toward the beloved, in the context of which she is conceived independently of her relation to the lover, and as deserving respect, care, and compassion, regardless of how she addresses, or fails to address, the lover's interests. It is crucial that such an attitude is exercised alongside self-affirmation. After all, in the context of the latter the lover is driven by his interests and desires and conceives the beloved as addressing these, so that without self-denial it may easily collapse into egoism and selfishness.

Loyalty is a clear case of such a twofold position of denial and affirmation. While it is self-denial that guides the lover in his submission to the relevant commitments, in loyalty this submission is not motivated by an adherence to an impersonal rule or a universal law, but rather by the interest of the lover to maintain a significant relationship with the beloved. Accordingly, wholehearted assent to commitments (as opposed to the mere fulfilment of them) manifests an acknowledgment of the lover's *own* interests: his will to have the beloved in his life. In this sense, the loyal lover is not detached from himself; he does not act unwillingly out of a sense of obligation or because he feels forced to do so out of a sense of duty from which he might be alienated. When loyal, the lover is willing to set aside his own interests, while at the same time acknowledging how important and valuable *for him* is that for which he sets these interests aside: the relationship with his beloved.

Now, the merit of this 'work'—namely, of such a complex position of self-denial coupled with self-affirmation—is that it yields a clear-sighted vision of the beloved (say, June). In what way?

Arguably, it is natural for us to be motivated by our own interests, desires, aspirations, and so on, which often affects (in an undesirable way) our attitude to the beloved. The work of self-denial targets this, by being the kind of position that tears the veil of self-focused attitudes that, like a cobweb, envelops the beloved and prevent us from focusing directly on her. At the same time, however, in the context of love, to truly see the beloved is to see her value not just in herself—but also for the lover. The latter requires self-affirmation. After all, to see the value of the beloved *for the lover* is to discern those traits, particular to the beloved, that provoke the lover's attention, the lover's *interest*. Accordingly, to let one's interests be involved (by virtue of self-affirmation) means a fuller encounter with the beloved, where the lover perceives not only the beloved's 'objective' value but also her 'subjective' value: her particular importance *for him*. Both 'denying' and 'affirming' himself in this way, then, the lover sees not only the value of the beloved in being who she is but also how her being *who she is* is particularly valuable for him—given who *he* is.

Such a vision of the beloved is crucial, because it allows the lover to discern the beloved's 'kernel of individuality' (no matter whether and how she has changed) and the way in which this kernel informs her present 'persona.' In this way the lover gains an *attentive* correspondence by which he continues to experience the correspondence that provoked his love in the first place. In other words, seeing the beloved's value from both an objective and subjective point of view enables the lover to be attentive to the correspondence between him and the beloved: namely, it enables him to see her value as a self and experience her positive affect on *his* selfhood. This is so because the clear-sighted vision of the beloved uncovers the metaphysical correspondence that endures as a potential no matter how the lovers have changed.[17] Given that the correspondence between the lovers always exists in its *potential* level, a clear-sighted vision of the beloved is needed for maintaining the correspondence in its

---

[17] As was explained earlier, one's selfhood, one's individual essence, has two aspects—potential and actualization—and it is therefore equally *both*. Hence, although it is the actualized aspect of the beloved's selfhood that is immediately experienced by the lover, the potential is always present, and discernible, in the actualization. In the same way that the breakability of a thin glass cup is present in our experience of the cup although it is not broken, so (in principle) the potentiality of one's selfhood is present in the actualization.

actualized level. Only when correspondence exists on *both* levels can love endure.[18]

To conclude, as a wholehearted assent to commitment, loyalty involves both self-denial and self-affirmation. Hence, inasmuch as self-denial coupled with self-affirmation yields a clear-sighted perception of the beloved, loyalty yields a clear-sighted perception of the beloved. A clear-sighted perception of the beloved is what is necessary in order to attain attentive correspondence with one's (metaphysically correspondent) beloved. Hence, inasmuch as correspondence is the reason for love, loyalty—by enabling this correspondence—is indispensable for the endurance and flourishing of love.

When love lacks loyalty: the case of Black Dogs

To clarify further the connection between loyalty and attentive correspondence—and thereby the virtue of loyalty (being a necessary condition for the endurance of love)—let us now turn to examine a case of *dis*loyalty: a story of lovers who *fail* in their love.

Considered in the context of marriage (or romantic love more broadly), disloyalty is paradigmatically conceived in terms of the lover conducting an intimate (erotic) connection with a person other than the beloved. This is an affliction to the beloved, and a threat to love, because the lover turns her back (as it were) on the beloved, preferring the presence of someone else. After all, in being with the other person—whether physically or only in yearnings and thoughts—the lover is *not* with the beloved, as against the

---

[18]   Here it should be clarified: my position is that once two lovers correspond, they never lose the *potential* to be romantic lovers. This, however, does not, of course, mean that once two lovers correspond, they necessarily *remain* romantic lovers. As the reason for love is rooted in the actualization no less than in the potential, poor actualization may lead to a failure in attentive correspondence and result in a weakening of the existing correspondence and thereby to a failure in their romantic love.

expectation that she be (in such context) *only* with the beloved. In this sense the beloved is replaced by someone else, and a replacement of the beloved (if only tacitly) is antithetical—and hence destructive—to love.

However, disloyalty to one's beloved can take other, more implicit, forms. One such form is when the lover acts disloyally not by letting another *person* replace the beloved, but by letting an idea take the place of the beloved; preferring a way of life that does not make real room for the beloved's presence in the lover's life. This is the kind of disloyalty at the center of *Black Dogs*. Ian McEwan's short and poignant novel tells the story of the unhappy love between an estranged couple, June and Bernard Tremaine, as told by their son-in-law, Jeremy. Deeply fond of both Bernard and June, and happily married to Jenny, their daughter, Jeremy attempts to take a neutral stand in his reflective account of the profound breach that sundered his parents-in-law's relationship. Jeremy, however, has a more significant role than a mere narrator. Listening to the spouses' opposing positions in a nonjudgmental way, while nevertheless expressing skepticism in the face of their absolute confidence regarding the truth of their respective positions, Jeremy's written narrative reveals the nature of their failure to love each other properly.

In the preface to the Tremaines' story that serves as an explanatory background to the writing of this (fictional) memoir, Jeremy briefly relays his own story and, in doing so, implicitly presents the two major themes of the novel. Jeremy lost his parents in a car accident at the age of eight and, as a teenager, lived with his older sister, her abusive husband, and her little daughter, Sally. Compensating for the absence of parental love, he became something of a substitute parent to Sally, who was unintentionally neglected by her young, lost mother. After finishing high school, Jeremy quickly left this miserable home behind and started a new life as a student at Oxford, although this meant leaving Sally behind. Knowing that he left her with a mother who could not really take care of her, the guilt of feeling that he had betrayed Sally never left him, even long after she became an adult. Despite the change in his circumstances, at Oxford Jeremy continued to feel estranged from the world, and his misery only abated when he met Jenny: "This sorry madness came to an end with my marriage, in my mid-thirties, to Jenny Tremaine. Love, to borrow Sylvia Plath's phrase, set me going. I came to life for good."[19]

And so, in a nutshell, are the two themes of the novel. On the one hand, disloyalty toward a beloved person in the form of choosing a life in which the beloved cannot take a central part and, on the other, love as really the only possible answer to human suffering. Despite being a skeptic who—by his own admission and in strict opposition to his parents-in-law—lacks the passion to believe in anything whatsoever, Jeremy nevertheless admits that "I would be false to my own experience if I did not declare my belief in the possibility of love transforming and redeeming a life" (15). And he dedicates this memoir to his beloved wife, Jenny, and to his beloved, but betrayed and still suffering, niece. Regarding the latter he expresses the wish that she finds "this love" (15); the kind of "transforming and redeeming" love that will help to bring an end to her misery. With these two themes in mind, we can turn to the story of June and Bernard and inquire into the failure of their love.

On the face of it, the breach in their relationship had to do with the dramatic change in June's worldview. When Bernard and June met and fell in love, during the Second World War, they were both passionate idealists who shared a belief in materialist communism. Deeply concerned about the suffering in the world and earnestly enthusiastic about ideas that could potentially bring an end to this suffering, they were optimistic about the prospect of advancing together both personal happiness and political goodness. However, in their honeymoon in postwar France, June underwent an experience that served as a crucial turning point in her—and

---

[19] McEwan 1992, 12. Further references to this work will be provided in the main text.

Bernard's—life. When walking alone in a deserted field (Bernard, who was an amateur entomologist, was far behind her, preoccupied with exploring an interesting insect), she encountered two enormous black dogs—later she learned that they used to belong to the Gestapo—that attempted to attack her. This is how June, in retrospect, described the profound significance of that event:

> Despite what Bernard says, I don't actually believe they were Satan's familiars, Hell Hounds or omens from God . . . What I saw that day, and on many days since, was a halo of coloured light around my body. But the appearance is irrelevant. What matters is to make the connection with this centre, this inner being, and then extend and deepen it. Then carry it outwards, to others. The healing power of love . . . (62–64)

But Bernard—ardent rationalist as he was—could not grasp this experience and was impatiently intolerant of its articulation in these terms. He could not understand why and how June became indifferent to communism, and took this as a betrayal of both him and herself. He could not understand what he perceived to be her magical thinking, and he was hostile to her developing spiritualism. The loving couple grew more and more apart until years later June decided to leave for France with their children. Although they remain legally married, she lived apart from Bernard, who experienced this as yet another aspect of her disloyalty toward him.

However, although it was June who underwent a change and June who left, the disloyalty was not only on her part. In his refusal to respect something of such deep significance to her, in his stubbornness not to open himself to that which did not straightforwardly align with his beliefs and worldview, Bernard, in fact, failed to see her, *who she is*. In other words, he was intentionally blind to the June that she had become, a version—a better one, in her judgment—of the same June he fell in love with. He refuses to value the change that is so important to her; a profound shift in how she views and understands the world and determines what counts as a good life:

> The evil I'm talking about lives in us all. . . . My own small dis-covery has been that change is possible, it is within our power. Without a revolution of the inner life, however slow, all our big dreams are worthless. The work we have to do is with ourselves if we're ever going to be at peace with each other. (205–206)

However, there is, of course, no little irony in the fact that June's change, rather than allowing her to be at peace with Bernard, caused the opposite, and that "the healing power of love" that she has found within herself could not heal the deep injury in their loving rela-tionship.[20] Thus, her disloyalty was rooted neither in her change nor in her decision to live away from Bernard per se. Rather, it was rooted in the refusal on her side to understand Bernard's difficulty to accept her change and in her deep contempt for *his* worldview. Scorning his scientific rationalism and ungenerously reducing it to petty narrow mindedness, June failed to see Bernard no less than he failed to see her—and both failed to acknowledge the great value that each had for the other. Hence, if loyalty is a wholehearted as-sent to fulfil one's commitments, then both Bernard and June failed, because both rejected the implied commitment of love: to let the beloved be who the beloved is and to help the beloved become who he, or she, can be.

There is an evident correlation between the spouses' disloyalty to each other (in the sense just explained) and the failure of their love. In terms of the correspondence between them, it is the failure of attentive correspondence that explains why their love could not

---

[20] To her credit, June indeed acknowledges and regrets this: "Making a good life, where's the point in doing that alone? . . . why should I expect millions of strangers with conflicting interests to get along when I couldn't make a simple society with the father of my children, the man I've loved and remained married to?" (53–54). However, she makes this confession only near her death, and only to Jeremy, her sympathetic listener.

flourish. Attentive correspondence, recall, is the kind of correspondence that the lover (say, Bernard) experiences when, thanks to the double stance of self-denial and self-affirmation, he discerns the beloved's 'kernel of individuality' and appreciates its value for *him*—even if the beloved is changed in a way that is not appealing to him. Succeeding in 'seeing' the beloved in this way[21] makes the initial correspondence—the beloved's positive affect on the lover's becoming who he is—discernible again, and so the reason for the lover's love for the beloved is again available.

Of course, the metaphysical correspondence of June and Bernard, which is a crucial part of their spontaneous, initial, correspondence, is intact. They are still the same selves, although changed and impatient with each other's current actualizations of those selves. Being metaphysically correspondent means that each of them is capable, in essence, of helping the other become who he, or she, can potentially be. On a deeper level, beneath the disagreement, they still understand each other; they still correspond. Their respective qualities, which affected each other in the beginning, are still apparent in each. They both remained idealistic, passionate about ideas, earnest in their projects. They still share the same acute responsiveness to sorrow and suffering.

In fact, even when it comes to their deepest disagreement—the possibility of being swayed by the inexplicable and susceptible to experiencing that which strict reason cannot explain—they are closer than it seems. While June has her 'black dogs', Bernard has 'the woman in black'—a significantly meaningful memory from their honeymoon in France of a young woman, overcome by the grief of losing her husband and two brothers in the war. The grim, not to say ghostly, encounter with her—that June has no recollection

---

[21] For example, such a success would be for Bernard to see that June is still as caring about the flourishing of human beings and as passionate about alleviating suffering as she was when he fell in love with her.

of, and that has no circumstantial evidence—prompted in Bernard something of a revelation:

> For the first time he sensed the scale of the catastrophe in terms of feeling; all those unique and solitary deaths, all that consequent sorrow, unique and solitary too, which had no place in conferences, headlines, history, and which had quietly retired to houses, kitchens, unshared beds, and anguished memories. (196–197)

Sorrow and evil are of a real concern for the two lovers. Hence, if only they were loyal to each other, they could continue to help each other address that which is of crucial importance to each, and in doing so help each other become a better version of themselves. To be loyal, in their case, would have been for each to continue seeing, through self-denial, who the other still is—despite the changes, regardless of the real faults; and to appreciate anew, through self-affirmation, the value that each has for the other, the positive *effect* that each has on the other. When listening once again to Bernard's complaints over June, Jeremy loses his temper:

> What struck me then was not simply the injustice of Bernard's remarks, but a wild impatience at the difficulty of communication, and an image of parallel mirrors in place of lovers on a bed, throwing back in infinite regression likenesses paling into untruth. (102)

Because there is truth: the truth of their being (metaphysically) correspondent, and of continuing to love each other. But in order to keep *experiencing* the correspondence, and, accordingly, for their love to flourish, they needed to work, and in this they failed. Here is Jeremy's reproach:

You never listened to what she was telling you. She wouldn't listen either. Two softies!... She told me she'd always loved you. You've said the same. How could you waste so much time...? (102–103)

The *failure* of loyalty in this story, then, serves to elucidate the virtue of loyalty. Loyalty is a way of truly being with the beloved as it allows for truly seeing the beloved and her value for the lover; it is to keep available, by means of the double stance, the reason for love—correspondence—and in doing so enable not only the continuation of love but also its flourishing.

Bibliography

Frankfurt, Harry. *The Reasons of Love*. Princeton, NJ: Princeton University Press, 2004.

Jollimore, Troy. *Love's Vision*. Princeton, NJ: Princeton University Press, 2011.

Kierkegaard, Søren. *The Sickness unto Death*. Translated by Howard V. Hong and Edna H. Hong. Princeton, NJ: Princeton University Press, 1980.

Kierkegaard, Søren. *Works of Love: Kierkegaard's Writings*, vol. 16. Translated by Howard V. Hong and Edna H. Hong. Princeton, NJ: Princeton University Press, 1995.

Kolodny, Niko. "Love as Valuing a Relationship." *Philosophical Review* 112 (2003): 135–189.

Krishek, Sharon. "The Focus of Love." *Canadian Journal of Philosophy* 51:7 (2021): 508–522.

Krishek, Sharon. *Lovers in Essence: A Kierkegaardian Defense of Romantic Love*. New York: Oxford University Press, 2022.

McEwan, Ian. *Black Dogs*. London: Vintage, 1992.

10

A Dubious Virtue

Tony Milligan and Heidi Cobham

Attempts to understand loyalty are partly shaped by political concerns about subservience, inequality, and alignment. These feed into broader worries about what we might be loyal to and whether loyalty can be regarded as a virtue. It does seem to be more equivocal than truthfulness, a commitment to justice, or moral courage. Nonetheless, we contend that loyalty can be seen as a virtue, when the appropriate conceptual machinery is put in place to help us understand the difference between claims about virtues and the recognition of mere traits of character. Our discussion will begin with an attempt to tease out the grounds for concern about loyalty and how these are politically inflected. The second section will set out a familiar distinction between character traits *simpliciter* and such traits operating as virtues. The final substantive section will try to deepen the point by focusing upon a problem case where loyalty fails, in Iris Murdoch's novel, *The Bell*. The problem case will help to draw out the idea of *conditions for loyalty* and to sharpen up the concept of loyalty as a virtue that accommodates sacrifice but also requires that such sacrifice does not simply pander to the egocentricity of others.

Loyalty as a dubious virtue

Loyalty, when thought of as a virtue, can be ambiguous and problematic. The reason for this ambiguity is because the borderlines

Tony Milligan and Heidi Cobham, *A Dubious Virtue* In: *The Virtue of Loyalty*. Edited by: Troy Jollimore, Oxford University Press. © Oxford University Press 2024. DOI: 10.1093/oso/9780197612644.003.0011

between being loyal and being submissive are not always clear, and the reason it can be problematic is because it touches upon important ethical questions about what it really means to be in a loving relation with another person. The extent to which we are really committed to the relationship and to the person may be tested when something goes badly wrong. If nothing goes wrong, there is no need for loyalty. (Routine and habit may do just as well.) Such applies not only with familiar and familial relations but also with political engagement and professional life. Among peer groups, we may be loyal to one another, or we may fail to show such loyalty, and the demands of loyalty may also speak with several voices rather than one. That is, we may find ourselves expected to compromise our commitment to being a certain kind of person out of loyalty to colleagues, a political party, or friends. Loyalty is so routine and so built into our ways of relating to others that it is easy to imagine that it may involve nothing deeper or more virtuous than sheer alignment, picking sides in a world of friends, enemies, and neutral parties.

Thinking of matters in this way may be regarded as a form of skepticism about loyalty, specifically its standing as an actual virtue. Consequently, we may be drawn to think of it, instead, as a dubious virtue, or as no virtue at all. The reason is because loyalty, as alignment, looks very different from truthfulness, practical wisdom, courage, or any familiar virtue. What drives skepticism about the standing of loyalty as a virtue is a combination of the ease with which counterexamples can be given and a background picture of virtue itself. This is a background picture within which various character traits (such as loyalty) are relational but not relational all the way down. In this background picture, the standing of a trait of character (such as loyalty) as a virtue remains overly dependent upon internal factors, rather than circumstance, contingency, and factors beyond the control of agents. Even to the extent that an agent who longs to be loyal, and would happily be so *under the right conditions*, may find that any way for their loyalty to operate as a virtue is blocked or otherwise not available. The *conditions for a virtuous loyalty* may not be realized. An agent may wait patiently for a better opportunity (and their patience might well be a virtue), but no exercise of will can remedy their predicament. This approach, within which an act of will cannot suddenly propel us into a situation where a virtue is available, owes something to Iris Murdoch, and our primary exemplar herein will be drawn from one of her novels.[1]

Saying this much is a way of giving skepticism about loyalty its due, without ourselves falling into such skepticism. In what follows, we are committed to upholding the standing of loyalty, or at least doing so *up to a point*. There are clear cases in which loyalty functions as a virtue, as well as cases in which it fails to do so. Loyalty as mere political allegiance looks like a potentially dangerous thing—something akin to a love of some cause or leader. Loyalty on this score looks like the kind of thing that drove Hannah Arendt to say that she loved only her friends, because any kind of political love, love for cause, country, people of the great leader, would be too dangerous.[2] We may think along similar lines about loyalty: about its risks and pitfalls within personal life, politics, or in organizational contexts.[3] Yet there are loyalties which seem admirable, because they are more personal, even if they have political dimensions. In Japanese culture, Mori Ranmaru has long served as an image of loyalty, for his death alongside Oda Nobunaga, while enemies circled outside, and the flames inside the burning temple crept closer. This points to a romantic image of loyalty, one that survives unto death, which portrays it as something both dangerous and at the same time attractive. On this score, loyalty is not depicted as a Western construct, or as something destined to fall away as hegemony shifts from West to East.[4] Yet we can say this

[1] In terms of the relevant philosophical writings, see especially Murdoch (1981).
[2] See Arendt and Scholem (2017); see also Nixon (2015).
[3] See, respectively, Agassi (1974), Cohen (2019), and Irwin (2014).
[4] See Foust (2012, 2015).

while noting significant cultural differences and the option of disagreement about the choice of exemplars. For example, in England, Piers of Gaveston, Edward II's loyal lover, has not enjoyed a similarly favorable reception. Yet we are in little doubt that in both cases images of *loyalty* are in play, loyalty until the last sword is drawn.

Exemplars of this sort serve to remind us that loyalty can be dangerous, dubious, and indistinguishable from fealty or mere political alignment, where it exists as something akin to love or even something that involves love. Consequently, loyalty can rise to the level of virtue, or function as something else, something more neutral, base, or reprehensible.[5] And so, when we describe a pattern of actions and responses as loyalty, whether we are praising these actions and responses *as a virtue* can remain an open question, something still in doubt.

We have been considering the common view that understands loyalty in terms of political and factional alignment, of being on someone's side. Such political themes help to drive a skepticism about loyalty that spans both its political instances and its more personal dimensions. On the political side, behind dated conceptions of fealty, sits the prospect of subservience, an attitude incompatible with autonomy of a sort that we have come to value in broadly liberal societies (whatever their faults). According loyalty too high a value might then seem to be a regression to things past, to attitudes proper to another and earlier time. Here, we may reflect upon classic and Stoic-influenced representations of loyalty in the literature of antiquity. We envisage scenarios within which someone who should not be a slave finds themselves in that tragic condition, and they overcome this mistaken ordering of things by rising above their position. This is achieved not through churlish disobedience, but through loyalty; through an embodiment of virtue, which is, in and of itself, anything but servile.[6] This disturbing theme of loyalty

---

[5] See Jollimore (2012) and Milligan (2020).
[6] See Vogt (1974).

within inegalitarian contexts is carried over into colonial-era literature with its fondness for mimicking the classical. It is there in the case of Kipling's water carrier Gunga Din, who we may imagine as upright and bold, but in the poem has been belted and flayed by his British masters. Yet he is the better man. It is there, too, in Rosemary's Sutcliffe's *Eagle of the Ninth*, an even later mimicking of classical times, written in 1954 and read by generations of public schoolchildren across Britain. This is a tale within which Esca, a captured but noble Celt, again rises above his now servile status by betraying his own people and helping to recapture the Eagle that means so much to Marcus, his master. He could leave at any point and melt into the woodland. He could even have his master killed or enslaved in turn. To some of us, this may seem like a missed opportunity. But he remains loyal and only in this way can he prove a true inner nobility of character, an inner character that no chains can reach, and no mere bodily harm can take away. It is apparent that Marcus sees and understands this nobility in a way that other Romans do not. When Tribune Servius Placidus asks, "Are you sure that you can trust that barbarian of yours in a venture of this kind?' Marcus replies in the briefest of terms that he can. "Doubtless you know best," says the Tribune, "Personally I should not care to let my life hang by so slender a thread as the loyalty of a slave."[7] But Marcus is not in the habit of thinking of Esca as a slave. The relation of master and slave has evolved into something else, yet it is an evolution which has not actually erased the troubled relation.

What is striking about cases of this sort is not only the attitude toward loyalty itself (its insertion into an obviously inegalitarian order of things) but the attitude taken toward virtue more generally, as something inner, personal, and beyond reach. The Tribune cannot see what is inside of both Marcus and Esca—a thing which is wholly owned by those who have it and in no way dependent upon the actions of others. The loyal are loyal no matter what the

[7] Sutcliffe 2020, 92.

context, whether it be that of master and slave or friend to friend. This is a worrying picture not only because of the inequalities of power (Aristotle notoriously worries about the possibility of friendship between master and slave, but there is a different concern at stake) but also because of the way in which it represents virtue as decontextualized or separable from the contingencies of the world, that is, something other than a fully social and interpersonal phenomenon. It is as if virtue exists apart from the world, as if it is immune to and unaffected by it. This portrayal suggests that virtue might exist as nothing short of an inner perfection, because there appears to be no outer event or circumstance that could possibly depreciate or enhance it. Marcus understands loyalty in these terms. It is a sort of inner gold that does not tarnish and whose luster is independent, not only of social standing, but also of actual states of affairs concerning the worthiness or suitability of persons in whose direction it is turned. It is relational, but only *up to a point.* The idea that Marcus, or Esca, or both, might want their loyalty to be a virtue, but find this option blocked by circumstances beyond their control, has no place in this understanding of *what virtue is* and *what loyalty is.*

Nonetheless, despite reasonable doubts and outright skepticism that it might ever play the role of a virtue, loyalty has generally been seen as one. It has been seen as a way of relating toward others that we ought to strive for or, better still, inspire and also as something that, in turn, helps us to strive for good things. And this applies even in the face of a recognition that people can be loyal to bad causes, to dangerous organizations, or to oaths which come into conflict with our care for people. Many of us have accepted troubling cases without feeling that we need to abandon the very idea that a virtue is in play. Others have viewed the troubling cases as more damning. R. E. Ewin claims that such cases undermine the claim that loyalty really is a virtue, because there is an internal conceptual connection between the very idea of a virtue and the idea of good judgement: loyalty is not always a good thing, but surely virtues are, more times than not, good things (or so the hope goes)?[8] The common expectation is that virtues are always good, because they are ideals for which most, if not all, reasonable persons strive, in order to obtain their idea of the 'good life'. Virtues, we want to believe, enhance, rather than detract from, our lives. Virtues are the vehicles within which we become morally excellent individuals. Virtues, by and large, are seen as good for us, at least most of the time, as they are viewed as the tools necessary to curate a morally praiseworthy life. If we are Aristotelian, and *eudaimonistically* inclined, in our understanding of virtue, we will say that virtues tend to promote our good. If we are less Aristotelian, and more *aretaically* inclined, we may say that goodness or admirability is already built into virtues themselves; otherwise we would not pursue them. One way or another, we set out to become virtuous *because* virtues are the better option, even if bad things can happen to good people.

While this idea, that virtue and good judgment are conceptually related, may seem plausible, it draws upon an understanding of *what philosophy is* that we might now question. It leans a little toward a treatment of philosophy as conceptual analysis. And this is something we may have been more comfortable with in the recent past than we are now. The idea that concepts (such as virtue, loyalty, character, and love) have a fixed essence that we might crack open, allowing us to say what might and might not fall under them, seems a little remote from how we actually work with them, and the different kinds of work that they might do. And so, while it makes sense to say that virtues are good things, and that this really is built into the very idea of a virtue, we know very well that many traits of character that we think of as virtuous can also serve bad ends. They can facilitate great wrongs as well as great goods.

Courage is like this. And love too (even if not a virtue, but virtue connected) can be misdirected and dangerous. The character traits that we call virtues do not come with any internalist guarantee that

---

[8] Ewin 1992.

they will aim always for the good. The idea of such a guarantee really does seem like a Platonism too far. It is also a Platonism which is easily adapted to modern, and rather egocentric, ways of seeing the world. Virtues become inner traits of a sort whose presence can be entirely divorced from one's place in the world, and from the way in which they function. This is a way of thinking which is also associated not only with the classic stoic image of invulnerable inward commitment but also with folk tales of holy fools and innocents who go around triggering havoc, but who are inwardly pure of heart. Such is a picture of things which again makes it seem as if we ourselves can do all of the work that is required for virtue. In contrast, we want to stress the way in which virtues have an *ongoing vulnerability to the other*. Our character itself depends, in multiple respects, upon ourselves, but never ourselves alone. Character and virtue depend also upon contingencies which reach beyond the self, that is, matters outside of our control. And this is a point familiar from the literature on moral luck.[9] This is a view which may also be familiar from certain accounts of grace as a restriction to the *will* of individual agents, but it might also be presented in more secular terms. Virtues are moral accomplishments, but they are accomplishments of a sort which involve various kinds of dependence upon other agents. Loyalty is not only a dubious virtue, it is also a dependent virtue, as all virtues are, at least up to a point.

Having said this, of all the virtues which we argue are dependent, loyalty, unlike the others, seems to be one of the more obviously dependent virtues. Loyalty inevitably ties us to the judgments, behaviors, and reactions of those to whom we are loyal, thus rendering us vulnerable and exposed to the other in a way that is not the case with, for example, compassionate agency, which often thrives upon the failings of others and is not blocked by them. Unlike many virtues, loyalty is also contrastive. Loyalty, unlike other virtues, appears to necessitate that one pledges allegiance to only certain

---

[9] See Walker (1991).

people at the exclusion of others. That is, loyalty, by its very nature dictates that we be loyal to *these* people to the exclusion of *those* people. The same is true only of certain kinds of loving agency, and it is difficult to place in relation to the virtue of honesty (which extends out in all directions). A relation to one group of people may shape an apparently separate relation to someone else. It depends upon shifting configurations of attachment, only some of which are within our control.

By emphasizing the constraints upon loyalty (its restriction to some and not others, the dependence of its role upon the actions of others), we can do at least some justice to skepticism about the standing of loyalty as a virtue by allowing that there clearly are many cases of nonvirtuous loyalty. There may even be cases of loyalty that look like a virtuous loyalty but are not. Yet we depart from such skepticism by denying that all cases are like this. Often loyalty *is* a virtue, and occasions on which we no longer feel able to remain loyal, or where the option of a virtuous loyalty is blocked, can be suitable occasions for regret.

Character traits and virtues

To allow for multiple contexts in which loyalty is not a virtue, we will draw upon the standard distinction, associated with Philippa Foot, between character traits and how they function.[10] Such talk about how traits function may itself be a kind of shorthand for a more complex relational story,[11] but for our present purposes it is a convenient shorthand. In brief, it is only when a character trait functions in the right way that it is a virtue. Although we will use this move to help make sense of loyalty, it is courage that is the standard exemplar. For instance, the courage of Gandhi looks more

---

[10] See Foot (1978).
[11] See Rorty (1986: 399).

like a virtue than the courage of Reinhard Heydrich, a planner of the Holocaust. Yet both really do look like courage rather than anything else. Heydrich flew almost one hundred combat missions, was shot down behind the Russian line, and managed to escape capture, for which he was decorated and ordered to stop risking his life. It is difficult to deny that he was courageous, even if we think of him also as monstrous or evil in some more banal way.[12] The risks habitually taken by both Gandhi and Heydrich were 'reasonable' given a strictly means-ends assessment of the goals they pursued. Neither acted routinely on the basis of something like an adrenaline rush. And we may still say this, even though both ended up being assassinated.

Exactly what it is that makes the courage of Gandhi a virtue, while the courage of Heydrich was anything but virtuous, obviously depends upon something larger, or broader, than the character trait of courage itself. But we can say a little more than this, more than pointing to context and social embeddedness. Eudaimonists like Foot and Hursthouse will say that the vital factor is a connection between the character trait and flourishing (*eudaimonia*).[13] And so courage must have this tendency; otherwise it is merely a character trait and not a virtue. Those, like Michael Slote, who defend a more aretaic conception of virtue will appeal instead to personal excellence (*arete*) and admirable traits of character, irrespective of whether they have any tendency to promote a life which is good in the fullest sense.[14] Here, a 'good' life includes a life enjoyed and not only lived.

Virtues, on the latter (more *aretaic*) view, need not tend to benefit their successor. And this is a persuasive thought. Happiness and virtue do not always seem to go together, and we have known this for some time. In De Sade's *Justine: Or The Misfortunes of Virtue*,

---

[12] See Dent (1981: 576).
[13] Foot 1978; Hursthouse 1999.
[14] Slote 2001.

twins are separated at birth.[15] One (Justine) embraces virtue and still all manner of terrible things happen to her before she is finally killed by a bolt of lightning. (Virtue seems to offer poor protection from natural disasters and falling masonry.) The other (Juliette) embraces vice and has a thoroughly enjoyable time committing terrible deeds. The debate between eudaimonistic and aretaic conceptions of virtue will not be settled here—perhaps it will never be settled—but in any case, we will remain officially neutral about its outcome. Our intention is only to point out that there are disciplined ways to run the claim that character traits sometimes *do*, and sometimes *do not*, function in the right way for them to operate as virtues. That is, there are plausible, nonarbitrary ways of making sense of their functioning, sometimes in one way (as a virtue), and sometimes in another way (more neutrally, or even as a vice).

Yet we may wonder about how well such extreme scenarios or extreme comparisons work. Consider, again, the contrast between the courage of Gandhi and the courage of Heydrich. Few if any of us will ever be tempted to the morally repellent extremes of Heydrich or capable of the political goodness of Gandhi. Can we, then, legitimately draw a large conclusion about our lives from theirs? We can, if the same point can be made, even if a little less forcefully, in cases of a simpler sort. Here we are thinking of cases in which agents may defend bad causes with a courage that is worthy of some far better cause. Confederate soldiers defended racist institutions, and in all but a few cases, they may well have been racist at a more personal level. But it would be odd to imagine that they were less courageous than their counterparts on the other side, that is, soldiers whose courage has a better claim upon being a virtue because of the cause at stake.

We may also wonder how far we get by appealing to courage or to any other cardinal virtue as an exemplar of virtues in general, given the far broader range of virtues that are conceivable and the cultural variability of the repertoire of the virtues, and of the preferred

---

[15] De Sade 1787.

exemplars. But, in this particular case, when we use courage as a comparison case to help illuminate the concept of loyalty, the carryover from one character trait to another seems to hold. Loyalty, like courage, looks like the kind of thing that is not, per se, a virtue or a vice, but something that can function as either.

To say this is to accept that, up to a point, skepticism about loyalty as a virtue seems to hold. But it does not hold all the way. If we accept the distinction between loyalty as a character trait, and *the way in which it then functions in particular cases* (with regard to the good life, or excellence, or something else), then examples of loyalty to bad things need not undermine the standing of loyalty as a virtue in all cases. This simple move serves only to open up just enough shifting conceptual space for loyalty to be a virtue; it does not quite do justice to a skeptical doubt which may help us to always keep in mind the downside of loyalty, its risks and our susceptibility to them. If we are seeking a better understanding of this downside, the analytic move of distinguishing between trait and function may seem little more than sleight of hand unless it is backed up by some deeper kind of reflection. That is, as something that touches upon familiar experiences of what it is like to care for other beings, to want to be loyal to them, and for loyalty to fail. It is our contention that the suspicions, or what might be called 'the skeptical stance', really do touch upon matters of depth in our relations with one another. While loyalty can be a virtue, any oversimplified defense of loyalty is bound to be ethically problematic, not just mistaken, intellectually, but geared to a defense of things which should not be defended.

Loyalty in Iris Murdoch's The Bell *as a problem case*

So far, considerable weight has been given to politically inflected concerns about alignment, subservience, and the apparent availability of loyalty for bad causes as much as for good ones. Some conceptual machinery has been put into use, to distinguish between having a character trait and that character trait functioning as a virtue. And these things are all well and good. Enough has been said to avoid the charge that we are trying to make sense of an elusive and shifting concept by appeal to conceptual analysis alone (as if it had a fixed essence, that we might crack open). But avoiding the charge of a lapse into mere conceptual analysis is one thing, and presenting a case that touches upon matters deep within our lives is something quite different. To try and make headway on the latter, we will, in a more sustained way, engage with a case of failed loyalty set out in Iris Murdoch's *The Bell* (1958), which is both more personal than the earlier examples, and more sustained and thought through. Nonetheless, as before, we try to do justice to the skeptical stance, and to doubts about loyalty, while sustaining the view that it really can be a virtue.

In the novel, Murdoch gives at least some traction to the skeptical stance toward loyalty. The text is appropriate for our purposes because one may reasonably argue that the entire novel rests on the loyalties of its characters, not only toward one another but also to traditions of religion, *and* to themselves, too. In classic Murdochian fashion, a mixture of Platonic and existentialist themes helps to build an account of loyalty, as well as its breakdown. The text is set within an unlikely lay religious community attached to Imber Abbey in rural England. (We say 'unlikely', because communities of this sort are less familiar in England than in France, where they are well represented in literature, notably in J. K. Huysman's pilgrimage novels beginning with *Là-Bas* [1894] and ending with *L'Oblat* [1903].) Scenarios of this sort invite a particular set of themes that Murdoch also repeats, up to a point. Huysman's central character is torn between mutually unlivable loyalties to himself (a felt need for sincerity) and to a religiosity which runs deep within his being, but is at root about aesthetic sensibilities rather than ontology. It is religiosity, but without any actual sense that a living God can be placed within it. He slowly moves away from the demi-monde and torturously shifts toward becoming a lay community brother, but simply cannot hold on through the familiar phase of spiritual crisis, void, or dark night of the soul. The inner workings of belief in a deity are missing, with only the shell of religious traditions in place. He experiences difficulties (and ultimately failure) in transitioning from a love of plainsong, and the mystical aura of Catholicism, into actual acceptance of Church teachings, and belief in things unseen. Everything seems part-time, not quite the real thing.

Murdoch's comparable scenario focuses not upon the classic isolated individual, but upon a mismatched marriage that is thrown into the context of a far more makeshift, but equally male-dominated, high Anglican community. The community is well-meaning, but the reader has the same sense that spiritual commitment is being played with rather than fully inhabited. This is not because all spiritual commitment must be like that, but because the real thing (exemplified by nuns in the nearby Abbey, where there is no audience to watch) is slightly too difficult for humans, or for *humans like these*. The community is, in Platonic terms, an imitation of the Good. In other words, there is more Fire than Sun. The mismatched marriage between Dora Greenfield and Paul Greenfield is equally marked by pretense. The young Dora is married to the middle-aged, slightly underachieving, stuffy, and overly formal Paul, who is thirteen years her senior (not an original theme by most standards). It is difficult to avoid recognition of some echoes from Terrence Rattigan's *The Browning Version* (1948) and the film that was based upon it shortly after its publication. The text fuses themes of the time and themes about the erosion of norms. Its setting alters the dynamics, and Murdoch's Paul is far less endearing than Rattigan's ageing classics master (although both are pained by the open infidelity of their wives).

Paul is a well-off, educated, mature man who owns a flat in Knightsbridge. This is almost a complete statement about his character. Dora, however, comes from a lower middle-class family and lacks self-confidence and self-identity. The contrast is significant because it implicitly gives Paul the impression that he has the right to educate and undermine Dora. He plays the fatherly role to his wife, which is even more significant because she lost her father at the age of nine. Paul is continuously portrayed as an oppressive and insulting character toward Dora—many a time Dora is reported as afraid of Paul's reaction and afraid to look at him. There is deep imbalance, inequality, and miscommunication between the married couple. There is a lack of common ground on which they might stand and where communication might occur. Dora repeatedly tries to talk to Paul, to sort matters out, but his choice of moment, and ways of speaking about their life together, run along fixed tracks and pathways.

The faltering relationship sits in the foreground. In the background, there is loyalty to a spiritual and ethical ideal of God, in times when the idea of a real personal being is no longer easy to place. As indicated, it can perhaps be placed, but not *here*, and not in a community like this. Things will fall apart—not just for Paul and Dora, but for the lay community itself. It is about to come undone in a dreadful way. But this no more engages the reader's sympathies than the unravelling of their marriage. Supposedly a place of contemplation and prayer, it is shown mostly as a group of people arguing about agricultural machinery and building repairs, before sitting down to talk about the chief requirement of the good life. (Oddly, for a Murdoch novel, the framing of talk about virtue is strongly Aristotelian.)

To further set the scene, Dora has slept with someone else, and, to make matters worse, not just *any* someone else, but a frivolous 'someone else', specifically Paul's best friend, Noel Spens. This is not just infidelity, but the wrong infidelity. The collapse of the relationship between Paul and Dora has been accelerated by the inappropriateness of her choice of sexual partner: inappropriateness by acquaintance, inappropriateness by frivolity, and by sheer embarrassment about it being so publicly known. Yet, in Paul's eyes, this is exactly the sort of error that Dora is prone to make. She would mess it all up and err in the wrong way. And yet, Paul condescendingly tells Dora, "You are fortunate to be able to know that my love for you remains unaltered."[16] Even with allowances made for the times, Murdoch invites the reader to see why Dora should *not* be loyal to Paul, and certainly not in the way that he expects—that is, in a way that is based upon the solemnity of the marriage as a contract rather than a way that connects loyalty in any deep way with flourishing of a familiar sort. In spite of his sense of solemnity, Paul is not even a full member of the community and is even further removed from anything like actual *imitatio Christi*, even on a softened pastoral and Anglican understanding (rather than Huysman-style) of what this might involve. Above all, there is a disconnect between his interest in the spiritual life and his life with Dora. They seem entirely separate, like pieces of different jigsaws. Paul listens intently to the successive talks about the good life, yet it is difficult for the reader to picture Dora ever having any sort of good life with him. She "left her husband because she was afraid of him. She decided six months later to return to him for the same reason [. . .] She decided at last that the persecution of his presence was to be preferred to the persecution of his absence" (7). Although the persecution does not take the form of anything so clear cut as bodily violence, it is still damaging because it involves a dull superiority and sense of expectation. The reason that Dora remains loyal to Paul is *because* he is her husband, because of a kind of inertia in the shift between loyalty and something else, and also because of Paul's own helplessness and her sense of this helplessness. Loyalty in this instance has not arisen because his actions toward her have made him in any obvious way worthy or deserving of her loyalty.

What is going on here, in Murdoch's text, involves more than the usual trick of engaging our sympathies with the party who, by a set of received social standards, does wrong. Of course, the usual

[16] Murdoch 1962, 12. Further page references to *The Bell* will be given in the text.

literary tricks are still there. Ordinarily, we would distance ourselves from the adulterer and sympathize with the other partner.
But novels rarely work in that way: we like Anna from Tolstoy's
Anna Karenina (1878), and we may like Fontane's Effi Briest from
the 1895 novel of the same name. Flaubert's Emma Bovary from
Madame Bovary (1856) and the disloyal and slightly murderous
Therese from Zola's *Therese Raquin* (1868) may be a bit hard on their
husbands, but we can at least understand that this is not the life they
need. If we sympathized most with the supposedly wounded party,
novels of infidelity could be dull and unsurprising, and much of the
nineteenth-century literary canon would never have been written.
We all know that the standard move in situations of this sort is to
shift the reader's sympathies and to dispose of husbands as any sort
of object of interest. They are rendered dull or overly conventional,
or both. However, there is something about Paul which is different.
He is dull and conventional, but *not just* dull and conventional.
Something else is in play, and this something makes us sense that
Dora is not actually committing any sort of mistake. If she has any
pathway to a good life, it is the path she is already on. It is a pathway
in which loyalty to oneself, one's needs and longings, can outweigh
a historically transmitted and strongly gendered conception of loyalty that she has had no part in forming. And, in this respect, Dora
is unlike the aforementioned women who, in line with the inexo-
rable laws of nineteenth-century morality, have their fun and must
then come to a bad end. She arrives within the story by train, but,
unlike Anna, we do not expect to see her depart at the nearest train
station.

But, one way or another, Dora must get away. She is, in a certain
sense, still trapped inside Paul's conception of the world, inside his
conception of *what loyalty is* and *what she is*, such that her lack of
role in shaping the former relates to a lack of role in shaping the
latter. When with Paul, Dora has no sense of identity. By this, we
do not mean that she has the ordinary gaps in her picture of herself;
rather, we propose the stronger claim that she possesses a lack which

is more pronounced: she lacks interest in the things that would establish her identity and subjectivity in the world. She does not work, has given up painting, and is superstitious but has no belief in God. Her only loyalty is to her husband, Paul, for it is "one of the few facts that remained in her disordered existence quite certain" (18). Dora constantly feels trapped "as if she were merely a thought in his mind," such that she becomes the very embodiment of the butterfly that she clasped (for its own good and safety) on the train to Imber (40). Dora is defined only by the fixed perceptions that Paul has afforded her, meaning that she is trapped by, and subservient to, his vision of her. In her commitment to Paul, she becomes loyal to his perception, to his Pauline view of the world. And here, in appealing to such a view, we are suggesting that Murdoch's naming, her use of "Paul" rather than "Matthew," "Mark," "Luke," or "Jane," is far from accidental. Were Dora to attempt to break free from Paul's view of the world, she would be violating the contract he has assigned to her. This is a contract endorsed through his preferred way of articulating Christianity, a way which has drawn him to Imber, and to a lay community seeking to escape from worldly and personal flaws.

These are all familiar Murdochian themes of attraction and repulsion, exemplifying the faintly masochistic tendencies which Murdoch sees as built into love, longing, and human character. Such themes are not, in and of themselves, reasons for disloyalty, given that they are normal within Murdoch's conception of the world, and normal within Murdoch's sense of Christianity as something which is beautiful, but at the same time vulnerable to a lapse into various kinds of puritanism. Our point here is not that Murdoch's reading of Christianity is particularly good, but rather that she captures the phenomenology of being trapped in a relationship quite well. Dora's lived experience of being trapped, and Murdoch's depiction of Paul's awkward and accusing response to it, do look like reasons for disloyalty or for *an absence of loyalty*. What is personally experienced makes a difference, and it can run deep. Dora's sense of the impossibility of being loyal in the way that is expected runs deep. It involves more than the mere lack of happiness in what she shares of her life with Paul. It is not simply that the marriage is making her miserable; rather, she comes to feel that unhappiness itself is what loyalty is all about. Her ability to see it as anything else is compromised. When she finally leaves Paul, she feels "intense relief" (12). But this is not simply because she can now, in good conscience, sleep with someone else. Rather, she can come to see a range of things in a different way, and these things include love and loyalty itself. At the risk of being slightly paradoxical, *an understanding of what loyalty might be only becomes possible for her through her disloyalty to Paul*, and ultimately through her separation from him. It is only through her disloyalty that she can get outside of Paul's own constricted view of things. In this particular instance, the action comes before the vision of what loyalty might be, yet it draws upon a way of picturing the relationship as unworkable, while she remains trapped inside of it. Dora sees that she must break the contract Paul has assigned to her by leaving him. She cultivates not only physical and mental but also emotional distance from Paul as a way of distancing herself from her loyalties to him. In cultivating this newfound distance from Paul, Dora is, inadvertently, able to foster closeness to *herself*, by finding herself and rediscovering a sense of who she might become and what a different kind of loyalty might involve. By so doing, Dora creates the means to live without the control of Paul. The irony being that, it is only by first being disloyal to Paul that Dora was able to finally become loyal to herself, which is something that is not directly available within the relationship. There is the possibility of acceptance, as a kind of submission, but that is something very different from *what loyalty might be* if it is to be thought of as any sort of virtue.

However, Paul does not see matters in this way. He remains a man with notebooks, but without epiphanies. His conception of loyalty remains categorical rather than conditional or richly attuned and finely responsive to the particularity of situations.

It lacks any connection to practical wisdom. He tells Dora that "your escapes have diminished you permanently in my eyes" (41). Comparing her to the spiritual seekers at Imber, he remarks that he does not think of her as "capable of anything so serious" (42). Such remarks raise some disturbing but obvious concerns about his binary division of people, and of women in particular, into two kinds, with Dora placed as the wrong kind. (We may also suspect that he loved his mother a little too much, and is liable to be confused when looking at paintings by Titian, in which sacred and profane love look suspiciously alike.[17]) In more theory-friendly terms, he does not see the norms of loyalty as in any way internal to relationships and varying with relationship. Not in the sense that one party can simply make up the standards, but in the sense that reasonable expectations emerge out of ways of relating and are not fixed textually, by the quasi-promises made during wedding vows or by the public disproval of those who break them. Yet vows of this sort are difficult to read as literal promises about a future that remains largely unknown.[18] When someone promises to love another forever, they are not promising to slip free of the bonds of time or to presently control the person they will become at a more distant point in time. Expressions of love and commitment may look like contractual obligations of a difficult or impossible-to-meet sort, but that is not what is going on when we utter them. They may occur within a service, but they do not concern the delivery of a service. They are not commerce.

Paul cannot see matters in this way. Vows are vows, whether uttered in a marriage ceremony or in the figurative marriage ceremony of the nuns in the nearby Abbey. He has, in a sense, caught Dora under law, the law of contract, and now feels that she is unfairly breaking the agreement. According to Paul's contractual view of Dora, she would not have been justified in any circumstances

---

[17] See Wind (1969).
[18] A point raised by Marquis (2005) and Moller (2003).

whatsoever to leave him, for this would be to cross the boundaries that the solemn vow of marriage affords her. For this reason, Paul's sense of deep hurt is inflected by a sense that he is the wounded and wronged party. Yet it is also inflected by a realization of his own awkwardness, and by a vague awareness that Dora's less rule-bound capacity for navigating the world may be better than his own. His reaction involves commitment to a contractual view of loyalty in which it need have no connection to a sense of the good life or some separate admirable traits. Yet the reaction is also shaped by something other than a sense that the rules have been broken. It is shaped by a new and unwelcome self-knowledge. Paul wishes that he could forever subject Dora to his fixed perception of her, one in which he is forever the teacher and she the pupil. But Dora's lack of autonomy under such an arrangement is something that Murdoch invites us to reject. And so we witness Paul hurt also by the loss of the esteem that goes with *being loved by another*. The latter, in particular, matters a good deal. It is Murdoch's main licensed mechanism for valuing the self, not directly but through the eyes of another who loves us when they might love any number of other people instead.[19]

In Paul's pastoral vision of the world, flourishing is always a requirement. But his underlying grasp of the thing that loyalty is seems curiously independent of any notion of the good life. It is cut off from any viable conception of flourishing. But is it not only difficult to square this understanding of loyalty with a eudaemonist (good life) conception of virtue, it is also difficult to square with a more aretaic (admirable trait) conception of the sort that Murdoch herself inclines toward in her more directly philosophical texts. By this, we mean a conception of virtues as *admirable character traits which aid 'unselfing'*, that is, a sacrificing of ego for the sake of others, and in ways that do not simply pander to the character flaws of others but address their real needs. The second clause can easily be

---

[19] See also Milligan (2013).

lost sight of, leaving us with only a plausible imitation of unselfing, sacrifice as submission to another's will and not for the good—not even for the sacrificing agent's good, for the apparent beneficiary's good, nor for the sake of some more reified conception of the Good. What this means is that Paul's understanding of the virtue of loyalty as requiring sacrifice on the part of Dora is not itself wrong. Virtues often do tend toward sacrifice, at least on any plausible aretaic conception and arguably on more eudaimonistic conceptions, too. But Paul's understanding of what that sacrifice might be, in Dora's case, is far more problematic. It looks suspiciously like a surrendering to him that is most likely to feed his own weaknesses and faults. It is difficult to see how a plausible conception of sacrificial virtue would allow this. Put bluntly, Paul demands the wrong kind of sacrifice, and Dora can see that there is something wrong with it. Paul himself is loyal, but he is also petty, pompous, and spiteful. But these are not competing traits. They are non-admirable aspects of his character which are strongly connected. His loyalty (whether it is to a failing marriage or to a faltering traditional religiosity) is of a piece with everything else, a dogged holding onto what he knows. It is a rejection of personal growth. Any virtuous loyalty on Dora's part would have to help Paul overcome these things. *Virtuous loyalty assists the other, but not necessarily in the ways that they want. And it is only in this relational dynamic, within which sacrifices can be called for, made at the expense of our default egocentricity, and made in ways that tend to assist the other, that virtuous loyalty is to be found.* Where any of these conditions break down, loyalty is something other than a virtue. And while formulated in aretaic terms (in terms of admirable traits), this conception of loyalty as a virtue has an obvious connection to the eudaimonistic (good life) understandings of virtue within personal relationships (such as friendships) that Aristotle writes about, and that Plato writes about and also depicts.

This is a world away from Paul's more puritanical grasp of matters. Dora cannot lead. She must come to where he is. He will not chase after her. On such an understanding of the virtues, loyalty along Paul's lines will still not count as a virtue because we simply cannot admire it. He wants Dora to abandon any pathway that might make her the kind of person that we could admire or allow her to become such a person. And what does Murdoch suggest an admirable Dora looks like? The simple answer is this: a more substantial, and more real version of Dora than Paul is ready to deal with. That is, an admirable Dora might well be capable of sacrifice (and leaving Paul itself *is* a sacrifice of comfort), but she would also be free from Paul's vision. Confident, assertive, and courageous enough to make the right kind of sacrifices, in the right way, in the right context, and with regard to the right things. This is precisely the version of Dora that Paul rejects.

Thinking about loyalty in the light of the problem case

In the problem case, Paul's conception of loyalty looks familiar, but it does not look at all like a virtue. To frame matters in more Murdochian terms, it is not connected with any sort of improved vision of the world, recognition of others, or a partial overcoming of egocentricity. Virtues, from a Murdochian point of view, lead us to look away from self and attend to the particularity of both people and things; otherwise they are not virtues but something else. While there may well be a certain level of eudaimonism in Murdoch's view of the world (a connection between being virtuous and enjoying a good life), the overcoming of egocentricity and its clouding of vision is more obviously pivotal to her conception of *what a virtue is* (Jollimore 2011). Paul's conception of loyalty cannot, on this approach, count as a virtue. It is flawed in part because it is entirely independent of who Dora is and entirely independent of the particularity of the relationship between them. It is not about overcoming egocentricity in order to see the other person more clearly. It is not formed through, or reshaped by, their sharing of a life (Rorty 1986).

What we are suggesting here is that a virtuous loyalty in personal relationships is the kind of thing that depends upon situational factors and that Murdoch is sensitive to this aspect of what allows loyalty to operate as a virtue. Loyalty depends upon various contingencies which allow loyalty to operate in the right way, as well as depending upon factors which are internal to particular relationships and depend upon the unique and particular people involved. Factors such as the mutual expectations that emerge out of a shared life, rather than out of familiarity with the terms of a contract. Loyalty of this sort is also entirely possible. Indeed, it is often available within marriage as much as within relationship of other sorts. Murdoch's approach also runs along these lines. She is not, after all, suggesting that every marriage must be like that of Dora and Paul, or that marriage itself is a vicious bourgeois institution that we ought to be rid of. Whatever we or she might choose to say about other kinds of relationships, as contexts within which virtue may flourish, marriage for Murdoch remains such a context within which loyalty can be a virtue . . . if various other things are in place. It would, after all, be odd to say that marriage makes a virtuous loyalty impossible. That would set up a nice paradox, if it was true, but it is unlikely to be true, and so unlikely to generate any sort of paradox. Indeed, our grasp of *what loyalty is* may itself be shaped in part by the phenomenon of marriage, or by narratives about marriage, just as much as it is by political exemplars of remaining true to a cause. This understanding of things also seems to be built into Murdoch's picturing of the relationship between Dora and Paul as a marriage that has gone wrong rather than her picturing of it as a marriage that has run along the usual tracks of failure. Similarly, the collapse of the lay community at Imber should not lead us to imagine that it says anything about the silent continuity of the nearby Abbey, where a far truer spiritual life continues.

This approach to loyalty draws upon the familiar machinery of virtue theory by using the distinction between merely having a character trait and the trait in question functioning as a virtue. But Murdoch gives an experiential depth to this familiar distinction. *The Bell* conveys a sense of what it is like to feel the pull of loyalty but at the same time to be aware that there is something not quite right about the loyalty in question. Dora senses that the loyalty Paul wants would suffocate her and still do him no good. It would simply reinforce his inability to really see her. In more Murdochian terms, it would reinforce his egocentricity. This makes it something other than virtue. However, Paul admires the sacrifices of the lay community, the ability of its members to set various things aside. And he is not entirely wrong to hold that there may be a connection between a capacity for sacrifice and virtue. However, again, the conditions under which loyalty is able to operate as a virtue are closely linked to whether egocentricity is reinforced or undermined. A readiness for personal sacrifice of a sort that will simply reinforce egocentricity will hardly qualify as a virtue in the Murdochian sense. Whether it is possible to be sacrificially virtuous by being loyal can depend upon factors beyond the control of agent themselves. The possibility of such a sacrificial loyalty will depend upon the other person, and upon the multiple contingencies of the predicament in which a couple, such as Paul and Dora, find themselves. Sometimes the predicament may be such that the standing of the loyalty will be dubious. But to say this does not bar the possibility of a virtuous loyalty on all occasions. Where a generalized skepticism about loyalty as a virtue goes wrong is in assuming that a virtuous loyalty must *always* be available or else loyalty must always be dubious. We have defended the less demanding view that the conditions for a virtuous loyalty need only be realized some of the time. The rest of the time, what is available to us will be a loyalty that is other than virtuous.

Bibliography

Agassi, Joseph. "The Last Refuge of the Scoundrel." *Philosophia* 4 (1974): 315–317.

Arendt, Hannah, and Gershom Scholem. *The Correspondence of Hannah Arendt and Gershom Scholem*. Edited by Marie Luise Knott. Chicago: University of Chicago Press, 2017.

Cohen, Kate. "Loyalty Is Dumb. Party Loyalty Is Dangerous." *Washington Post*, November 12, 2019. https://www.washingtonpost.com/opinions/2019/11/12/loyalty-is-dumb-party-loyalty-is-dangerous/

Dent, N. J. H. "The Value of Courage." *Philosophy* 56:218 (1981): 574–577.

Ewin, R. E. "Loyalties and Virtues." *The Philosophical Quarterly* 42:169 (1992): 403–419.

Foot, Philippa. *Virtues and Vices*. Berkeley: University of California Press, 1978.

Foust, Mathew. "Loyalty in the Teaching of Confucius and Josiah Royce." *Journal of Chinese Philosophy* 39:2 (2012): 192–206.

Foust, Mathew. "Nitobe and Royce: Bushido and the Philosophy of Loyalty." *Philosophy East and West* 65:4 (2015): 1174–1193.

Hursthouse, Rosalind. *On Virtue Ethics*. Oxford: Oxford University Press, 1999.

Irwin, Julie. "Loyalty to a Leader Is Overrated, Even Dangerous." *Harvard Business Review* (online) December 16, 2014. https://hbr.org/2014/12/loyalty-to-a-leader-is-overrated-even-dangerous

Jollimore, Troy. *Love's Vision*. Princeton NJ: Princeton University Press, 2011.

Jollimore, Troy. *On Loyalty*. London: Routledge, 2012.

Marquis, Don. "What's Wrong with Adultery?" In *What's Wrong?*, edited by G. Oddie and D. Boonin, 231–238. New York: Oxford University Press, 2005.

Milligan, Tony. "Abandonment and the Egalitarianism of Love." In *Love, Justice, Autonomy*, edited by Rachel Fedock, Michael Kuehler, and Raja Rosenhagen, 167–182. London: Routledge, 2020.

Milligan, Tony. "Valuing Love and Valuing the Self." *Convivium, Revista de Filosofia* 2:25 (2013): 109–122.

Moller, Dan. "An Argument Against Marriage." *Philosophy* 78:1 (2003): 79–91.

Murdoch, Iris. *The Bell*. London: Penguin, 1962.

Murdoch, Iris. *The Sovereignty of Good*. London: Routledge, 2001.

Nixon, Jon. *Hannah Arendt and the Politics of Friendship*. London: Bloomsbury, 2015.

Rorty, Amelie Oksenberg. "The Historicity of Psychological Attitudes: Love Is Not Love When It Alters Not When It Alteration Finds." *Midwest Studies in Philosophy* 10 (1986): 399–412.

Slote, Michael. *Morals from Motives*. Oxford: Oxford University Press, 2001.

Sutcliffe, Rosemary. *Eagle of the Ninth*. Oxford: Oxford University Press, 2020.

Vogt, Joseph. *Ancient Slavery and the Ideal of Man.* Oxford: Basil Blackwell, 1974.

Walker, Margaret Urban. "Moral Luck and the Virtues of Impure Agency." *Metaphilosophy* 22:1–2 (1991): 14–27.

Wind, Edgar. *Pagan Mysteries of the Renaissance* Revised Edition. New York: Norton and Company, 1969.

Index